Not Only, But Also
MY LIFE IN CRICKET

'Somehow one sensed that something extraordinary was going to happen when Sobers sauntered to the wicket.'
Wisden

'You know, sometimes I wish I'd never done it ... If I go from here to Hong Kong, if I go from here to South Africa, if I go to Germany or wherever I go, all I hear is: "Tell us about the six sixes".'
Garry Sobers

Not Only, But Also
MY LIFE IN CRICKET

Malcolm Nash

with Richard Bentley

ST DAVID'S PRESS

Cardiff

Published in Wales by St. David's Press, an imprint of

Ashley Drake Publishing Ltd
PO Box 733
Cardiff
CF14 7ZY

www.st-davids-press.wales

First Impression – 2018

ISBN
Paperback: 978-1-902719-71-9
eBook: 978-1-902719-72-6

British Library Cataloguing-in-Publication Data.
A CIP catalogue for this book is available from the British Library.

Typeset by Prepress Plus, India (www.prepressplus.in)

CONTENTS

*To my mother and father
who started, and always supported,
my wonderful cricketing journey.*

FOREWORD

always loved my cricketing visits to Wales. The first was in 1963, at Margam, for Cambridge University. The wind was blowing across from the adjacent steel works, and for a while red dust stopped play. Jim Pressdee scored a painstaking 50 (or a lot more?) and was barracked by the crowd. He walked over to them and invited them to 'Go home and watch the telly'. The pitch was so slow and low it was hard to hit the ball off the square, especially when Don Shepherd was bowling. In 1965 I played for Middlesex at Swansea. We won by an innings, I scored 0, and had a thoroughly good time. The match being over in two days, I drove back to London in my Morris Minor via the pretty route. I think it took ten hours. Harry Latchman was very patient. In 1969, again at Swansea, we were part of Glamorgan's home run to the Championship title. What a day it was, the final day, with the crowd singing the songs of the valleys. Majid Khan, I remember, playing Fred Titmus beautifully. I also scored my first Championship century against Glamorgan, at Cardiff, in 1973, 163 not out.

In one of these matches the umpire was Dai Davies, and we got him talking about his batting exploits when, during the 1926 miners' strike, he batted for a day and a half in solidarity for his friends the pit-workers. He vowed, he told us passionately, he wouldn't get out until the lockout was over!

Wonderful days, great characters, the sense of a world where the globalisation to come had hardly touched the quality and style of life. The only other place you got this feeling was in Yorkshire.

Then, from the mid-1960s, there was Malcolm. Tall, lithe (not, I would say, gangly as he describes himself!), Malcolm Nash was an elegant, stylish bowler. He looked born to the game, and to the art of bowling. He had an easy run-up, short but fluid. His action was perfect, side-on, high arm, good follow through. A model for any young aspiring bowler. And of course he bowled left-arm over, something that was a nightmare to some right hand batsmen – I remember Eknath Solkar of India getting Geoff Boycott out for a pastime! Malcolm swung the ball sharply, and bowled across the batsman. He was hard to leave, and one was always worried about lbws. He was not quick, but a bit quicker than he looked. As he says, he learned (partly from Fred Trueman, whom we were always encouraging to bowl his cutters, as he was less likely to hit you in the teeth) not to sacrifice movement for speed. On the often slow wickets in Wales, there was rarely much help for out-and-out fast bowling (which is also even more hard work!). In county cricket he was like Chaminda Vaas in Test cricket – the Sri Lankan also brought up on unfriendly pitches, also not fast, but always threatening to take wickets, always reliable and economical.

Malcolm was a bit of a nightmare to me too. In the 1977 Gillette Cup final he got me out first ball of the innings, poking away from my body, worried about (on this occasion non-existent) in-swing. I was reminded of my only pair in cricket, on the Saturday and Monday of a match between Middlesex and Kent at Lord's in 1964. On the Saturday I was lbw to John Dye – left arm over, the ball swinging in – on Monday c Cowdrey b Dye (at second slip) the ball going straight across. Classic stuff. Embarrassing too, as on Sunday it had been announced that I was part of the MCC touring squad for South Africa.

Malcolm was a fine cricketer. Dangerous with the bat, elegant too, with an easy top-hand-in-control swing. And he played cricket with a smile, or at least a wry grin, on his face. He enjoyed it, and conveyed that to the opposition as to his own team. But of course it was as a bowler, and especially a new ball bowler, that he excelled. He had that quality that my early Middlesex coach Jim Sims spoke of, when he told me, with immense seriousness, that a 'straight ball has a certain lethal quality about it – if you miss it you've had it: do you follow me, Michael?'

But by 'straight' I don't mean undeviating. I mean homing in on middle and off stumps – unless it was the one that slithered straight across towards the slips!

It was a pleasure to play against you, Malcolm. And I haven't even mentioned that over – until now!

Mike Brearley OBE

PREFACE

I recall writing an article in 1976, as cricket correspondent of the *Sunday Telegraph*, arguing that Malcolm Nash should be considered for selection by England. He was included in the Test trial of that summer, the least I thought he deserved at the peak of a successful career.

He was never picked, and I knew why. The chairman of selectors at the time was Alec Bedser and in 1976 he was aided by Sir Leonard Hutton, Ken Barrington and the Test match umpire Charlie Elliott. Fixed in their minds, I know, was the belief that a Test class left-arm seamer was someone who propelled a new ball faster than Malcolm, got higher bounce and was of bigger physique; something like Alan Davidson of Australia or Richard Collinge of New Zealand.

I understood their view because when I first saw Malcolm bowl in 1967 I too wondered if he could actually shake up opening batsmen, especially abroad where there is no juice in the pitch. It did not take me long to see him as an expert practitioner of seam and swing. In fact, every member of the Glamorgan side saw that the young man from Abergavenny who had wandered into their dressing room was a genuine wicket-taker, but how would he fit into our plans?

Long before the 1969 Championship season, I spent time trying to match the talents we had available with the changes in playing conditions. Batting bonus points would come within 85 overs of a first innings: increasing points for every 25 runs above 150 runs onwards, and they would be limitless, in order to prolong attacking play: 250 runs would bring in 4 points. Batting bonus points would be our main aim, I decided on a cold and snowy January day.

Alan Jones and Roger Davis would be our solid start, while Majid, Bryan Davis and A.R. Lewis would be kept together to keep the innings moving at a lively tempo. Peter Walker at six could play as an attacker or defender, as required, and then the blast of attacking all-rounders – measuring their progress according to bonus points, not runs alone – notably Eifion Jones, Tony Cordle and Malcolm Nash. Don Shepherd and Lawrence Williams would quickly learn to block their way to any extra batting point on offer. My plan looked good: in January!

As for Malcolm, he proved to be expert at launching a flurry of strokes, especially slashing cuts to the off-side, cover drives and all manner of lofted drives for six or four. Tony Cordle was just as aggressive while Eifion could either join in or steady the ship when needed. These three, batting at seven, eight and nine, became the envy of every other county.

We also had great catchers. Left-arm seam bowlers who genuinely swing the ball late into the pads always need expert close catchers: some balls swing, some go straight on.

Preserving his skill at swinging the ball Malcolm cared about his action: the feet position, the rotation of the hips, and the high arm with the wrist behind the ball. He always acknowledged the wonderful catching of Bryan Davis and Majid Khan at slip, the high skills of Eifion Jones keeping wicket and the short leg-side catching of Roger Davis and, perhaps above all, Peter Walker.

What I could not guess at that formative stage was how Malcolm's temperament would stand up to Championship cricket. In short, within a few games, not only did he demonstrate his attacking ability with the bat, but a serious skill in taking the wickets of the very best batsmen.

By the close of that '67 season he informed me that he was prepared to open the batting, open the bowling, and take over the captaincy too.

I loved it. Far better for the team that we did not have to wait a season or more for a new boy to settle in. Malcolm Nash stepped onto his stage without a nervous twitch, and the rest is history. Our Glamorgan scored their runs and bowled their overs faster than anyone else over the whole season and had the highest total of batting points.

Most importantly, as I see it, was Malcolm's disposition in the long aftermath of the Sobers day. He did not slink away from the experience, but embraced it, went off to the United States to spread his coaching-skills wherever he saw he could propagate the great game.

Tony Lewis CBE

INTRODUCTION

As always, Malcolm and I were chatting about cricket as we sheltered during a rare rain-break at the Swansea Cricket Festival. Malcolm, with my enthusiastic encouragement, was sharing some of his memories of playing at the famous St. Helen's ground.

The gentleman next to us could contain his curiosity no longer. Apologising for interrupting, he explained that he realised from our conversation that Malcolm must be an ex-Glamorgan player, but didn't know who he was.

"I'm Malcolm Nash."

"Oh, really? Malcolm Nash." The penny dropped. The connection was made. "Garry Sobers hit you for six sixes."

"Yes, I know," was Malcolm's patient response.

I asked him later if he was tired of what must be endless references to 'the Sobers over', and to people always making that link.

"No," he replied. "What happened, happened. I don't regret it, and don't forget, my name is in the record books too! But I hope it's not the only cricketing achievement I'm remembered for. I'd be disappointed if that single over defined my career. I'm not just the guy that Sobers whacked out of the park."

From that conversation the plan for this book emerged, as did its title – *Not Only, But Also*. That is, not only the bowler dispatched by Garry Sobers for a world-record six sixes in a single over, but also a talented and widely respected cricketer who graced the county cricket circuit for 17 seasons and whose achievements with bat as well as ball were so significant for Glamorgan and for the county game in general.

Over the following months, as we recalled and researched his cricketing exploits, it became increasingly evident that Malcolm's choice of title was most appropriate in many other respects, too.

For example, Malcolm was not only a talented left-arm seam bowler whose ability to swing the ball saw him on the edge of international selection, but also a very able and aggressive batsman with a first-class century before lunch to his name. Not only an opening pace bowler, but also a more than useful spin bowler when the conditions and match situation demanded, and not only a talented and enthusiastic all-rounder on the field, but also a thoughtful and active advocate of players' rights off it, playing a significant role in the formative years of the Professional Cricketers' Association.

In addition, Malcolm was not only a talented player but also an excellent coach, and not only a very able cricketer who had a trial for England, but also a talented all-round sportsman who captained Wales under-23 at hockey. Finally, and very importantly, not only a tough, hard-playing and confident competitor, but also a sensitive, self-effacing and thoughtful teammate and opponent.

Malcolm's reflections on his cricketing life, and on his many experiences and achievements in the game, are made against an affectionate and nostalgic backcloth of county cricket – and the life of a county cricketer – during the late 1960s and through the 1970s. They do, indeed, demonstrate that there is a great deal more to Malcolm's story, and to his place in cricketing history, than that duel with Garry Sobers at St. Helen's in the late summer of 1968. Not only that record-breaking over, momentous though it unquestionably was, but also so much more.

Richard Bentley

1

Garry Sobers is Playing

'Genius. It's an over-worked word and it is too often used in talking about people who don't deserve it. But in the case of Garry Sobers there can't be any argument about it. He must be the greatest instinctive genius, with bat or ball, there has ever been.'
John Arlott and Fred Trueman

"**S**o Garry Sobers is definitely playing then?" I asked, trying not to sound too excited.

Wilf Wooller nodded. "They've got a hell of a team on paper."

I'd got to the ground early and bumped into the ex-captain – still referred to as 'the skipper' by those who had played under him, and as Mr Wooller by the rest of us – in the car park. Officially Wilf was now club secretary, but unofficially was 'Mr Glamorgan', organiser of everything behind – as well as in front of – the scenes!

We walked into the small pavilion together. The ground looked immaculate and the views in every direction were outstanding. The ground staff were busy on the square and chairs had been borrowed from somewhere to ring the outfield. The beauty of the scene was spoilt only by the ugliness of the makeshift scaffolding for the TV cameras but, as far as I was concerned, that was a price worth paying. I had already phoned several people at home to tell them to make sure they tuned in for my first appearance on television!

*Wilf Wooller –
'Mr Glamorgan'.*

I couldn't believe my good fortune. I was actually going to play against my boyhood hero, Garry Sobers, but this wasn't the match at St. Helen's when Garry broke the world record for the number of runs scored in a single over – off my bowling. That unexpected pleasure was still to come!

This game was a little over a year beforehand – on June 18th, 1967, to be exact – in the unlikely cricket setting of a military camp at the edge of the beautiful Brecon Beacons National Park and in the shadow of Sugar Loaf, the southernmost peak of the Black Mountains. It was my first full season as a professional cricketer and things were going well for me. I had a handful of Championship games under my belt and had already experienced the excitement of playing at historic grounds like Hove, Harrogate, Chesterfield and Grace Road – as well as Cardiff Arms Park, of course, and the new Sophia Gardens.

I felt I was making progress with both bat and ball, usually opening the bowling or coming on first change, and batting at six. I'd managed to amass a couple of hundred runs, including a 69 and a 42 not out, but I knew I'd got out cheaply too often after getting a decent start. In addition, I had a clutch of wickets under my belt – 14 or so, with 6-64 against Sussex – including the prize scalps of Jim Parks and Tony Greig: my best figures to date. I'd also got out David Steele – a solid batsman who would memorably go on to play for England – twice in our game against Northamptonshire at Cardiff.

I felt I'd benefitted from bowling to a range of batsmen with differing batting techniques, including some famous names and significant talents, and I'd had the advantage of watching some very experienced players, too. You can learn so much from watching! I'm not sure that young cricketers watch enough these days. Really watch, I mean. Watch, analyse and learn! I'd seen Fred Trueman at close quarters – perhaps too close: Nash b Trueman 0 – as well as players of the quality of Colin Milburn, Geoff Boycott, Roy Marshall, and Peter Willey. I'd also had the added experience of playing for Glamorgan against the Nawab of Pataudi's 1967 Indian touring side, with world-class performers like Farokh Engineer, Bishan Bedi and, of course, 'Tiger' Pataudi himself. What an elegant batsman he was. He oozed class, despite the handicap of having lost the sight in one eye following a car accident some years before.

I remember so clearly the special feeling of playing against an international team for the first time. That Indian game was particularly significant for me – a sort of rite of passage – competing against players who would themselves take part in a Test against England only a few weeks later. It was a real thrill. I'd had Indian players in my 'Owzat!' Rest of the World team as a kid, and now here I was sharing the field with their next group of internationals.

So, all in all, it had been a wonderful start to my first-class career, the start any young cricketer would dream of, and it was an unexpected bonus to hear that I was included in the side to play against the International Cavaliers on the Sunday – the rest day – of our three-day match against Essex at Sophia Gardens, Cardiff. We had a 13-man squad for the Championship game and I had anticipated being left out so that one of the more established guys could enjoy the excitement of the televised match but, just when it felt as if nothing could be better, I was presented with the chance to meet – and play on the same pitch with – my hero Sobers!

I've always been a bit uncomfortable with the word hero being used in a sporting context, but it is a reasonable one to use in terms of Garry's significance to me as a young cricketer growing up with aspirations to be a professional player – and a left-handed all-rounder, at that. For a long time I'd been excited by his achievements with both bat and ball, and by his positive attitude to the game. Garry's approach was a perfect match for the International Cavaliers side – he always played cavalier cricket!

In the seasons before the start of the John Player League in 1969, Sunday was traditionally a day off for professional cricketers. We played two three-day games a week – Wednesday, Thursday, Friday, and then Saturday, Monday, Tuesday. Sunday was a day for putting your feet up or playing some golf, but live televised limited-over cricket was fast becoming popular. The BBC's coverage of the Cavaliers' games drew big viewing figures, and attendances at the matches were high, too. It was all very new and exciting, and a great way to spend a Sunday afternoon – watching international stars you would never otherwise see. The Cavaliers, sponsored by Rothmans

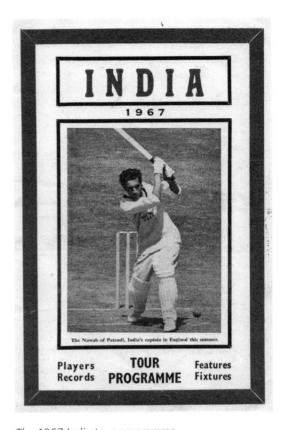

The 1967 India tour programme.

Garry Sobers – one of the 'greats', and a cricketer I had admired since boyhood.

and organised by ex-England legends Denis Compton and Godfrey Evans, played a full fixture list of 40-over games against county sides for several seasons until they were disbanded following the start of the televised John Player League.

The Cavaliers' line-up was always a strong one, made up of star players from this country and overseas. The counties responded accordingly by also fielding decent sides, apart from the occasional resting of some tired muscles or a key bowler. So these were very much 'proper' matches, played to be won and with a lot of excellent cricket. At the same time, they were played in true cavalier style with the emphasis firmly on enjoyment – for spectators, a significant TV audience and, very importantly, for the players themselves. The fact that there was some prize money at stake for both batters and bowlers probably helped, too!

So, on this June Sunday, at the picturesque army camp ground at Cwrt-y-Gollen, near Crickhowell, Glamorgan put out a decent team – not our strongest, but very respectable! Of course, we were all new to limited-overs cricket and tactics then, and although we fielded our usual openers in Bernard Hedges and Alan Jones, there were some significant changes to our Championship batting order. Tony Cordle was at three, and I was at four. Don Shepherd – another big hitter captaining the side on the day – was batting at five. Len Hill - who top-scored for us in the game - was next, with Peter Walker pushed down the order to bat at nine. This was one of only a handful of occasions that I played with Glamorgan's long-serving batsman Bernard Hedges before he retired at the end of the 1967 season. I wish it had been more.

I saw Bernard Hedges open the Glamorgan innings, partnered by Gilbert Parkhouse, when I watched Glamorgan as a teenager.

We had the added interest of including local 19-year-old rugby prospect, Keith Jarrett, in our side. Keith - whose father, Harold, had turned out for Glamorgan in 1938 - was a very handy cricketer who played two first-class games with us that same summer. Keith had already won his first Welsh cap, against England, at the age of 18, and he went on to have a distinguished rugby career, representing Wales at both union and league. There was very much a south Wales sporting community in those days. We got to know a lot of the rugby boys, as well as some of the snooker and soccer guys, too. Trevor Ford, centre-forward with both Cardiff City and Swansea Town and winner of 38 caps for Wales, once volunteered to field for us at St. Helen's when we were briefly short of a twelfth man!

The International Cavaliers' line-up was daunting. Brian Close was captain. The fact that he was also captain of England at the time shows you the status and quality of the Cavaliers' set-up. It also tells you a lot about Brian himself and his love of the game. He had led England against India in the first match of the three-Test series the previous week, and would return to Test duty four days after playing at Crickhowell. He would also captain England in the second three-Test home series against Pakistan later

Newport's young rugby union star Keith Jarrett played two first-class games with us in 1967, against the tourists from both India and Pakistan.

that same summer. Yorkshire's Jimmy Binks was behind the stumps for the Cavaliers, with Geoff Boycott, Keith Fletcher, Lance Gibbs and Trevor Bailey (in his final season as a player) some of the other familiar names. Then, batting five, was Garry Sobers, the current captain of the West Indies.

I still remember the excitement of playing in a match with Sobers for the first time. Bowling to him and facing him were incredible experiences. It was – literally – a dream come true. I had imagined it so many times as we had starred together in boyhood games of 'Owzat!' on my bedroom floor or the kitchen table! In my imaginary World XI team to challenge the might of England, his was always the first name I pencilled in – alongside my own, of course. Well, Garry may not have had a statistically outstanding day at Cwrt-y-Gollen – no blistering century or eye-popping cluster of wickets – but he was nevertheless outstanding, a huge presence on the field, and I was in no way disappointed.

Glamorgan batted first and scored what for those days was a very respectable 40-over total of 198 for 7. I was deceived by the quality spin of West Indian international Lance Gibbs: stumped, for what would not be the last time in my batting career! Now, I know you are not supposed to enthuse too much about the opposition's achievements on the pitch but, for me, a highlight of our innings was a stunning catch at cover by Garry Sobers to dismiss an astonished Tony Cordle. He was horizontal, hanging in the air! Garry was one of the best fielders you could hope to see, agile and with incredible reflexes. A fine out-fielder, he was equally good close to the wicket. This

Brian Close was the youngest man to play for England when, at 18, he was selected against New Zealand in 1949. In 1967 he was captain of England as well as the Cavaliers.

Lance Gibbs, one of the great West Indian off-spinners, had me stumped by Jimmy Binks (Yorkshire and England).

all-round fielding ability was a significant part of what made him a truly great all-round cricketer – in the eyes of many, the greatest all-rounder there has ever been.

Our opening attack of Cordle and Jeff Jones - who had already been capped by England and who would, during the next winter, play a significant role with both ball and bat in England's eventful Caribbean tour - soon got amongst the visitors, quickly reducing them to 23-3. Obstinate opener Boycott wasn't sure what to do at the other end – he hadn't got over being dropped by the England selectors for slow scoring in the first Test of the summer – and it was whispered that it was Brian Close who had given him the unwelcome news. Although reinstated for the final Test, being dropped for what was termed 'selfish play' affected him badly. Things only got worse for him at Cwrt-y-Gollen. He didn't know whether to stick or twist and on 29 was run out – not for the last time in his illustrious career (once, it is rumoured, deliberately and on team orders)!

Sobers top-scored with 33 – enough for us to see at first hand the power and timing we had heard so much about. I didn't manage to get him out on this occasion – I wish I had – but it was so exciting to find myself bowling to him, and I did, at least, get the final Cavaliers' wicket to end the match and give us a Glamorgan victory by 59 runs.

Because we played this match at the army camp ground near Crickhowell there was nowhere obvious for us to gather for the traditional drink at the end of the game. I suggested that we all head back to the

After the Cavaliers' game we all went back to the Abergavenny clubhouse for a few drinks.

Abergavenny clubhouse – it was only a few miles down the road and I knew they would be delighted to see us – so everyone, including Frank Bough and all the other BBC staff, made the short trip – except for the unhappy Boycott, that is – and we had a smashing evening.

It was a strange experience sitting with all these guys in the familiar old clubhouse that had been my cricket 'home' since I was a nine-year-old – and before that if you count all the visits to watch my dad. We enjoyed a few drinks, and then a few more! There were some songs and party-pieces, too. We signed some autographs – word soon got around - and we talked and talked about cricket. Of course, no food had been laid on because it was an impromptu gathering, but I think we got through the club's entire stock of crisps and nuts!

Leaving Abergavenny that evening, I was still in awe at meeting – and sharing the pitch and pavilion with – Garry Sobers. I'll admit it was very significant to me, and hugely enjoyable. As most people in the cricket-playing world know only too well, this wasn't to be my last encounter with the great man!

However, it was the first time we had met in person, I had come across Garry and his cricketing exploits a number of years earlier. In fact, I was an eight-year-old schoolboy when I first became aware of the exploits of Garry Sobers. It was when he hit the news playing his first Test for the West Indies at the age of just 17. His was a remarkable introduction to the world of first class cricket. He had played only two games – both for his native Barbados – when called in to the West Indies team to play in the fifth and final Test against Len Hutton's mighty England side at Sabina Park in Kingston, Jamaica in March 1954.

Can you imagine that? A first first-class game at 16. Then just one other senior game at the beginning of the next season, followed by an international call up. It was a cricketing version of a *Roy of the Rovers* storyline, and Garry was instantly and unshakably my hero. I don't think I ever told him that as such but, as we sat with a beer at the end of another memorable encounter at St. Helen's some years later, I did rather sheepishly admit that I'd been inspired by his teenage exploits with both bat and ball – pointing out, of course, that I was still in short trousers at the time!

I can remember watching some highlights of Garry's Test debut on our little black and white TV at home. There was not much televised cricket then, and during these foreign tours it was perhaps just a short filmed report on Peter Dimmock's popular weekly *Sportsview* programme, but it was enough. I was hooked. We had one of those large magnifying glasses – like a giant, flattened goldfish bowl – that you stood in front of the screen to make the picture a little larger – though, as I remember, no clearer! Through the grainy fuzziness was Garry, a schoolboy more than holding his own against Hutton's all-star England. In the first innings he took 4-75 in 28.5 overs, including a wicket in his first over in international cricket (and despite a majestic double hundred from Hutton). He also scored a handy 14 not out and 26.

Sobers' first Test wicket was that of Trevor Bailey, who had himself already turned the match very much in England's favour by taking seven first innings wickets for only 34 runs, including sending back the first three batsmen – John Holt, Jeff Stollmeyer and Everton Weekes – with only 13 on the board. This was Bailey's best bowling

Signing autographs with Garry Sobers after the Cavaliers' match.

performance in international cricket. It was a very unusual day for him because he opened both the bowling and batting for his county before stumps were drawn! A rare feat!

In one of those strange coincidences which cricket seems to produce so often, England's all-rounder Trevor 'Barnacle' Bailey had not only been in the Cavaliers' team at Cwrt-y-Gollen – Don Shepherd bowled him for a duck – but he was also playing at Sophia Gardens in our three-day Championship game against Essex. He was in the last of his 22 first-class seasons, but was still a fine player. He'd knocked over Bernard Hedges early in our innings on the Saturday, and it had been a great experience for me to face him in the middle.

By another coincidence, I'd lost my first innings wicket against Essex to the cunning leg spin of Robin Hobbs – bowled for a duck. It looked so tempting and hittable, but he beat me (as he beat so many over the years) in the flight. I didn't feel too badly because, only the week before, Robin had been playing for England against India at Leeds – the first of his seven caps – and I did get hold of him a few times in the second innings, scoring 62 not out. The coincidence? Well, later in my career I would be captained by Robin after he moved to Glamorgan, and then I would take over from him as captain for another two seasons. But that's another story for another chapter…

I drove away from Abergavenny that day thinking how good this cricketing life was! I'd played against some of the most talented and well-known cricketers in the world. I'd met my boyhood idol Garry Sobers, and I'd taken a wicket on TV. I tell you, I felt ten feet tall and, to cap it all, the next day I would be back at Sophia Gardens proudly pulling off my Glamorgan sweater again and bowling to Trevor Bailey. Surely it couldn't get better than this, could it? Talk about living your dream! As I drove, I reflected on how quickly it had all happened.

Less than two years previously I had been playing for Abergavenny and working with the family firm of Robert Price and Sons, our local builders merchants and very significant in supporting my cricket development. I knew there was always a job with them if and when I needed it, and their flexibility and understanding were crucial. I'd had no significant contact with any county team or been part of any academy or youth structure but now, having played for Glamorgan in the first

Trevor Bailey – Garry Sobers' first Test victim (in Jamaica, 1954) – and later his biographer! In 1967, Trevor, with 61 England caps, was in his final first-class season with Essex.

game of the season to cover an injury, I seemed to have become a regular with ten consecutive Championship appearances already under my belt.

I had become what I had always wanted to be: a professional cricketer. I felt I was starting to be established as part of the team. I was beginning to feel comfortable in the role, and it was all because I'd plucked up the courage to write that letter to Mr Wooller.

I felt I was becoming established.

2

'Dear Mr Wooler'

*'Just 15 years old, this tousle-haired batsman has
extreme promise. He has a richness of strokes which
puts most of his Abergavenny Seconds colleagues
to shame. The only thing lacking in his make-up
at the moment is bags of confidence and bags of
experience. With those two factors tucked beneath his
belt he will become a batsman to be reckoned with.
Mark my words!'*
Abergavenny Chronicle, 1960

It goes without saying that you don't get far in professional sport without putting in a great deal of hard work and effort. At the same time, you are also unlikely to get very far without the support and active involvement of a number of other people, too. All this with a few slices of good fortune as well, of course.

I often think about, and recall with huge gratitude, those people who helped and encouraged me over the years, and who were significant in shaping my cricketing life.

For example, Bill Voce, the ex-Nottinghamshire and England left-arm fast-medium bowler, was a very significant influence on me. He had become well known as Harold Larwood's partner in the controversial 1932-33 'Bodyline' series against Australia, but there was so much more to Bill – and to his career – than that. His first-class career, spanning the War, had lasted an astonishing 25 years, during which he took 1,558 wickets. That's a lot of experience to pass on! He won the first of his 27 England caps on a tour of the West Indies aged only 20. It was the harder, faster Caribbean pitches that convinced him that he should stick to his newer fast-medium style, though he sometimes reverted to his original slower style when conditions suited and, later, when age dictated! Bill was also a useful hard-hitting lower-order batsman. So, all in all, we two 'lefties' had a number of things about our game in common.

It was such a stroke of luck to come across Bill at the MCC England Schools' Fortnight at Lord's just before the start of the 1969 season. I was one of the youngest of 12 MCC coaches working with the schoolboys. It was a tough course and included us having to make a practical presentation for the examiners – including Bill Voce, one of the senior coaches working with us. We really clicked from the first day and, from my point of view, there couldn't have been a better time to meet him.

Having got my MCC coaching badge at Lillishall the previous autumn (on the same course, incidentally, as Geoff Boycott, Bob Taylor, and my Glamorgan teammate Kevin Lyons) I had signed up to coach in South Africa from October 1969. Alan Jones had coached and played at Springs, a small city in Transvaal, on the Reef between Johannesburg and Pretoria, for the two previous winters but, when he decided not to return for their 1969-70 season, he very generously recommended me as his replacement. It was an amazing opportunity, so it seemed sensible to take the more advanced coaching qualification before going. It would be useful in Africa and, at the same time, would help me in the analysis and development of my own cricket, so when I found myself in the company of Bill Voce I wasted no time in tapping his brain – usually in our lunch-breaks.

Bill Voce gave me reassuring advice about swing bowling!

My main concern was that, playing at altitude and in a warm climate, I would find it difficult to get the ball to swing, but Bill had toured with the MCC in South Africa during the winter of 1930-31 and his response was reassuring. "Rotate your hips – focus on that hip rotation – and you will always swing the ball." Simple but sound advice that has stayed with me – and that I have in turn passed on many times.

The fact that Bill had achieved so much, and had been such an outstanding player himself, made his thinking on the game worth its weight in gold, especially coming so early in my career and with my South African adventure looming. The timing was just right for me and I have never forgotten our conversations, just the two of us quietly chewing over cricket! I certainly got a lot more than an advanced coaching qualification – invaluable though that would prove to be over the years to come – from my two weeks at Lord's.

Of course, there were also current players who would willingly share their thinking and pass on advice. Two that had a particular impact on me were fellow new-ball operators, Wes Hall and Fred Trueman. Like Bill, not a bad pair to be picking up bowling tips from! Interestingly, both Wes and Fred, at different stages in my career, emphasised the need to stick with my action, and not to risk losing my ability to swing the ball in a quest for more pace.

Teammates, too, were invaluable in sharing ideas. As well as skipper Tony Lewis, Eifion Jones and Peter Walker were two who invariably had some useful thinking to pass on, but everyone contributed in this respect. It was a team where shared thinking, and mutual support, were key characteristics. Guys were always chipping in with ideas and observations – often very small points, but almost always worth thinking about.

It's interesting now to note that these ideas weren't only coming from your own side, sometimes they were from the opposition too, and occasionally from an umpire. Ex-keeper and ex-bowler umpires were the best in this respect. Wicketkeepers like Hugo Yarnold (Worcestershire) and Barrie Meyer (Gloucestershire), for example, and bowlers like Ron Aspinall – a big, tall medium-quickie who had retired early through injury after a very promising career with Yorkshire. Eddie Phillipson (Lancashire) and Arthur Jepson (Nottinghamshire) were two other very talented right-arm fast-medium bowlers who were always prepared to talk when they were wearing the white coat! David Constant was another. David was unusual in that, having been a very promising schoolboy cricketer who then went on to play for Kent and Leicestershire, he gave up playing to achieve his ambition of becoming a first class umpire in 1969 at the age of only 27 – not much older than me! A slow left-arm orthodox spinner, he was another always prepared to help another bowler – especially a fellow 'leftie'. I'd ask if my foot was pointing in the right direction. If his answer was "Yes", then all was good, but if it was "No, you're a bit fine leg," then I'd know straight away what adjustment to make.

Teammates, opposition and umpires alike, we'd often analyse some aspect of bowling action or fielding positions or batting technique over a beer or two at the end of a long day's play. St. Helen's was always a favourite place for that – on the flat roof of the old pavilion, gazing out over Swansea Bay. I remember Gloucestershire's Arthur Milton saying how much he looked forward to a drink and a yarn there after stumps. One of the best batsmen I ever bowled to and a wonderful judge of line, Arthur could leave it an inch outside his off-stump.

I talked with umpires all through my career. Here Barrie Meyer, one of the most thoughtful, gives a decision in my favour against Somerset's Peter Roebuck.

At Glamorgan, Phil Clift was also influential, both in his capacity as club coach and as 2nd XI skipper and mentor. His shared experiences taught us a lot about cricket and conducting ourselves as cricketers. Very importantly, he also taught us how to succeed. We saw a lot of Phil at the indoor nets at Neath and the Arms Park, but although a very competent bowling coach, his role was primarily with batsmen.

An even bigger Glamorgan influence on me personally was Wilf Wooller, not only while he was club secretary but long afterwards, too. He was second to none on the technical side of bowling, and on analysis, and was someone I often turned to for advice over the years. If I wasn't bowling well I would have a word with Wilf, and he was always very happy to share his analysis. He would remind me of the basics: front foot in the right position, sideways action, rotation of the hips. Not rocket science, I know, but so important. When bowling goes wrong, it is these basics you need to go back to and refocus on.

Wilf was club captain when I supported Glamorgan as a boy. In some ways I wish I'd played with him – I'm sure it would have been an interesting experience, if not always a comfortable one – but he had already retired as a player. I did, however, have the chance to be on the field with him just once, and I'm grateful for that memory. I think it was in a game against Welsh Universities at Barry in 1966. Wilf would have been 55 or so by then. Never the speediest between the wickets, he had slowed considerably and was in no position to get home safely when called for a sharp run by a young and eager Jeff Jones. Back in the dressing room, we could tell from Wilf's face that he was not a happy man, but he seemed to be doing better than might have been expected in not allowing his irritation to boil over. However, if Jeff thought he had got away with it, he was wrong. After post-match handshaking and showers, he was one of a group of young players moving cheerfully towards the dressing room door when Wilf's gaze fell upon him.

"Where do you think you're going?"

"A few of us are going to grab a pint and something to eat at …."

"Oh no you're not, my lad. You're practising calling, and running. Get changed …"

So, a hapless Jeff Jones spent an hour – it must have seemed an eternity – on his own in the middle, fully padded up, running enthusiastically (but not too enthusiastically) between imaginary sets of stumps, and calling plaintively through the increasing gloom to no-one in particular.

Probably top of the list of those who influenced me most would be the former Somerset and England opening-bat Harold Gimblett, who coached me when he was engaged as the professional at Ebbw Vale for the 1955 season. Most league teams in those days hired a professional to strengthen their side. Like Bill Voce, Harold had achieved so much in the game and had a wealth of cricketing know-how to pass on. His three Test caps had been won in the 1930s, but it was in 1953, only a couple of years before he and I came across each other, that he had been one of Wisden's five 'Cricketers of the Year' – alongside Tom Graveney, David Sheppard, Stuart Surridge and Fred Trueman. Illustrious company indeed!

I was only just approaching my tenth birthday when I had the good fortune to be coached by Harold and, as you can imagine, it was an amazing experience. I learned so much. Harold always said, "Go for your shots", and he never tried to change anything that came naturally and worked. He used to do throw-downs, and I remember one day when he threw a wide one, just short of a length. I waited for the ball to pass me, and then flat-batted it through square cover off the front foot. He was surprised, and asked me if I could do it again. I said that I could – and then did! "Never stop playing that shot, son", Harold instructed. Sure enough, it became a firm favourite of mine. I could play it off the back foot, too.

As well as benefitting from Harold's coaching, I enjoyed listening to his stories, too – it was real *Boy's Own* stuff! At the end of a two-week trial, during which Somerset told him he had no future in first-class cricket, Harold was rushed into the first team as a last minute replacement to cover illness – and scored an undefeated century in just over an hour with a borrowed bat. It was the fastest 100 of the Championship season. The next year he was opening for England against India at Lord's! Harold's trade-mark was his quick scoring and love of hitting sixes – he once got three in an over during the course of which his partner appealed against the light! Then, in 1948, he set a new Somerset

The Welfare Ground at Ebbw Vale.

record score of 310, against Sussex at Eastbourne. It was no surprise that the first ball of the first over Harold faced in his first innings for Ebbw Vale was dispatched for a huge six, which was still talked about years later.

The previous – and first – professional at Ebbw Vale was another ex-Somerset player, Bill Andrews, a big, tall opening bowler, and one of Gimblett's batting partners in his record-breaking debut innings. I was still only seven years old – nearly eight – when I started working with Bill. So, at a very impressionable age, I had the benefit of three years of coaching from two outstanding and experienced cricketers. Once a week, after coming out of Hereford Road Junior School in Abergavenny, I'd catch the bus which would drop me outside the Welfare Ground where the nets were located. Dad worked in Ebbw Vale so he'd pick me up after finishing and we'd travel home together talking about what I'd done that afternoon with Harold or Bill.

Dad never interfered in the technical aspects of my game, leaving that side of things to those he felt knew better – and to me. He was not a pushy parent and could even seem un-interested at times, but I realised later just how much cricket, and in particular my involvement in cricket, meant to him. When I was playing professionally, his emotional involvement – and his concern that I should perform well and do myself justice – meant that he found it difficult to watch, especially in the early days. I can add my father, Ted, to the list of influencers too, and for two reasons.

PLAYER'S CIGARETTES

THIS SURFACE IS ADHESIVE. ASK YOUR TOBACCONIST FOR THE ATTRACTIVE ALBUM (PRICE ONE PENNY) SPECIALLY PREPARED TO HOLD THE COMPLETE SERIES

CRICKETERS 1938

A SERIES OF 50

9

H. GIMBLETT
(Somerset and England)

On making his début in 1935, against Essex at Frome, Gimblett caused a sensation by getting a hundred in 63 minutes. Incidentally, this feat won him the Lawrence Trophy. Essentially an attacking batsman, he excels with the drive and cut and is a fearless hitter of all types of bowlers. Gimblett is a Somerset farmer and with broad shoulders and powerful physique he is well equipped for punishing methods. In 1936 he went in first in two Tests against India. In the 1937 season he scored 1,558 runs, average 30·54, although an injury kept him idle most of June. Born October 19th, 1914.

JOHN PLAYER & SONS
BRANCH OF THE IMPERIAL TOBACCO CO. (OF GREAT BRITAIN & IRELAND), LTD.

H. GIMBLETT

I was fortunate to be coached by Bill Andrews (left) and Harold Gimblett, two ex-Somerset stalwarts to whom I owe a lot.

The first is that, from as early as I can recall, he was an enabler – always there when a cricketing lift or some other practical assistance was required. It was my father who, from an early age, immersed me in cricket and gave me the freedom and support to follow my interest in the game. Dad played for Abergavenny for many years and, in the period just after the war, was 2nd XI captain. He was a very useful medium-pace seam bowler – with best figures of 7 for 35 – tall and gangly like me, and an undisputed number 11 batsman. I remember visiting the ground on match days and watching him play. We never played on the same side, which is a pity, and he'd called it a day by the time I started. Dad also took me to see Glamorgan play – my first experiences of professional cricket.

Glamorgan played a Championship game at the Welfare Ground in Ebbw Vale every season until 1967, and Dad was a Glamorgan member – a vice president, in fact – so we always went to watch our 'local' match and would sit in the members' area, close to the players as they came in and out of the pavilion. I'd catch the bus from Abergavenny and see the rest of the day's play, or go for the whole day if it was a Saturday or in the school holidays. I was very proud of my Coronation autograph book with a picture of the Queen on the cover, and I can vividly remember asking Glamorgan players like Haydn Davies, Jim Pressdee and Jim McConnon for their signatures. The trouble was, sitting close to their route to and from the crease, my enthusiasm would sometimes get the better of me and I'd choose the wrong moment to ask – so occasionally the answer would be: "Not now, son, see me at the end

I grew up with cricket! In this picture – to commerate an Abergavenny CC v Worcestershire CCC match – my father is in the centre of the middle row (in a long-sleeve sweater, next to Don Kenyon with his sleeves rolled up).

of the day," They always cheerfully signed in the end, though. Later, when I played professionally, I tried always to remember how important it was to give an autograph and how much it could mean to an enthusiastic youngster – and even not-so-youngster!

So, with my older brother, Colin, also a junior member of Glamorgan and a regular with Abergavenny CC, and my mother, Marie, an enthusiastic tennis player at the adjacent club, I grew up in a sporting environment. However, it was largely from my father, and his obvious enjoyment of all things cricket, that my own excitement for the game grew.

The second way in which my father was significant in shaping my cricketing career was more specific. It was his suggestion that I should write to Glamorgan requesting a trial. I remember writing the letter as if it was yesterday, and the circumstances leading up to it. It was January 1966. I'd left school and was back in Abergavenny, living at home, working for a living and enjoying the novelty of having wages to spend while at the same time playing as much club cricket as I could manage to fit in, which was a lot! I was putting in some decent performances with both bat and ball, usually opening the bowling, batting at number three, and was getting good reviews in the local press. It was a very comfortable existence,

The autograph hunter becomes autograph giver! When I played professionally, I never forgot how exciting it had been to get a signature.

but begged the question: what was I going to do with the rest of my life? I suppose the simple answer was – more cricket, if possible, but where?

I had played in my first match for Abergavenny – for the 1st XI – in 1955 when I was only ten years old. It was a Thursday afternoon, so either it was the school holiday or I must have had an afternoon away from the delights of the classroom! I only played because one of our guys didn't show up. So, like many youngsters before me – and since – my first appearance owed more to a mix of pragmatism and skipper's desperation than it did to selectorial foresight! I always had my kit with me, just in case, and needed no second invitation to change and get on the pitch. Funnily enough (and continuing the theme of getting an unexpected chance as a 'stand-in') my first Championship match for Glamorgan would also be as a result of another player's unavailability – as my hero Garry Sobers' first Test appearance had been, too.

Our opponents were a touring side called 'The Mayflies'. Abergavenny used to entertain a number of touring sides and the team from Birmingham came every year. I did nothing of note against them. In fact, I didn't bat or bowl, I just fielded, but I played, which was the main thing. I tasted my first experience of playing in a proper, competitive, grown-up cricket match: and I loved it!

At the time of this first experience of adult cricket, I was playing regularly with the club's junior side. In fact, I had been playing regularly for a couple

With the Abergavenny 1ˢᵗ XI in 1959 (that's me sitting on the grass).

of years against other junior teams linked to local clubs, as well as against teams from one or two local private schools and, although Abergavenny was my team and my home town, I'd sometimes play for other sides, too. I played on occasions for Crickhowell Colts and Ebbw Vale Colts. If there were three games with three different teams on three different nights I'd willingly play in them all! As a youngster it didn't matter where I played cricket or who I played for. The main thing was to play. I'd not come across the notion of club loyalty at that age. It really wasn't an issue. My loyalty was to cricket!

The junior team at Abergavenny was run by Lewis White, the 1ˢᵗ XI captain for many years and a very useful number three batsman and off-spin bowler. Lewis, an affable Welsh-speaking west-Walian, was in charge of net sessions, too, and would be someone else high on the list of people who influenced and supported my cricketing development.

I used to go to the nets every day of the week. Official net sessions were Tuesdays and Thursdays, but I would go over to the nets every evening – earlier in the holidays. If there were people there I'd bowl to them and if there was no-one there I'd bowl on my own. In the end, I could drop the ball on a sixpence. I'd get to bat occasionally, too, as a reward for my hard work with the ball!

Helping to roll the wicket was another favourite pastime. In fact any job around the club – anything to do with cricket!

As well as the daily visits to the nets, I'd spend hours on my own bowling against the garage door, or in the garden, batting back against a wall. I'd also practise picking up and throwing, and I'd make good use of all these skills playing in the street with my brother and his friends. They were all older than me – my brother Colin, by five years – and I had to do exactly as I was told if I wanted to be allowed to play. As well as sharpening my skills, playing with bigger, older and stronger boys and having to hold my own toughened me up, too – not only in terms of what I found I could do with bat and ball in hand, but also in learning to get my head down, scrap when necessary and not give up. At the same time, I learned not to be bullied into always being the one to have to go and retrieve distant far-hit balls or get talked into conceding my wicket! I remember that they often found it difficult to get me out. One of my innings lasted for two weeks and caused particular irritation and resentment. All sorts of new rules were introduced in an effort to get me out quicker from then on – caught one handed off a roof or left-handed one-bounce off a wall – but the more the rules changed, the more I concentrated and dug my heels in, more determined than ever not to give away my wicket. I learnt to become very determined and to hate losing or coming second. It was good training.

Back in the house, any spare moments when I wasn't playing or watching or practising – or on rainy days – would be spent day-dreaming cricket with the aid of the game 'Owzat!' in my bedroom or on the kitchen table. I'd usually play my World XI against England, and the name of Garry Sobers would be the first on my team-sheet. Always!

I used to have Hanif Mohammad in there as well. I think it was because he held two world records at the time – the highest first-class innings of 499, and also the longest innings in test history (337 in 970 minutes). Then there were always a few of my Australian heroes such as Keith Miller, a great all-rounder and another tough competitor, and Neil Harvey, an attacking left-handed batsman and a great fielder. When Harvey retired, only Don Bradman had scored more runs and more centuries for Australia. Another name also included on my team sheet was that of Alan Davidson, Australia's opening left-arm bowler, who had made such an impression on his first tour to this country in 1953. Those were the regulars who joined me, as I was, of course, always in my own Rest of the World team – the second name written in after Garry Sobers!

Already showing the benefits of good coaching – and plenty of practice!

Other team members depended on who was doing particularly well at the time. Occasionally I'd poach one or two of the England players like Peter May and, later, Fred Trueman. I loved watching Peter May – even though he was a right-hander – because there was something elegant about him that made batting look easy, but my Rest of the World team against England was usually a variety of very talented players (lots of them fellow left-lefthanders) from around the world, and one very enthusiastic young Welshman from Abergavenny!

So, one way or another, what with nets and matches and coaching and helping on the ground and games in the street – and 'Owzat!', of course – you could say my life at home was largely cricket! The endless hours spent at the cricket club or playing with a ball in the road or rolling 'Owzat!' dice may have been a contributory factor – I don't know. Anyway, I didn't pass the 11-plus.

I managed to pass the entrance examination for Wells Cathedral School, though, and found myself being driven down to Somerset by my parents for an interview with the headmaster, Frank Cummins. This was conducted in his drawing room in The Cedars, the Junior House at Wells. After chatting for a while, he suggested showing us some of the facilities, and before I knew it we were walking towards the playing fields and a game of cricket. Mr Cummins obviously noticed my eyes light up and a large smile cross my face.

"Do you play?" he asked innocently. I assured him that I did. "Would you like to join in for a few minutes?"

Would I heck! I just took my tie off and played in what I was wearing. It was only for one or two overs, but long enough for me to startle a few batsmen. The head had obviously seen enough, and the interview came to an abrupt end.

"You're in," he said. "We'll see you in September." That was it! Ten minutes joining in a games lesson and I had a place at Wells – and a whole new world of wonderful sporting opportunity was about to open up.

The sports facilities were exceptional, with three separate grounds. The Cedars had two cricket and rugby pitches, Tor Furlong had cricket and rugby pitches, but our best cricket field, with a real 'belter' of a square, was at Mundy's Meadow. This had hockey and tennis facilities, too, so you can see that we were spoilt in terms of sporting opportunities.

We had some very good games teachers as well. Geoffrey Lewis was our history teacher and house-master of Plumptre (I was in De Salis); he also ran the 1st XI cricket team. Years later, after joining Glamorgan, I discovered that Geoff was involved in the hospital broadcasting of Somerset cricket. Alan Whitehead, who played for Somerset but gave up first-class cricket at the age of only 20 (and who went on to have a long and distinguished career as an umpire), joined the School as cricket coach shortly before I left.

When I started at Wells, the winter terms – Michaelmas and Lent – were largely given over to rugby. I enjoyed it very much and developed into quite a handy scrum-half, playing through the various age groups and then for several seasons regularly in the 1st XV. I had good hands, good feet, a good kick but wasn't quite quick enough to be fly-half. With hindsight, full-back would have been perfect – I could drop-kick between the posts from halfway.

As well as playing cricket and rugby, Wells also introduced me to what would become another sporting passion – hockey. I was 15 or so before I started playing, and it was a totally new experience. Of course, it was tricky being left-handed so I had to train myself to become right-handed whenever I had a hockey stick in my hand. That was difficult, a real challenge, but I'd known about 12 months in advance that I would be playing hockey for part of each of the next few winters, and thought: 'OK, I've got to be a good hockey player, left-handed or not – so I'll practise. I'll practise in the street. I'll practise in any spare moment I can find.' So that's what I did, on my own, hitting the ball against a wall, stopping it, hitting it again, stopping it – again, and again, and again. They were similar routines to those I'd employed in front of the garage with a cricket bat and ball. For hours and hours, day after day. I guess I used to drive the neighbours crazy but it worked. When the time came, I could more than hold my own on the hockey field, and before long I was playing for the school. I loved hockey and after I left school I played for Abergavenny and got into county and regional sides, going on later to get my Welsh under-23 cap.

Despite the huge enjoyment from rugby and hockey, cricket remained the main focus of my sporting life at Wells. In my first summer there I was playing cricket for the under-13 side, and for the under-15s, and for the 1st XI, too! I think I was the youngest boy in the history of the school to have played for the first team, and I held my place for the six summers I was there – usually opening the bowling, and batting at number three or four. I was already very much an all-rounder at that stage.

The match against Millfield School was always a key fixture for us. The intense rivalry was prompted partly because they did not rate us highly enough to warrant a two-day fixture. Ours was always restricted to a one-day match, though most of their games were two-day affairs. That discrimination hurt, it really did. Umpiring in one of our needle matches against them was my old coach from primary school days, Harold Gimblett. I had a fairly good day with the bat – I think I got 50 or 60-odd – and then found myself bowling from Harold's end. I'd knocked a couple over and then shouted for an lbw and he said "Not out". I looked at him but, of course, didn't speak or show dissent. We had been too well-trained for that. He hadn't given it out and that was fine. We won the game and I grabbed a word with him afterwards: "Thanks

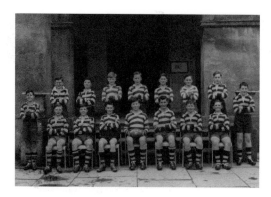

I was an all-round sportsman at Wells – playing for the school's rugby team ...

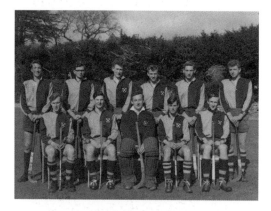

... the school's hockey team ...

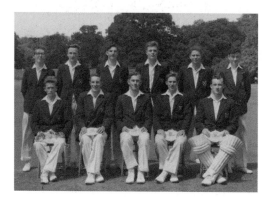

... but cricket dominated, and I was a member of the 1st XI early in my school career.

very much, Mr Gimblett." He looked at me quizzically. I said, "I remember you, but you won't remember me." He knew I looked familiar, but couldn't place me. "Ebbw Vale," I said, and his face lit up.

"Yes, I do remember. Unbelievable. We could do with you at this school." It was great to see him again and we had a good chat. I was so sorry to hear some years later that he had died in tragic circumstances. He didn't always enjoy the easiest of relationships with cricketing authority, but to me he was an inspirational coach and a lovely, gentle man to whom I owe a lot.

While I was still at Wells I went to some of the regular cricket weeks at Millfield. Colin Atkinson, another ex-Somerset cricketer – and a good hockey player, too – had taken over as headmaster. I got to know him quite well, and later I was invited to join in some of the Somerset schoolboys' coaching sessions that he organised. As had been the case in my primary school days, I took the chance to play, and to learn more about the game, wherever and whenever the opportunity arose.

I played whenever I was home from school, too, and in the summer holidays, and was putting in some decent performances for the

NASH TAKES 25 WICKETS IN SIX DAYS

YOUNG BATSMAN WITH PROMISE

My final season with Abergavenny was an incredibly exciting one.

Abergavenny 2nd XI, with both bat and ball. Then in 1959, when I had just turned 15 and following a particularly promising innings for the 2nd XI against Usk, I got my first real chance to show what I could do in the 1st XI. I was selected for the visit to our neighbours and great rivals Panteg, at that time one of the strongest sides in the area. Effectively, this was my first team debut because in the game five years earlier I had played only to make up the numbers on the field. The Panteg match was a good day for me as I was able to help to save us from defeat with an unbeaten innings of 61. Over the next few seasons my first team appearances increased and I was soon a regular whenever home from Wells.

It would probably be fair to say that I enjoyed the freedoms of the cricket field more than the confines of the classroom. In fact, I took every opportunity to play (at school and at home in the holidays), and seemed hardly ever to be out of a pair of whites – unless it was to swap them for a hockey or rugby kit! Unsurprisingly, though passable, my academic work did not shine. The head summed things up on one of my last reports: "If Malcolm could only bring his powers of concentration from the cricket field into the classroom, his academic achievement would be considerably greater!" Anyway, I decided to leave Wells after my first year in the sixth form and in 1962, aged 17, I returned to Abergavenny.

Back in Monmouthshire, working as a trainee accountant with the local builders' merchants, I enjoyed having some wages burning

I enjoyed my time at Wells, but always preferred to be in sports kit than school uniform!

a hole in my pocket, and revelled in the new-found freedom which enabled me to play and practise regularly for my home town club. My cricket continued to improve and I hit some good, consistent form, usually batting first wicket down and opening the bowling. Before too long, I went from being seen as a regular first team player to being a key first team all-rounder, and in 1964 got tantalizingly close to completing the 'double', finishing the season with 944 runs and 85 wickets.

My form continued into the next season, too, and I was in the wickets early. A highlight of the summer was getting a memorable '10-for' (10 for 29) in our Whitsun Bank Holiday Monday fixture against Lydney, another great local rival. This was to prove to be the only time in my career that I took all ten wickets in an innings, though ten seasons later I was to come very close to doing the same for Glamorgan. I still remember how exciting the achievement at Lydney was, and how much attention it received in the local press. It was the beginning of an amazing run of bowling form and a productive week. In four games, over six days, I took 25 wickets for a total of 110 runs.

Ready for one of my last games as a fully-fledged Abergavenny player – the return fixture against Lydney. Brian Shackleton, the captain, is seated in the centre of the front row.

When we played Lydney in the return fixture at Avenue Road on August Bank Holiday Monday, I had already passed the 100 wickets mark for the season. I was still in good form with the bat, too, and my innings of 70 saw me pass 1,000 runs for the season – the first Abergavenny player to achieve the double for ten years. I ended my summer with 126 wickets and 1,143 runs for my hometown club. It was a great season in a talented team well captained by Brian Shackleton, opening batsman and very good skipper and motivator – and our local chemist!

In fact, there were a number of very able cricketers in that Abergavenny side. Geoff Richardson was another key batsman, and an excellent hockey player too. Mike Farr was another hockey-playing cricketer, a bowler of prolific off-cutters who, on a wicket with a bit in it, could be unplayable. Mike was good enough to have played first-class cricket. We also had the services of Bob Jennings, Lewis White's brother-in-law, who bowled orthodox slow left-arm, and two players who were particularly important to my efforts with the ball – John Powell, our very capable wicketkeeper, and Alan Lloyd, a reliable opening bowler who would often share the new ball.

The 1965 season was significant for me for another reason, too. I had the chance to 'guest' outside my home environment and to test myself with a different set of cricketers. Also, very importantly, to get feedback from people outside my local club community and, quite unexpectedly, this experience almost opened the door to professional cricket – and the opportunity of a new life over the border!

At Abergavenny we didn't play league cricket. We did at Ebbw Vale – that was the South Wales and Monmouthshire League. But at Abergavenny it was all friendlies – against local Welsh teams and also against sides from neighbouring counties like Herefordshire, Gloucestershire and Worcestershire.

A fixture we always particularly looked forward to was against Worcester City. I remember the excitement of playing on the New Road ground in a fixture against them – though their base was at Norton Barracks. I played at both venues several times. The Worcester match was almost always a tight and exciting contest. They were a good bunch, and I always got on well with their guys. That's what the game is all about: you make friendships, some of them lifelong. I invariably did well against Worcester City and during the 1965 season was invited to join them on their annual tour to England's south coast. We were based near Portsmouth, and spent a wonderful week in July just playing and talking cricket – and having a few beers! We played United Services, we played Havant, and we played a couple of games in Sussex, one being an incredible tied match at Horsham – a super game of cricket. It was all great fun!

I had a pretty good week with the City, getting some runs and wickets. I hadn't realised it at the time, but a couple of the guys on the tour had

In 1965, at the Avenue Road ground.

strong links with the county side. They were Worcester City skipper Mike Powell, who would become a life-long friend, and Mike Jones, a member of the Worcestershire CCC committee who would go on to serve a term as chair of their cricket committee. During the course of our final game of the tour they came up with an amazing suggestion. They asked if I would be interested in the possibility of coming up to Worcester the next year and being part of the county set-up. They offered to make all the necessary arrangements for me to have a trial at New Road if I wished. Of course, I was excited by that possibility. It was a massive compliment and a great chance, especially as Worcestershire were such a strong and successful side at that time. I said I'd like time to think it over and check a few things with my folks. Several times during the autumn of 1965 I was on the verge of following it up, but I'll admit I was a bit over-awed by the idea, too. It was a big step.

Anyway, Christmas came and went and I still hadn't done anything about it. Then I found myself talking to my father one bleak January day: there was no live cricket from sunnier climes on TV then to brighten up the winter mornings! I told Dad I'd finally decided to try and make it in cricket, and to push forward with the idea of a Worcestershire trial.

My father was, as always, supportive. He had just one question, and one suggestion.

"Why don't you want to play for Glamorgan?"

I answered that I probably did, but that it was from Worcestershire that the opportunity had come.

"Well, if you want to play for Glamorgan – and Wales – why don't you write to their club secretary? You've nothing to lose."

Phil Clift, second left, coaching aspiring county cricketers.

To be honest I'm not sure that I expected much to come of my letter. I was quite well known as a promising young club cricketer in the local area, and had been for some time, but I had never been part of any Glamorgan academy-type or youth cricket set-up. I also had no contact at Glamorgan, though my father had met Phil Clift, the Glamorgan coach, when they had briefly served together as instructors at an Army camp in Brecon.

So, on January 24th, 1966, I posted my letter addressed to Mr W. Wooller at the Glamorgan CCC office, 6 High Street, Cardiff. Admittedly, more in hope than expectation!

3
1966 and All That

'Alan Jones remembers the winter nets at Neath ...
"If Malcolm got you out in the nets, you wouldn't stop
hearing about it. He'd be in the dressing room, telling
everybody he'd rolled you over."'
Douglas Miller

To my surprise and delight, a letter personally signed by Wilf Wooller, club secretary, arrived by return of post. I could hardly contain my excitement, but there it was in black and white:

'... on the question of playing County Cricket, Glamorgan would be interested in giving you a trial.'

This was to be at the Neath Indoor School. As I read on, it got even better.

'Assuming things go satisfactorily for you, you would be offered a Summer Contract probably on the basis of £10 a week, and your future then would depend entirely on how you progressed that season.

Assuming you made satisfactory progress and the County thought there was a future for you in the first-class game, you would then be offered a more permanent Contract on an annual basis.'

So now it was up to me to show what I could do.

As Wilf suggested, I telephoned him at the High Street office to accept the offer of the April trial, together with his offer to meet in Cardiff. The upshot of these conversations was a suggestion that I should join the regular winter Wednesday evening net sessions for Glamorgan's 'up-and-coming' young players – people like Eifion Jones, Euros Lewis, Billy Slade, Tony Cordle, Ian Morris and Roger Davis who were soon to become good friends and teammates.

So, every Wednesday evening until the trial itself I borrowed my mother's Ford Anglia and made the round trip to Neath, driving like the wind. I thought I was Stirling Moss! These net sessions were always a big thrill and Wednesdays

GLAMORGAN COUNTY CRICKET CLUB

All correspondence should be addressed to
THE SECRETARY
Telephone No. 29956

6 HIGH STREET
CARDIFF

27th January, 1966

M. Nash, Esq.,
Lydstep,
Windsor Road,
Abergavenny,
Mon.

Dear Mr. Nash,

In reply to your letter of the 24th instant, on the question of playing County Cricket, Glamorgan would be interested in giving you a trial. It seems to me the best and fairest way of carrying this out would be for you to report to the Glamorgan nets at the start of the season, which will be the 13th April, at the Neath Indoor School by 10.30 a.m. Nets are then a continuous process right into the season with practice games, etc. During this period all your travelling expenses will be covered and an allowance will be made for your meals, but in practice most of the boys find it more convenient to take sandwiches and coffee. Tea is brewed up down there if required.

Assuming things go satisfactorily for you, you would be offered a Summer Contract probably on the basis of £10 a week, and your future then would depend entirely on how you progressed that season.

Assuming you made satisfactory progress and the County thought there was a future for you in the first-class game, you would then be offered a more permanent Contract on an annual basis.

This should clarify some of the points which must arise in your mind, but no doubt you would like to have a chat with me at some point in the future, and I will be happy to see you any time you wish when you are in Cardiff. I am usually in this office between 10.00 a.m. and 5.00 p.m. Mondays to Fridays, and it would be simpler for you, when you have the opportunity, just to ring up and see if I am in and you can then drop in for a chat.

Phil Clift sends his kind regards to your father with whom he served in the War and, of course, knows on the cricket field.

Kind regards,

Yours sincerely,

Wilfred Wooller

Wilfred Wooller
Secretary

The secretary's offer of a trial with Glamorgan CCC.

could never come round quickly enough. They were a good opportunity for me to get to know Phil Clift and the guys, and to get used to the facilities. So, when April 13th finally arrived and I moved to digs in Skewen, I felt quite at home with the set-up at Neath.

By modern standards the indoor nets, housed in a dilapidated old hangar-like red-brick building beside the pavilion, were not an amazing facility. The building itself was spartan and damp, and the nets always seemed cold and noisy, but they certainly did the job and had some positive features. In

Wilf Wooller.

particular, I was impressed by the range of surfaces on offer. I loved this concept – and, looking back, it was ahead of its time.

We had three quite different nets.

One had a teak wood floor – quick and bouncy. That was the end net, right in front of the senior dressing room. There was a big canvas screen from ceiling to floor which was the backdrop, the sight screen. There was a two foot gap outside the changing room, for you to walk round the nets.

The middle net was a green linoleum. Low bounce and slowish. The ball didn't do an awful lot. Nothing. Zippo!

The surface in the third net was rubberised, a bit like the material on a conveyor-belt. Again slowish, but it turned. It turned a lot, in fact.

So I knew the score when, as instructed by Wilf's letter, I reported to the Neath Indoor School for the first morning of the season – and the first morning of my official Glamorgan trial. It was April 13th, 1966.

There were two distinct groups, and two changing rooms. The first team players – the senior players – used the changing room just behind the 'fast' net. The others – 'first team challengers' – were a mixture of club and ground players, new recruits, and others – in fact, all of us who were not regular first-team players. We were ushered into the second changing room – the colder one!

Of course, I knew which net I wanted to bowl in but I also realised that I was in the junior camp. So, which should I go for? I needn't have worried. Ossie Wheatley, Jeff Jones and the other senior bowlers were straight on to the wooden floor, and I was directed to the middle net. Fair enough. After all, I was a young newcomer, and someone who was there essentially as a batsman who could bowl a bit, too.

Thankfully, I managed some pace and bounce out of the green lino – I'd had plenty of time on it during the Wednesday evening sessions – and after only one over Phil Clift said: "Right, Nash, you come into this net." I swapped

The Gnoll at Neath, showing the indoor nets to the left of the pavilion. Very basic in some ways, but ahead of their time in others!

places with Euros. Now I was on the teak boards – where I had wanted to be. I'd been upgraded – economy to first-class!

The first team batsmen were batting in order so I found myself bowling to Alan Jones and getting him in some trouble. In fact, I had him in trouble a couple of times – I beat the outside edge and got a couple of nicks – and I never moved out of that net again.

In a very short time, the balance had changed. I had become a bowler who could bat a bit. It was a good feeling. I remember giving myself a talking to. 'Enjoy yourself, son. Don't screw anything up now.'

It might sound big-headed, but I found I could give all the batters a difficult time. Not from a pace point of view, but because of sideways movement. I'd swing the ball late and beat the outside edge. Or I'd bowl them. Or rap them on the pads.

Looking back, it was an interesting model and one that, although I enjoyed it at the time, I wouldn't advocate as good practice. In hindsight, it probably wasn't the best way to organise net practice. Years later, when I coached in the United States, I wouldn't let our bowlers bowl at our batters. They were good bowlers, and I didn't want them upsetting the batsmen or shattering their confidence by playing and missing too often. So, for the batsmen, it was always throw-downs - concentrating on getting the ball in the middle of the bat - and, for the bowlers, I'd get them bowling at a six inch deep rectangle. "I don't want you bowling at batters – you can bowl at that instead."

I have to admit, however, that bowling at the batters at Neath was a good experience, especially getting them in difficulty sometimes – and reminding them about it later. Alan Jones has spoken of the battles with Don Shepherd and me, and what he remembered as 'real competition and satisfaction on both sides'. It was great fun and my enthusiasm obviously left an impression on the batsmen, but nets were serious, too. You were bowling for your place in the side. If you could get these guys into trouble, you'd get the opposition into trouble, as well.

Of course, there's a huge difference between bowling in the nets and bowling out in the middle. It's a totally different feel – chalk and cheese – and that applies whether you're a batter or a bowler. Either way, your experiences are limited because you aren't out – or you haven't taken a wicket – unless the stumps are knocked over. So nets are great for getting you into nick, and to iron out any technical problems you might have. That's what they are for. They aren't there for you to score 150 or get '5-for', and, of course, they can't ever properly replicate that competitive element out in the middle – however hard you try. You have the mental exercise of converting what you've done indoors to a game situation.

I was a good net bowler. Could never get enough of it. I'd very rarely get a bat, though. I asked Phil Clift one day: "Coach, is there any chance of me getting a knock here?"

"Maybe next week," was the reply. You didn't argue about these things. You were a junior player. "You're here to bowl at these boys. Get plenty of practice. Then we want you bowling in the middle. Whatever you get with the bat will be a bonus."

It didn't take Glamorgan long to decide they liked the look of me. I had been expecting to wait for weeks before hearing how they rated my trial but, only two days later, I had a letter saying they'd be pleased to offer me a contract for the summer of 1966.

Nor did it take me long – even less than those two days – for me to decide that this was what I wanted. I knew straight away that a career in cricket was for me. I felt completely at home. I talked things over briefly with my folks, applied successfully for leave of absence for the summer from Robert Price and Sons, and became a professional cricketer.

Soon we moved from Neath to the Arms Park in Cardiff – and outdoor nets. We reported to the pavilion on the first floor, half-way up the old North Stand that was shared with the rugby ground next door. It was a good pavilion – I liked it despite its awful corrugated tin roof. Club captain Ossie Wheatley was there, together with every member of the playing staff. Ossie led a general chat about our goals and ambitions for the season, outlining what was expected of us as players, and as a team – what were we realistically aiming to achieve that summer? Then he threw it open to us all to join in – well, to the senior players, really. "Does anyone want to ask any questions or make a comment?" offered Ossie. 'Better not say anything,' I thought, 'or should I?' Anyway, in the end discretion proved the better part of valour. I didn't say a word.

I was simply delighted to be involved in that meeting. To be part of the squad. My life had changed so much in such a short time. I was a professional cricketer, and my first season was about to start. I couldn't wait to get out on to the field. We were already changed into whites, looking very smart and business-like, but there were no nets up.

"Ok," says Phil Clift, "Nash, Davis, Lewis, Jones – you come with me." We followed him to the depths of the old North Stand where the nets had been stored – not very carefully – for the winter. Six months of filth and dust and grime. "See those nets. Take them over to the field and get them up, okay?"

We struggled across with the nets and posts, managed to put them up and, for good measure and to impress the coach, cut and rolled the practice wickets at the edge of the outfield.

Phil Clift had played nearly 200 games for Glamorgan before becoming coach (and later, on Wilf Wooller's retirement, secretary)

You can't imagine that happening today, can you? Anyway, having put the equipment away, we returned cheerfully from under the rugby stand, ready to at last show what we could do on grass with bat and ball.

We were intercepted by Phil Clift. "Where do you boys think you're going?"

"Going to play in the nets, coach."

"You're joking! You look like you've been sweeping chimneys."

"Well, the stand and the nets were filthy, coach, but we've got it all sorted," I reassured him. "They're up and we're ready to have a bowl."

"Not today, you're not. Not unless you've got clean kit with you. You're not playing cricket looking like that."

So that was that – until the next day, anyway. We looked on, disconsolately, as the others practised across the other side of the field. It was an important lesson Phil felt we had to learn, and perhaps it sunk in as I've certainly always been a stickler for being properly turned out on the field.

1966 was a wonderful year for me. From April onwards, I think I must have played cricket every day of the week! What a life! But it was a steep learning curve, too. One of the important things I learnt was what was required from a physical point of view, but I was fortunate in that respect. I was pretty fit, and built like a bean-pole in those days. I never got tired. The more I bowled or batted, the better I felt.

Most weekends I was back playing for Abergavenny CC – but now as a Glamorgan pro on loan! In those days, Glamorgan used to attach all their uncapped players to a local league club. I had spells with Swansea, Gowerton and Llanelli, but for the first year they let me keep the link with my hometown club. It was a good scheme for a young cricketer. You were the professional and expected to put in a hard shift and a decent performance in each game. You'd open the batting or go in number three, or you'd bowl 25 overs, and there was an expectation that you'd be good for a half-century or better, or at least a '5-for'. On the following Monday, Phil would ask you how you'd done and we all had to report back – in detail. Sometimes, if the 1st XI had a home match, the skipper would sit in too. If you weren't doing as well as you should be, Phil would want to know why and, of course, if the club you were attached to contacted Glamorgan with any critical comments you'd be in very hot water indeed!

Then during the week, back with the squad in Cardiff, we had plenty of outdoor netting and a full programme of practice games, club and ground matches, and 2nd XI fixtures.

I remember the excitement of my first appearance for 'the Twos', and the first time I wore the Glamorgan cap and sweater. Unlike the blooming daffodil motif of the 1st XI, the 2nd XI's cap reminded us of our place in the club's pecking order with just a daffodil bud, while the sweater had no motif at all – just the navy and gold trim. It was a two-day game at Bridgend's Newbridge Fields ground at the end of April 1966. Our opponents were Warwickshire Seconds.

We won the toss and batted. Our side was a typical mix of some of Glamorgan's ground staff – Billy Slade, Roger Davis and Eifion Jones – plus some more established cricketers like University of Wales student Hamish 'The Dutchman' Miller and our captain, Phil Clift, who, at 47, was more than double the age of most of his charges!

Eifion batted number three. He was very well regarded as a batsman from the outset, and two of his earliest appearances for the first team would be as a number five batsman – with David Evans behind the stumps – but at Bridgend he was keeping, too.

I did okay with the bat, going in at number seven. I got into double figures in each innings, but lost my wicket twice to the slow left-arm spin of Ronnie Miller.

I also got a wicket, the first to go down in Warwickshire's first innings, and my first wicket ever for a Glamorgan side – B.A. Richardson c &

b Nash 2 – only eight minutes into the game. Bryan Richardson was, perhaps, not such a prized victim as either of his elder and more famous brothers would have been (Dick and Peter both represented England) but Bryan was certainly no mug with the bat and played 40 first-class matches for Warwickshire – and scored a couple of centuries.

Another familiar name in the Warwickshire team was Eddie Hemmings – a raw 17-year-old off-break bowler and, like me, making his way in his first season as a professional. Eddie, of course, went on to play for England, though he didn't get the first of his 16 caps until he reached the ripe old age of 33!

There were no wickets for me in the second innings. With the pitch taking spin the two Lewises, David Wyndham and Brian, ran through Warwickshire, sharing seven wickets. A solid, workmanlike victory for us by 75 runs, and a good start for me in Glamorgan's colours.

The hard work of a professional cricketer kicked-in, with more practice, more nets, more friendlies, and more club and ground and 2nd XI games. I was thrilled and excited at being part of the set-up, and all the time hoping that before too long the chance to swap my 2nd XI sweater for one with the daffodil of the 1st XI would present itself. Then suddenly it happened. Well, nearly!

Almost two months after the Bridgend game, I was named as 12th Man for the Championship match against Surrey at Cardiff Arms Park.

It was late June 1966, and soccer had encroached into cricket's short summer. Television screens and newspapers were full of the forthcoming World Cup in England, with the home team's opening match against Uruguay only a couple of weeks away. I was keeping an eye on the World Cup, of course, especially as I had played cricket against several of the England footballers including Martin Peters, Geoff Hurst and skipper Bobby Moore in a very enjoyable benefit match in Essex the year before, but now the focus of my excitement was very much Cardiff Arms Park, not Wembley Stadium.

Surrey, Championship winners three years in a row in the 1950s, were still a formidable team with some outstanding players – Micky Stewart, John Edrich, Pat Pocock, Graham Roope and Geoff Arnold. Down in Glamorgan, though, we were finding things tough. Some promising individual performances, but too much inconsistency. The rebuilding process under captain Ossie Wheatley was well underway, but we were not yet the finished article.

Simply put, we were awful against Surrey and succumbed to a heavy defeat by nearly 200 runs. We started our first innings right at the end of the first day, with Tony Cordle – much to his delight – opening the batting as night watchman. The plan was flawed, however, as 'Speedy' got out without a run on the board and a second watchman, a less enthusiastic Euros Lewis, being

I made my first-class debut at Cardiff Arms Park, but it was the only match I played there.

sent out to keep a bewildered Roger Davis company. This meant Tony Lewis eventually batting number six, and legendary opener Bernard Hedges number seven, in our re-jigged batting order.

As it turned out, our more illustrious batsmen didn't have to wait long the next morning to get their pads on. We were all out for 90, with Peter Walker scoring half the runs as seamers Stuart Storey and G.G. 'Horse' Arnold taking five wickets each. Even worse was to follow. Peter Walker was top scorer again – with 19 to his name – as we were ignominiously bowled out for only 83 second time round. Another five wickets for Storey, with Arnold and Roope completing the rout.

There was, however, some personal consolation in such a humiliating defeat as I found watching Surrey's three international fast bowlers in action a valuable learning experience and, although I don't think I got on to the field of play (unless it was to carry a sweater on or off), I got a real buzz from being in and around the dressing room, rubbing shoulders with some Glamorgan and Surrey stalwarts. The dressing room was, naturally, rather subdued, but I kept out of the way and soaked it all up.

I hadn't realised it at the time, but this 12th man experience was intended to get me prepared for my first team debut in Glamorgan's next match against Cambridge University.

So, two days later, I was in the same home changing room again, but this time as a player, a full participant, down to bat at number seven in a Glamorgan line-up that included several established first-team regulars like Alan Jones, Peter Walker and, of course, Tony Lewis, captaining the side in this match against his old university. There were also a number of other youngsters, like me at the start of their career – people I had got to know at Neath, like Eifion Jones, Len Hill and Euros Lewis.

I must admit, it was a strange feeling being in the dressing-room as a full member of the 1st XI. For a start, I had no idea which was my space to get changed. Nobody told you where to go, but they did tell you where you couldn't go, and where the regulars changed. David Evans, Ossie and Shep had their own spaces, of course. Thankfully it was a big room, so finding a spot wasn't a problem. I remember standing there half-changed and thinking of all the Glamorgan 'greats' who had used the same room, the same pegs, over the years. It gave me goose-bumps!

It was a gentle start for me. Tony won the toss and elected to bat. The first day was rain affected, and we lost two wickets in scoring an uneventful 102 by the close, but it gave me plenty of time to get used to being in the team. We declared early next morning, with 168 for 4 on the board and a half-century against the skipper's name. Tony Cordle and Hamish Miller took the new ball but

Ossie Wheatley was Glamorgan skipper in my debut season ...

... but Tony Lewis skippered the side in my first-class debut against Cambridge University.

Malcolme Nash, the Abergavenny all rounder made a promising first class debut, when he played for Glamorgan in their game against Cambridge University at Cardiff Arms Park last week.

He did not bat in the Glamorgan first innings which was declared at four wickets, but in the second innings he scored a stylish 16 before being bowled.

He helped Len Hill, the Newport County footballer, who compiled a half-century, to add 41 for the third wicket in half an hour.

There was great excitement in Abergavenny at the news of my Glamorgan debut.

I was longing to get it in my hands on it. Eventually Tony said: "You have a go next from the pavilion end, Malcolm." It was the right end for me at the Arms Park, with the prevailing wind coming across the ground from the river. At the start of the over, Tony tossed me the ball and just said: "Go and do what you're good at." Some of the other guys shouted "Good luck".

I'll admit I was pretty excited about the game. I had butterflies – but I had butterflies before every game I ever played! It's difficult to explain how nervous excitement gets to you. I'd already played hockey at quite a high level, so I had a feel for a bigger occasion. My knees weren't shaking or anything, but I certainly was nervous – at least until I'd got the first ball out of the way.

The University openers had passed the 50 mark and were looking reasonably comfortable but, with the total on 68, I pushed one down the leg-side and Eifion stumped opener K.P.W.J. (Keith) McAdam – an ex-Millfield Schoolboy. My first ever first-class wicket, and it felt good! It was a smart piece of wicket-keeping – and the first of many occasions when Eifion and I would combine to take a wicket. The Nash/Jones combination would become a familiar entry on Glamorgan score-cards in the years to come.

No doubt Eifion's glove-work was appreciated by umpire Hugo Yarnold, the former Worcestershire keeper who was standing with D.J. Evans – well known for officiating in 2nd XI cricket but appearing here in his only first-class match. Hugo went on to umpire in Test matches in 1967 and 1968, but was tragically killed in a road accident as he returned home from officiating at a county match at Northampton in 1974. I remember that if you bowled an outstanding ball or a particularly good over from Hugo's end he would always reward you with, "Well done, kid" and an encouraging smile.

I didn't have time to take in the excitement of my wicket before I'd got a second, Cambridge's number three, Anthony Gould, trapped lbw for a duck. The first of many lbw decisions to go my way over the years – a total of 261 (out of 991 wickets) over my career. If I'd bowled in the modern era of umpire referrals – and the greater willingness to give lbws that television replays have brought to the game – that wicket haul would have been a lot higher.

So, a decent start for me with the ball: 6-1-30-2. I was happy enough with that, though I would have liked to have done better, of course, and remember worrying later that perhaps I hadn't done enough.

When we batted a second time, I was promoted to number four to give me some time in the middle, so I now also got my first first-class runs – 16 before being bowled by David Acfield. 'Ackers' was also in his first first-class season, and we went on to play against each other many times in his long (400-plus first-class games) and successful career with Essex. David was also a very talented fencer, representing Great Britain in the 1968 and 1972 Olympic Games, and winning gold for England in the 1970 Commonwealth Games in Edinburgh. He managed to combine his cricketing and fencing careers, though all the time he was fencing internationally he could not be paid for playing cricket!

Eifion's smart leg-side stumping got me my first Glamorgan wicket – the first of many wickets we combined to take.

A particular memory for me from the game was the added excitement of bowling to the West Indian wicketkeeper Deryck Murray. Deryck, then 23, was captaining Cambridge University having already played in all five Tests in the 1963 series against England.

By coincidence, the West Indies were touring again while we were playing Cambridge University. In fact, the drawn second Test at Lord's had finished only the day before, with Glamorgan's Jeff Jones in the England side, for whom Basil D'Oliveira was making his debut. 'Jackie' Hendriks and David Allan shared the summer's wicket-keeping duties for the tourists in the absence of Murray. Captain of the formidable West Indies team was Garry Sobers who enjoyed an amazing series average of over 103, as well as taking 20 wickets. At Lord's he scored a brilliant second-innings 163 not out to save the match.

So the sporting pages of the south Wales evening papers on June 22nd, 1966, included the names of Sobers – acknowledging his outstanding innings at Lord's as captain of the formidable West Indies – and Malcolm Nash – mentioning

Deryck Murray, Cambridge University captain, had already been capped by the West Indies.

briefly my Glamorgan debut against Cambridge University. Before too long our names would be on the same page again, but this time interwoven in the same story.

That was the end of my first-class cricket for the season, and the end of cricket for me – and for Glamorgan – at the old Cardiff Arms Park. During the winter, we moved to our new home at Sophia Gardens.

I reckoned it had been a pretty good first season, and I was starting to feel comfortable and confident in my Glamorgan surroundings. A lot had happened in my first season, but ahead now was another winter of hard work – in the Neath nets, and back with Price's, the builders merchants, in Abergavenny.

Our 1967 pre-season work in the indoor nets included a couple of weeks at the nearby Afan Lido. It was a useful and very enjoyable part of our preparation. I thought it was great and really threw myself into it! Bryn Thomas was the main organiser, with Glamorgan's Alan Rees. We also saw a lot of Graham Jenkins, Richard Burton's brother, who was the council's link between us and the lido.

We'd use the facilities at Neath in the mornings, then use the lido for the rest of the day. Those of us living too far away to travel daily – the guys from 'the east' – slept in dormitories at the lido itself.

Our lido work was officially 'special training', and involved a whole range of activities both in the gymnasium and on the space outside – including the nearby beach. I can remember running on the beach and in the soft sand of

I thoroughly enjoyed our pre-season training at the Afan Lido. Here is the 1967 squad, with me third from the left in the middle row.

the dunes, running up and down steps, playing hockey and soccer, heading-tennis, badminton, basket-ball, and the inevitable circuit training, of course, but not weights – not the bowlers, anyway. Don Shepherd was very firm about not letting any of the bowlers on the weights in case they got muscle-bound – not a great condition for a bowler. He felt that a bowler got stronger – in all the right places – by bowling more!

It was a wide range of activities, all helping to get us into good physical shape. We went from one thing to another and we got fit, fit, fit! The programme was also designed, however, to help mental discipline by focussing on things like concentration, determination, endurance, identifying strategies – and trust and team work, of course. After all, those were qualities we needed as professional cricketers, and that's what I now was.

'Shep'.

I had to keep pinching myself, but it wasn't a dream. I was a professional cricketer. It may sound big-headed, but I knew I could make a go of it in the first-team and Championship cricket, and I wondered how long it would be before I got the opportunity to prove it.

That chance was to present itself sooner than I dared hope.

4

Baptism of Fire

'The difference between a fast bowler and a good fast bowler is not extra muscle but extra brains.'
Fred Trueman

A pre-season injury to Tony Cordle gave me my Championship debut.

"Speedy's' done his ankle. You're in the side for Harrogate."

What a prospect! Can you imagine how exciting it was to hear this news from our new skipper, Tony Lewis? My Championship debut was to be against the reigning County Champions, Yorkshire, who had won the 1966 title comfortably from chasers Worcestershire and Somerset. They would go on to make that a hat-trick, winning in '67 and '68, too – before we would break the sequence with our own Championship success!

Obviously I was sorry that my mate Tony Cordle had injured his ankle in pre-season nets, but this was the chance I'd wanted and it had come earlier than I had dared hope. The first game of the season. My first Championship game, away to the mighty Yorkshire.

Okay, so I was playing because of injury to our first-choice opening bowler. Barbadian Tony Cordle, the county's first overseas fast-bowler, had come into the Glamorgan side from club cricket with Cardiff and had established himself as a first-team regular after making his debut in 1963. However, I had been in and around the squad for a while, netting and practising with the first team, and I had a first-class match under my belt – even if that had been against more modest university opposition. So I felt the chance was deserved, and I was determined to make the most of it.

It wasn't the first time I'd stepped-in to replace an injured teammate. My first ever game for Abergavenny, as a 10-year-old, had been because the selected player had dropped out at the last minute. I recalled, too, how Garry Sobers, my boyhood hero, had got both his first match for his beloved Barbados and his first international cap as a late replacement for an unavailable player! In 1953, age 16, he had been pulled into the Barbados team – batting at number nine – because West Indian fast-bowler Frank King was rested at the request on the national selectors. Sobers' first Test cap had come just a year later, after only two first-class games for Barbados, as a late replacement for the indisposed left-arm spinner Alf Valentine. So perhaps me replacing 'Speedy' was written in the stars!

To make things even better, we were going direct from Harrogate, venue for our fixture against Yorkshire, to another three away fixtures – against Essex and Leicestershire in the Championship, and Hampshire in the Gillette Cup. Then, after a couple of free days, to Hove to play Sussex. This wasn't some unkind whim of the fixture-compilers. It was because the winter of 1967-68 saw us leave the Arms Park, our Cardiff base since Glamorgan had joined the Championship in 1921, and take up residence just across the main road and the River Taff at our new Sophia Gardens ground. We had prudently requested that the cricketing authorities give us a little additional 'good weather time' to get things fully ready at the new headquarters.

In contrast to our brand new ground, the historic St. George's Road ground at Harrogate had been hosting Yorkshire fixtures since 1882, the same season that it hosted a match between an England XI and an Australian touring side. I knew that guys who had played there before enjoyed the venue. It had a reputation for attracting a large and knowledgeable (though sometimes unforgiving) crowd, and we and our supporters always seemed to be popular visitors. In fact, five years earlier there had been a ground record Championship crowd of over 13,000 on a day during a match against Glamorgan. The pitch was usually pretty decent, too, though we were a little apprehensive as we drove up to Harrogate because, the previous season, Ray Illingworth had recorded the incredible figures of 7 for 6 in Gloucestershire's second innings (which, with his seven wicket haul in the first innings, had given him match figures of 14 for 65).

Whether or not the early-season surface would behave itself wasn't the main problem. What took the wind out of our sails was that, when we arrived for play on the first morning, the pitch was covered in snow! There was a delayed start while the field was cleared, but conditions were far from ideal. It was bitterly cold, even in the sanctuary of the dressing-room, and the umpires agreed before play started that hot tea would be brought out at regular intervals to all those shivering on the field.

Ray Illingworth, who had begun his long first-class career 16 years earlier and was already well-established at international level, was by no means the only 'big name' in the XI that Yorkshire, skippered by Fred Trueman, fielded against us when we batted on the first morning of the 1967 Championship season. Their scorecard read more like a representative XI than a county side: G. Boycott, K. Taylor, D.E.V. Padgett, J.H. Hampshire, D. Wilson, P.J. Sharpe, P.M. Stringer, R. Illingworth, J.G. Binks (wkt), F.S. Trueman (capt), A.G. Nicholson. What a team to make your debut against!

Eight of those players had already won England caps, and several were still very much in the selectors' minds. Another, medium-pace bowler Tony Nicholson, had been invited to tour South Africa with the MCC but had been forced to withdraw through injury. Tony went on to become a very good friend of mine. He was a terrific guy. He took me under his wing after that

Billy Slade played in the season's opener against Yorkshire. Billy could have been a very significant cricketer, but things didn't work out and he left the first-class game at the end of the 1967 season.

first meeting at Harrogate, and he helped me a lot. We talked a lot about bowling and I learned a tremendous amount from him.

A tenth player, John Hampshire, was already being discussed as a future England batsman and would win his first international cap the following season. (For the record, in the return fixture at Swansea six weeks later, Yorkshire had the luxury of adding the names of B. Leadbeater, G.A. Cope and emerging teenager C.M. Old to that already formidable list.)

Peter Stringer, a young right-arm fast-medium bowler who later moved to Leicestershire for a couple of seasons before giving up the professional game, was the only 'unknown' in their side. Like me, he was in his first senior season and was also making his Championship debut in the Harrogate match.

Stringer, however, had started his season a few days earlier – bowling as if he, too, was an international. He came into the

Glamorgan game straight from playing for Yorkshire, as Champion County, in the traditional season-opener v. MCC at Lord's. His victims were Colin Milburn, Peter Parfitt, David Steele and our own Tony Lewis (one of four Glamorgan representatives in the side). His figures were an astonishing 4 for 10 in 7 overs!

So, perhaps predictably, it was Peter Stringer, and not one of the array of England bowlers, who got my wicket – bowled for a duck. I wasn't doing myself justice with the bat, but these were still early days. At the same time, having started my trial with Glamorgan as an all-rounder – more batsman than bowler, even – I knew that something was expected of me at the crease.

Unfortunately, a number of my team-mates fared little better and we were dismissed mid-afternoon for a disappointing 130, with only Alan Jones and Billy Slade getting past the teens, and Fred Trueman enjoying an early-season '5-for'. To make matters worse, my duck was a first-baller – and Brian Lewis, coming in after me, went the same way. So the unknown Peter Stringer had the rare distinction of taking a hat-trick in his first Championship match – Morris, I., Nash, M. and Lewis, B., all bowled – and I had the dubious distinction of being the filling in the hat-trick sandwich. It wasn't a good feeling but it certainly added to the drama of the match.

The drama didn't end there. It wasn't long before I found myself, on my debut, sharing the new ball with England's Jeff Jones – and bowling to England's Geoff Boycott and Ken Taylor! Replacing Ken when he was run out early on (not the only batsman on the circuit to be run out partnering Boycott, by any means) was a third international, Doug Padgett, and then John Hampshire who was on the verge of winning the first of his eight England caps. It was a daunting start, but incredibly exciting. It was easily the biggest stage I had played on to date and I got a real buzz from it.

Unfortunately, I didn't get a wicket, though I did have Boycott dropped early in his innings – by Jeff Jones at mid-off – while he was on his way to a century. As a sympathetic Tony Nicholson quietly pointed out, what a first Championship scalp that would have been! My economy rate was decent and I felt I had by no means disgraced myself – finishing with figures of 22-8-58-0 – and I certainly wasn't being dispatched to all corners.

It was Don Shepherd, as reliable as ever, who got Boycott and the other three wickets to fall as Yorkshire eventually moved on to 217 for 5 declared. Their innings was punctuated by a second-day totally lost to rain, and in the end the match petered out in a tame draw.

We packed our bags in the van and set off on the next leg of our early season expedition – Essex at the County Ground, Brentwood – and I was to keep my place in the side!

Playing at Harrogate had been a significant part of what was turning out to be a steepish, but very enjoyable, learning curve, and I was increasingly being

Jeff Jones dropped Geoff Boycott off my bowling – what a first Championship wicket that would have been!

reminded that you learn off the field as well as in the heat of the action in the middle.

One way was by watching other people. In the nets, of course, but also – and crucially – in action in match situations. As at the Arms Park against Surrey the season before, here at the St. George's Road ground was a chance to watch at close quarters a string of high quality fast and fast-medium bowlers, as well as some of the best batsmen in county cricket. I watched and learnt.

The third way – and one that proved invaluable in this and other encounters with Yorkshire – was in conversation. There were so many opportunities in the county game to talk cricket – with the Glamorgan guys, of course, but also with opposition players, and a very important memory from the visit to Harrogate was coming across 'Fiery' Fred Trueman for the first time.

I'd been warned that he was likely to appear in our dressing room to intimidate the new crop of inexperienced young players – and some not so inexperienced or so young, too!

Fred didn't disappoint. We hadn't finished changing when he – together with by his pipe – appeared in our dressing room to introduce himself and to welcome us to God's Own County. Then, having ascertained who the new lads were, Fred helpfully pointed out that the pitch here was a quick one, a strip that some very good batsmen had struggled on, and some equally good batsmen had been injured on – especially when he was bowling. Also, that he was in prime form, faster than ever, having taken five MCC wickets for not-very-many a few days earlier – including that of our new skipper, whose middle stump had apparently ended up just inside the Lord's boundary – and so it went on before he wished us a cheery, "Well, good luck then, lads," and disappeared.

Once you got past Fred's traditional words of welcome, and had met him a few times, he proved so useful to talk to. Here was someone who had made his first-class debut the same year I went to infant school, who was starting his 19th season with Yorkshire, who had played 67 times for his country – and who was prepared to talk cricket with me. In particular, to talk about fast-bowling.

We didn't really chat on this occasion – I just listened – but we did talk a lot during the return fixture at Swansea, and from then on always when we came

F. S. TRUEMAN

Fred Trueman was Yorkshire's skipper in my first Championship match – and a very good person to talk to about fast bowling.

across each other, both before and after his retirement. I think Fred had a grudging liking for Welshmen and he seemed to enjoy his visits to Wales. I don't know if it was because he got lots of wickets against us but he certainly got on well with the Glamorgan guys. Perhaps it was because he was from a mining community – I don't know – but there was an affinity, that's for sure. I remember that I whacked him for four in the return at St. Helen's. I think he'd taken the second new ball, and this one was wide outside off stick – it whistled through cover. It was a super shot – I really enjoyed it. He looked at me and said, "You won't be doing that again, son," and sure enough, I didn't. My off-pole went flying soon after.

I never failed to benefit from those conversations with Fred Trueman. Although a formidable opponent running in to bowl at you, he was always prepared to share his ideas and experience and I would certainly add his name to the list of people who influenced me as a cricketer.

Over the years we talked about grip, shape, elbows – and the need to get some decent weight on your backside! Fred also emphasised the need to keep thinking when bowling – and to out-think the batsman. In fact, we talked about anything and everything that was part of a fast-bowler's trade. Of course, we were different types of opening bowler, but we shared the job in common – and the enemy the other end!

Another very important thing that Fred stressed to me over and over again was the importance of looking after your feet. It was so important for a bowler. Down at Glamorgan, we were fortunate to have the services of an honorary club chiropodist, Trevor Rees, who was very helpful with the bowlers' feet and who would always come to the ground if we needed him. Our own Don Shepherd also always emphasised the need to toughen up and take care of your feet, and more than once during a fixture at Swansea we'd cross the Mumbles Road to have a paddle in the sea. There was nothing better! The soothing salt water healed and hardened at the same time, and restored muscle power. When we were away from St. Helen's, we'd resort to a bowl of salt water.

I always wore two pairs of socks when we were in the field and would always change into dry socks between sessions. I always bought good socks, too. I knew that socks and boots were the most important items in a bowler's kitbag.

My boots were made by Whitings, the boot-makers in Northampton. On the recommendation of one of the guys, I had discovered Mr Whiting's little shop, not far from the County Ground, during one of my first games at Northampton. The small workshop was incredible, crowded with lathes and lasts, hammers and nails. Mr Whiting – I think it was Frank – was a real craftsman who took such pride in the beautiful, kid boots he stitched by hand. On this first visit, he made a template of my foot (with two pairs of socks on, of course) and kept it so that from then on I needed only to phone for new boots – though I often popped in to see him if we were playing up there. Eifion had his boots made there, too – for batting and for wicket-keeping.

I got Mr Whiting to put a sort of drag-plate on my left boot. It wasn't a toe-cap, as such, just a half-inch strip about two-and-a-half inches long pinned to the welt and protecting it, stopping it wearing away. I always had this fitted, and found it very effective in making a pair of boots last longer.

Of course, you were responsible for buying most of your own kit in those days. The club would give you sweaters – long and short-sleeved – as well as your cap, blazer and a tie, but the rest of it was up to you to sort out. You got used to looking after your kit, keeping it clean and smart and to packing and unpacking it, too – that was an important aspect of life on the circuit.

So, with our kit, including a good supply of sturdy socks, safely stowed in the club van and us allocated to cars, we set off for our three-day encounter with Essex at Brentwood. From a personal point of view, this proved to be another good out-ground to play cricket on as we were part of the annual two-match festival (held there until the following season). Festivals were usually good fun. I knew, too, from the chat in the car on the way that the guys looked forward to playing Essex. They reckoned it was almost always a good match.

The Glamorgan team at The Oval in July 1967, my first season of Championship cricket. I didn't play in this game – my first absence after an unbroken run of matches. Standing (l to r): Alan Rees, Len Hill, Roger Davis, Peter Walker, Alan Jones, David Evans and Tony Cordle. Seated: Bernard Hedges, Tony Lewis, Don Shepherd and Ossie Wheatley.

The rain and cold that had spoilt our Yorkshire game had not entirely cleared, but at least it didn't snow again and we were pleased to get through most of the first day's play. Alan Jones got another 50, and lots of us chipped in – I got 29 before being caught behind off West Indian international quick bowler Keith Boyce – to enable a declaration at close-of-play on 210 for 8.

I also managed to get the first Essex wicket to fall, that of left-handed opener Micky Bear, who had scored a century against Glamorgan the previous season. Don Shepherd, economical as ever, with ten of his 21 overs being maidens, got four wickets. Brian Lewis got the other five.

So, we started our second innings just before the end of the second day with a lead of 40. I was starting to feel more comfortable with the bat in my hand again and top-scored with 42 not-out in a disappointing Glamorgan total of 153.

Essex were left a very gettable 195 for victory in 210 minutes, and all-rounder Brian Edmeades nearly got them there single-handed, reaching 94 before becoming one of Jeff Jones' four wickets. While Brian batted, wickets were falling steadily the other end, Don Shepherd getting another four-wicket haul which included a smart stumping by David Evans.

It was a very tense finish. The umpires called 'time' with Essex requiring only 16 more to win but with only one wicket in hand. We were so close!

Then more packing, more driving and a strong Leicestershire side awaiting us at Grace Road.

This wasn't such a good team performance from us and we slid to our first defeat of the season on a poor wicket that suited the spin of Tony Lock who took 7-54 and 6-62. His first innings figures might have been even better, but my improved form with the bat continued and I cost him some runs. I was pleased enough with my bowling form and got a few top-order wickets, including the only hit-wicket dismissal of my career – Clive Inman, the Ceylonese left-hander, for a duck – but as far as I was concerned it was my batting that stood out in this game.

In fact, for me it was another game with a particular personal significance. It was a game that shaped another aspect of my cricketing life. My choice of bat!

When you first came on the Glamorgan staff you were directed to Bill Edwards Sports shop in St. Helen's Road, Swansea – just across from the ground. "Bill will look after you," we were told, so I popped over the road and acquired a couple of Gunn and Moore bats from Bill. He did a special 'two bats for the price of one' deal for young pros coming on to the staff – an early BOGOF promotional offer – but I soon changed to a Stuart Surridge bat, also supplied by Bill, who was a main Surridge dealer and supplied a lot of Surridge equipment to the club, including balls. The Surridge bat suited me better. It felt good when I got some runs at Essex, but I still wasn't sure it was right for me.

Then, when we were at Grace Road, I changed again. I hadn't planned to, but I was introduced to Jock Livingston, an Australian who was working for Gray-Nicolls after his first-class career with Northamptonshire had ended. I think he was in Leicester visiting Tony Lock who was still playing for, and captaining, Western Australia.

Jock gave me a couple of his bats to try, and immediately they felt just right. I used one in the Leicestershire

T. L. LIVINGSTON

COUNTY CRICKETERS

2
T. L. LIVINGSTON
Northamptonshire

Left-hand batsman and out-standing cover fielder. Can also keep wicket. Born in Sydney, Australia, in 1920. Played for New South Wales from 1941 to 1947. Captained the Common-wealth team to India in 1949-50. Scored 210 runs versus Somerset in 1951. He has run up 1000 runs in a season six times. His best season was 1954 when he totalled 2269 runs (average 55.34). In 1949, he achieved the remark-able feat of stumping three bats-men off consecutive balls.

PRESENTED WITH
The ROVER
THE FAMOUS BOYS' PAPER

Australian 'Jock' Livingston had eight seasons with Northamptonshire before turning his hand to bat-making.

6

G. A. R. LOCK
(SURREY)

Tony Lock, aged 26, has been a vital member of the Surrey Championship-winning sides of the last 4 years. A left-arm bowler who really spins the ball, he is improving as a batsman. He toured West Indies in 1953-54 after winning recognition by Wisden's as one of the Five Cricketers of 1953. Last year he took 216 wickets at 14 apiece. His bowling and fielding make him a hostile cricketer, and his enthusiasm is unbounded.

Issued by

G. A. R. LOCK

I got some big hits off Tony Lock at Grace Road – using my new Gray-Nicolls bat.

match and top-scored again – for the second innings running – with a hard-hitting 69. I put Tony Lock into the pavilion a few times, much to the appreciation of our side. I whacked the living daylights out of it! It felt great. It was a major turning point for me, finding a bat I felt really comfortable with and timing some big hits. I thought, 'Right, we'll have some more of this' and, from then on, I was a confirmed Gray-Nicolls man for the rest of my career. They supplied all my clothing, as well as pads and gloves and other things, too.

Soon after the Leicestershire match I went down to their factory at Robertsbridge, north of Hastings, and they made a couple more bats for me there and then. They kept a record of all the details so you could order another bat at any time, but I went down again on a number of occasions. I liked visiting the factory and seeing the bats being made. You could even select the willow you wanted. The bat-makers would look at the available helves with you, and using their experience would help you to choose the prime pieces. Helves with a lot of water-marks – known as butterflies – were best. More butterflies meant more 'zip' in the finished bat. I'd also look for grain that wasn't too narrow because narrower grain indicated harder wood and a bat with not quite as much 'oomph' in it, and I liked 'oomph' when I was batting! Jock and his team used only English willow, the best for bat-making, and I can remember them telling me that the ideal height of a tree was about 15 feet. Taller was probably older, and not so good. There was a lot of science in bat-making – and in bat-choosing, too.

As well as the excitement of the bat-making process itself, I always enjoyed a visit to Robertsbridge because it provided an opportunity to catch up with Jock who was the sort of director of operations there. Great character, Jock. He had been unlucky to miss selection for Australia's 1948 tour squad – Bradman's 'Invincibles' – but had enjoyed a successful career as a left-handed batsman, slow left-arm bowler and occasional keeper with Northamptonshire after a spell in the Lancashire League. Like me, Jock, who made four double-centuries for Northants, used to enjoy hitting the ball hard. From time to time, after a chat with Jock and picking up a few bats in the showroom, I'd have some tweaks done to try out, but essentially I kept to the same specifications – 2lb 7oz/8oz, occasionally as much as 2lb 9oz. All with a short handle and a double grip. Having the extra grip countered the extra weight, so you could use a slightly heavier bat which, with the extra grip or grips, made it feel lighter. It was rumoured that Clive Lloyd sometimes had as many as five grips on his heavy bats! The balance of the bat, as opposed to weight, was everything. It was all about pick-up and balance.

In the end, it was Jack Birkenshaw who got me out at Grace Road. I liked Jack, who was a very good bowler and underrated by some. He had me caught by Brian Booth in the deep, going for another big hit. It was a pity because I was going so well with my new bat. It felt good in my hands. It's amazing how so much cricket is about confidence. You get some runs and you feel you are indestructible – until your next innings, at least – and then you are rolled over for a duck or whatever. That brings you back down to earth with a bump.

Leicestershire took a first-innings lead of well over 100, thanks largely to 96 from opener Maurice Hallam who, two years later, would record his highest score of 210 against us, and also score a century in the same match – a rare achievement that he repeated against Sussex two seasons later. I added insult to injury for Tony Lock. After hitting the ex-England spinner for those big sixes, I got his wicket, too, but that was my only success with the ball that day.

The second time around we were all out for a disappointing 172, leaving Leicestershire only 48 to get – which they did for the loss of three wickets – but at least I helped my season's figures by getting two of them for 15 in six overs.

Championship defeat at Grace Road was followed immediately by Gillette Cup defeat by Hampshire at the United Services ground in Portsmouth – though by the tantalisingly narrow margin of 16 runs in a high-scoring game. Our season

Jack Birkenshaw, Leicestershire's talented off-spinner who went on to win five England caps.

was continuing to fluctuate but, from a personal point of view, I sensed I was becoming more and more embedded in the team, and felt increasingly comfortable in my role. I was more than holding my own.

After getting back to Wales and some proper Welsh rain, which all but wiped out our match with Gloucestershire at Pontypridd's Ynysangharad Park, we prepared for the first match at our new Sophia Gardens ground. Fittingly for such an important occasion, it involved a touring side – the 7th Indians captained by the Nawab of Pataudi – who had also led Sussex the previous season and was following in the footsteps of his father who had captained the 1946 touring side as well as playing so successfully for Worcestershire for a number of years before the war.

Overall, the event was a success, even though the weather was against us and restricted both final preparations and play. Some of the outfield was waterlogged, and although the square had been covered it hadn't settled properly and there was some uneven bounce and movement. There was also an issue with a drain which had mysteriously been laid east to west across the strips, just short of a length. It was the Indian spinners who caused us most trouble, with Erapalli Prasanna getting 5 for 21 off 10 overs with his right-arm off-breaks. When our visitors batted, it was Don Shepherd who excelled. His figures of 10.3-6-10-4 show how difficult the touring batsmen found him to deal with. The conditions were later described by Wilf Wooller as 'inhospitable for the visitors and indeed to any form of cricket'.

We were now, at last, in our new home, and our guests from India were the perfect opposition to celebrate the start of a new chapter in Glamorgan's history on the other bank of the River Taff. The additional time taken to get the ground and

Openers Alan Jones and Alan Rees taking the field for the first over of the first match at our new Sophia Gardens ground.

facilities ready – when we had been on our early season travels – had proved worthwhile. The changing facilities were good. It seemed that the attention to detail, traditionally such an important feature of Glamorgan cricket, had paid off. Well, nearly. Sadly, the same attention had not gone into the planning of the catering.

At Glamorgan we rightly prided ourselves on being good hosts and giving visiting teams, especially touring sides, a warm Welsh welcome but, on this occasion, a catering blunder resulted in both sides being served ham salad for lunch. It was an awkward moment to say the least, and we felt for Tiger and his team-mates.

After a whirlwind May and June in which I'd played 12 County Championship games on the trot, together with a Gillette Cup match and a tourist game, I found myself relatively inactive for most of July. Just a few outings with the 2nd XI, some 12th-man duty, and plenty of nets, while Jeff Jones, Tony Cordle and Ossie Wheatley shared the Championship fast-bowling duties.

Then I found myself back in the side for a spell of five more 1st XI games, including a draw with Pakistan at Swansea. It was an interesting experience bowling to their exciting Test batsman, Majid Jahangar Khan. His eye-catching second innings 147 not-out was scored in only 89 minutes and included 17 sixes. Wilf Wooller, a university friend of Majid's father, was so impressed that Glamorgan almost immediately signed the young right-hander for the next season – and that proved to be the first of nine seasons with us in all, during which he scored over 9,000 runs and made 21 centuries.

Five of Majid's sixes in his record-breaking 147 at St. Helen's were scored in one over off Roger Davis. I remember that some of us wondered at the time whether anyone playing professional cricket would ever score six sixes in an over. We agreed that it was very unlikely!

In this second spell of first-team action, which included the match against the tourists (0 for 48, and 0 for 65), I failed to do anything of great note with either ball or bat. I wasn't opening the bowling, and in our win over Nottinghamshire at Ebbw Vale I didn't even get a bowl! That was a disappointment, especially being back on my home turf. I also got my first 'pair' – against Derbyshire. So it wasn't a great surprise to find myself side-lined again for much of August, especially with team selection in part reflecting the number of real spinners' wickets being played on.

Looking back, I'd like to think my two spells out of the side were because the club didn't want me to bowl too much in my first real season. People have suggested that perhaps it was all too much, too quickly, and that those with responsibility for managing my progress didn't want to risk burning me out. There may be some truth in this, though if so it was never explained. On the other hand, I think that what seemed a reverse of fortunes might also have been because they wanted to keep my feet on the ground. Maybe they felt that I was getting a bit cocky. Who knows!

Overall, however, despite the two spells of relative inactivity, and the club's generally disappointing results – we finished 14th in the Championship for the second season running – 1967 had been a fantastic year for me. My breakthrough season. I'd made my Championship debut, played in over half the club's Championship games – more than I could have dared hope for – played against the tourists from both India and Pakistan, and had the thrill of playing against Garry Sobers in the Cavaliers match! Not a bad start, by any means!

I was now very much regarded as one of the first-team squad, and felt comfortable and confident in that role. I wasn't yet a first team regular – an automatic choice – but hopefully that would be the next step, and not too far away.

Majid Khan – snapped up by Glamorgan after his innings at Swansea.

5

A Sense of History

'The scenario, at the home of cricket, will remain with me forever. It was a breathtaking experience, especially as this was my first sight of the world's most famous cricket ground. I just stood there on the edge of the boundary and gazed in boyish wonderment all around me. Was this really Lord's – and was I about to play here?'
David Shepherd

If 1967 had been a great start to my professional career, 1968 was an outstanding season for me and it still amazes me that so many memorable things happened in such a short space of time.

The previous season, with my first Championship match, first experiences of playing touring sides, and my first bowl at Garry Sobers, had been incredible enough, but the new season, in which I was becoming fully established in what was emerging as a very handy Glamorgan side, was to provide several more exciting 'firsts'.

A first appearance at the home of cricket was followed by three other games – all at the St. Helen's ground at Swansea – which also saw my name linked in different ways with aspects of cricketing history.

I'd never been to Lord's before. I'd not played a junior match there. Nor a 2nd XI game. I hadn't even visited the ground to watch a game. The closest I'd got to Lord's was some televised Test matches when I was younger. So you can imagine the thrill of pulling on whites and playing there for the first time.

Because we won the toss and chose to bat I was able to enjoy a quiet start to proceedings, sitting on the famous balcony, feet up and taking in the setting and atmosphere. Alan Jones and skipper Tony Lewis had rescued things with a century stand after we had lost two early wickets, and now – after a rare Majid duck – Alan Rees and Eifion Jones were consolidating their good work.

Suddenly, Alan holed out to Mike 'Pasty' Harris, Middlesex's Cornish-born opening bat and part-time leg-spinner (who went on to have many successful years with Nottinghamshire before becoming a first-class umpire) in his only over of the innings! I sensed numerous pairs of eyes on the players' balcony shift in my direction as I gripped my bat tightly and set off on the long, lonely walk to the wicket. Two floors. Two flights of stairs. Through the crowded first-day Long Room, the members varying in their levels of concentration and enthusiasm for events unfolding on the field, but united in their lack of interest and sympathy for a young, unknown opposition batsman making his nervous way through their comfortable territory.

To be honest, I don't remember much about that walk but I do recall, very vividly, reaching the small gate in the white boundary fence at the foot of the shallow flight of pavilion steps, then pausing. Probably none of the spectators noticed, nor any of my teammates, but to me it seemed a long pause. A very long pause. My feet seemed momentarily rooted to the ground. I was used to feeling a tinge of nervous excitement before batting, but today it was more noticeable. It must have been the Lord's effect! I was struck by a strong sense of tradition and history, suddenly aware that some of the greatest players across so many years had passed through – and quite possibly had also paused at – this same gate. It still gives me goose-bumps just thinking about it again all these years later. It was a very important moment in my cricketing journey.

I walked across the historic turf to meet Eifion in the middle. I couldn't have chosen a better partner to be waiting there for me with his familiar smile and calmness, but I didn't last long. Nash, caught Price, bowled Titmus, for a disappointing four.

I didn't set Lord's alight with the ball, either, coming on second change after Jeff Jones and Tony Cordle had opened the bowling and immediately got Middlesex in trouble at 2 for 2, but I did get a wicket

I opened the bowling at Lord's with our England international Jeff Jones. A serious shoulder injury meant that 1968 would be his last season.

– my first Lord's success – as they struggled to 40 for 5. It was a good wicket, too. England's Peter Parfitt, caught Morris bowled Nash for a duck. I bowled 15 overs for 45 runs as, with Cordle and Don Shepherd getting three wickets each, we took forward a decent first innings lead of 68.

In our second innings, Eifion got his second half-century of the match – and the second of many half-centuries in his first-class career. Unfortunately, I failed again with the bat – Parfitt enjoying quick revenge by getting me caught and bowled for a duck – but we were able to set up a thrilling conclusion to the game, declaring at 173 for 8 and setting Middlesex 242 to win. When umpires Buller and Jepson eventually called time, they were only five runs short of their target but with an equally tantalising nine wickets down!

My first visit to Lord's had certainly not disappointed. It was a great place to play cricket – all that I had expected it would be, and more. Fittingly, it was also an enjoyable and exciting game which could have gone either way until the very last ball. From a Glamorgan point of view, there had been some good individual contributions and a strong team performance. Our positive and more attacking approach was paying off. Our Championship future was looking brighter!

From a personal point of view, I felt I'd held my own on a big stage. My brush with cricketing history at the Lord's gate had been an enjoyable experience,

Fielding off my own bowling against Middlesex. Not at Lord's this time, but in the more informal setting of The Gnoll in Neath. Mike Smith was batting, with Alan Jones at slip, John Hopkins on wicketkeeping duty and Don Shepherd backing up.

Bowling at Lord's in 1974. Norman Featherstone is the non-striker.

and one I would never forget, but it wouldn't be my only involvement with cricketing history that season. Far from it.

Lord's remained one of my favourite grounds. It was always special, and I always looked forward to going back. That was surprising, because I generally didn't like larger grounds. Places like The Oval, Headingley and Old Trafford left me cold, I'm afraid. I much preferred playing on smaller, more intimate grounds where we were closer to the crowd and there was more atmosphere. Most of the out-grounds – and there were a lot more of them in those days – provided this.

St. Helen's in Swansea was a perfect example, and a firm favourite with me and many other players. It was a ground where I always enjoyed playing and, without fail, felt at home. And it was at St. Helen's in mid-July, six weeks after Lord's and with us continuing to go well in the Championship race, that I enjoyed hitting the national headlines for the first time with my bowling.

Our opponents were a Somerset side in transition and with a new captain, Roy Kerslake, a Cambridge Blue who had come out of his law practice to lead the side for one season following the retirement of Colin Atkinson. They included a number of talented and established players in their line-up, including Roy Virgin, Mervyn Kitchen, Bill Alley, Ken Palmer, Graham Burgess and Brian Langford. Alley and Palmer were nearing the end of their careers. Bill was in his 50th year and his final season; Ken would play for one more year. There were also some youngsters and newcomers including Dickie Brooks, who had taken over from Geoff Clayton as wicketkeeper; it would be his only first-class season. Also playing in the side at Swansea was a promising Australian, still only 19, called Greg Chappell. Of course, I didn't know then that Greg and I would have a memorable encounter at Swansea later in our careers.

Interestingly, four members of Somerset's team went on to become long-serving and well-respected first-class umpires. I came across two of them, Messrs. Alley and Palmer, on many occasions while they were wearing their white coats. The other two, Mervyn Kitchen and Graham Burgess, didn't start umpiring until I had finished playing.

A sprinkling of enthusiastic Somerset supporters were enjoying St. Helen's in its colourful July glory. In the days before the building of the Severn Bridge, Swansea had meant a long and daunting road journey for them, via the ferry at Aust. For many years, the bonus of the P & A Campbell paddle steamer service – which used to sail in the summer to and from the Somerset coast from various south Wales departure points including Swansea and Mumbles Pier – had provided an alternative and more romantic route to cricket. Sadly, 1968 was the last year of the paddle steamers, the 'Cardiff Queen' being the only one operating that summer. By then the 'new' Severn Bridge was in its second

St. Helen's was a favourite ground for me and many other Glamorgan players.

year and more Somerset supporters were encouraged to make the journey to west Wales by road. Anyway, however these supporters had arrived at St. Helen's, they were a welcome addition as always, bringing an extra element of enthusiasm to a match, and enjoying good-natured exchanges with the Welsh crowd and players alike.

Syd Buller was umpiring again, this time with Ron Aspinall. Ron had been a very promising young all-rounder with Yorkshire – getting Bradman caught by Len Hutton for 86 in the 1948 tour match at Sheffield – before injury forced premature retirement as a player after only 36 first-class games. He turned eventually to umpiring and enjoyed 21 very successful seasons in this role. I often came across Ron on the county circuit.

The Somerset first innings lived up to expectation posting a score of 337 all out, Kitchen and Chappell top-scoring with contributions in the eighties. I got through 26 overs in getting my 3 for 67, with six maidens. As was often the case, I proved difficult to score off and was frustrating batsmen. Looking back, I'm surprised how many overs I routinely got through in a day. My 26 here at St. Helen's would, by no means, have been an unusual load.

We started our reply uneventfully, shortly before the close of play, but the second day saw us lose wickets too regularly, despite a half-century from Roger Davis and some support from Tony and Majid. We ended 133 short of Somerset's total with Brian Langford taking six wickets with his right-arm off-breaks and the St. Helen's strip apparently starting to show signs of taking spin – with us facing the daunting prospect of batting last in search of a big score.

We feared the worst but, thankfully, Somerset's second innings never got going. A poor start – 11 for 1, 16 for 2, 22 for 3 – only got worse. Three more wickets fell with the total on 29, and they disintegrated to 40 all out in 27.3 overs. No-one reached double figures.

Surprisingly, it wasn't our spinners that caused the mayhem. I started the rot by bowling Roy Virgin, then Tony Cordle got the next two. In fact, I bowled right through their innings and continued to take wickets, finishing with by far my best first-class figures to date – 13.3-7-15–7 – and this on a pitch that wasn't supposed to offer me much assistance, though I came to realise later – chatting to bowlers like Tom Cartwright – that if the ball turns it will also seam, and if it seams it will turn. It's obvious, really, when you think about it.

I remember, too, that in this game the pitch played differently after tea. Perhaps it was because the tide had turned after lunch and was now well on its way back in. I don't know how much difference it made to the sandy St. Helen's square, but Wilf Wooller used to think it did. It was rumoured that Wilf never tossed at Swansea without a copy of the tide-tables in his pocket! On that particular day, together with the incoming tide, an on-shore south-westerly breeze certainly helped with my lateral movement.

Peter Walker was a great mentor and motivator.

The turnaround in fortunes was duly completed on the final morning when Alan Jones (undefeated on 102) and Tony Lewis knocked off the required 174 to give us a resounding nine-wicket victory in a game we had initially struggled in. It was another powerful team performance and, of course, I enjoyed getting a new personal best, too. I improved on my previous best figures of 6 for 25 off 17 overs, achieved less than two months earlier against Gloucestershire at Lydney. I might have done even better, but they declared on 82 for 8 after battling through 46 troubled overs! My six wickets included England's Arthur Milton – one of the best batsmen I ever bowled to.

Following so soon after that match, my 7 for 15 against Somerset helped my confidence enormously. I knew I was getting good wickets, and that I could hurt teams early in their innings. It was Peter Walker, always a great mentor, who helpfully pointed out to me that I was regularly knocking over at least a couple of the opposition's top five. I felt real belief in myself as an opening bowler, comfortable in my surroundings and at competing at first-class level. For the first time, there was a realisation that I fitted into the scene. That I was part of it. That I belonged. It was a good feeling.

Just two weeks after the victory over Somerset we were back at St. Helen's for the then traditional August Bank Holiday fixture against the tourists – Australia.

The visitors were enjoying a successful summer, despite some awful weather in the early stages of their tour. By the time they arrived at Swansea, they had surprised the cricketing world by defeating England in the season's opening Test at Old Trafford and drawing the next three, all of which were rain-affected. Rain had also influenced the outcomes of several of their matches against the counties, but they had managed to register some impressive wins and had lost only once – to a strong Yorkshire side.

It was a young Australian tour party – the youngest ever sent to tour the UK – but it also included a number of very experienced players who were used to performing regularly at the highest level. Their aggressive batsman/keeper, Barry Jarman, was in his third tour. In all, five of the team at Swansea had toured the UK before and four of them, Ian Redpath, Neil Hawke, Alan Connolly and Jarman himself, had been in the side beaten by Glamorgan four years earlier.

A number of our regulars had also been members of the 1964 victorious side – six of our guys played in both matches – and, as the 're-match' approached, the famous victory over Simpson's side was increasingly mentioned and there was a growing excitement in the home dressing-room. The local press was full of reminders of 1964, too. You could say that the memory of it spurred us on, though to be honest no additional incentive or encouragement was needed when you were playing Australia!

The 1964 skipper, Bobby Simpson, had joked in his gracious post-match remarks to the crowd gathered in front of the players' pavilion that Australian players had long memories and that the next tourists would try to avenge this defeat in four years' time. Now, at last, the long-awaited day had come. St. Helen's was again the venue for the traditional August Bank Holiday fixture – the only visit of the tourists to Wales that season. This time the Australians were led by the tour vice-captain, Barry Jarman, captaining in the absence of Bill Lawry who had suffered a broken finger at the hands

of John Snow in the Third Test which had ended only a couple of weeks earlier.

With Tony Lewis going down with a throat infection just before the game, Glamorgan were skippered by the ever-reliable Don Shepherd who, now almost 37, had been a key member of the victorious 1964 side. The St. Helen's wicket looked a decent one to bat on, and was probably less likely to help spinners than in previous years. Don had no hesitation in asking the Australians to field after he won the toss.

Barry Jarman captained the Australian side at Swansea.

Glamorgan were also without their regular skipper, with Don Shepherd captaining us in the absence of Tony Lewis.

Alan Jones, not for the first or last time, was the lynchpin of our first innings with an outstanding 99 against a very good attack that included the quickies David Renneberg, Alan Connolly, and Neil Hawke, and spinners John Gleeson and Ashley Mallett. Alan was so unlucky to fall to Mallett, caught at deep mid-off as he went for his century. I fell to the same bowler, too, but for 99 fewer runs than Alan!

Such was the confidence in our side that we were all a bit disappointed with our score of 224. It was not as many as we had hoped for at the beginning of the day. The wicket had held no great alarms and it would be fair to say that several of us had got ourselves out with careless shots.

When Australia started to bat after tea, it looked as if they were using a different wicket. They began with a careless run out, always an unsettling start to an innings. My throw from the boundary to the bowler's end saw skipper Jarman out by a country mile! Then I got Ian Redpath and Bob Cowper in quick succession, bowling Redpath and having Cowper snapped up by the ever-reliable Peter Walker at second slip. A needless 3 for 1 had become 22 for 3. Our tails were up. Brian 'Bertie' Lewis, bowling his right-arm off-breaks, got some wickets too, and I carried on where I had left off on the same ground a couple of weeks earlier. Don Shepherd was kind enough to mention my performance in his post-match interview, calling it "brilliant bowling". I was certainly in the groove, and getting late lateral movement of the ball.

I ended with 5 for 28 in 15.3 overs, including six maidens. Brian got the other four wickets. Don bowled exceptionally well, too, and his very tight bowling frustrated the Australian batsmen and encouraged them to take more chances at the other end. His remarkable figures were 16 overs for only 11 runs.

Ian Redpath   Bob Cowper   Ashley Mallett

John Gleeson   John Connelly   John Inverarity

My six Australian victims, including the first-innings '5-for'.

The Australians were all out early on the second day for 110. That first innings performance of ours in the field was hugely significant in determining the outcome of the match. We took a lead of 114 precious runs, but it was vital for us to build on that as our visitors were unlikely to be rolled over a second time!

Bryan Davis, the stylish Trinidadian batsman who had played four Tests for the West Indies against Australia a few years earlier and who was now qualifying for Championship cricket with us, had a rare first-team outing and top-scored with 66. Roger Davis also got a good half-century, and Alan Rees a useful 33. A few of the other guys chipped in, too – I only managed 7 – and Don, to the crowd's delight, got a couple of hefty trade-mark sixes before declaring at close of play on 250 for 9.

We really wanted to win this game, and knew that this meant keeping the opposition in with a shout, too. The target of 365 to win in a full day

The off-spin of Brian Lewis played a significant role.

achieved that. We didn't want the Australians to simply put up the shutters, and Don took the view that if they chased down the target of 365, then they deserved to win. A great final day was in prospect. We were excited as we got changed and warmed-up – confident, too, but by no means underestimating the size of the task.

St. Helen's looked fantastic. It was at its Bank Holiday best, with temporary stands adding to the sense of occasion, and 10,000 people holding their breath. I opened the bowling once again, with Tony Cordle. As in the first innings, the Aussies suffered an early run out, and I bowled John Inverarity. It was 45 for 2 and looking promising, but Cowper and Sheahan dug in and took the score to 116 for 2 before Brian Lewis made the crucial breakthrough getting Cowper caught behind by Eifion. He and Don bowled a lot of overs – 32 and 27 respectively – with Brian's in a long unbroken spell from the Mumbles Road end. Don thought the less experienced off-break bowler would encourage Australia to stay in the hunt for runs. The strategy worked. Brian wasn't anything like as economical as Don, but picked up three more very important wickets.

The two skippers, Jarman and Shepherd, with some of the crowd that gathered at the end of the game.

AUSTRALIAN BOARD OF CONTROL FOR INTERNATIONAL CRICKET
AUSTRALIAN TEAM ON TOUR, 1968

R. J. PARISH, Manager.   L. E. TRUMAN, Treasurer.

AUTOGRAPHS

BILL LAWRY (Capt.)

BARRY JARMAN (Vice-Capt.)

IAN CHAPPELL

ALAN CONNOLLY

BOB COWPER

ERIC FREEMAN

JOHN GLEESON

NEIL HAWKE

JOHN INVERARITY

LES. JOSLIN

ASHLEY MALLETT

GRAHAM McKENZIE

DAVE RENNEBERG

IAN REDPATH

PAUL SHEAHAN

BRIAN TABER

DOUG. WALTERS

D. SHERWOOD (Scorer).   A. E. JAMES (Physiotherapist).

The autographs of the 1968 Australian tour party.

Then Peter Walker chipped in with the key wicket of Paul Sheahan when he had reached 137 and was starting to look as if he could win the match if he stayed in the middle. Peter was our outstanding fielder in a team of very good fielders and took a difficult return catch from a long-hop drilled fiercely back at him. He later admitted that it was one of the worst balls of the day!

Peter also got the final wicket, at around 4 o'clock, with Australia still 79 runs short. In scenes reminiscent of those four years earlier, the crowd swarmed across the field from all directions and gathered facing the players' pavilion. We got caught up in the crush and it took us quite a while to get off the field and up the long flight of St. Helen's steps. Then, players from both teams mingled outside the pavilion, listening to the singing and cheering, enjoying a beer and taking in the atmosphere.

For us, it was a great feeling. We were all very excited, of course. It had been another strong team performance and a Glamorgan side had once again beaten top international opposition. The Australians, though naturally disappointed, were generous in defeat. Barry Jarman, who had kept wicket as well as skippering the side, got the biggest cheer of the day when he started his post-match address by saying: "So we've been beaten by Glamorgan – what's new?"

For me, that game – and my performance in it, on that larger stage – was just as significant as the 7 for 15 against Somerset. I didn't get one of the stumps that all disappeared mysteriously into Welsh thin air, but I have still got the sheet of Australian autographs given to each of us at the end of the match as a souvenir of the occasion. There are some good players listed on there!

Although I'd played against the Indian tourists the season before, this match against the Australians was by far the biggest I had ever played in. It was my first match against an Australian side, several of whom had been players whose exploits I had admired at a distance for years. Now I was sharing a cricket field with them, playing against them and in some cases getting their wickets. I knew I had more than held my own in some very distinguished company. It was a great feeling.

What a summer it was turning out to be. I had been part of a historic win. The 1968 tourists lost only two games in a long and arduous tour – one of them the Final Test when the Ashes had already been successfully retained – and this was Glamorgan's second successive victory against them, only the second time a touring side had been beaten on successive tours by the same county.

The cricketing gods hadn't finished with me yet, though. More involvement in cricketing history – and another record – was not far away.

6

'You Couldn't Have Done It Without Me, Garry'

'People should remember that Malcolm was a wonderful opening bowler in his own right, but he always wanted to try out his spinners and he reckoned he could bowl slow left-arm as well as anybody in the country.'
Peter Walker

It was a surreal moment. I found myself walking down the famous flight of St. Helen's steps side-by-side with my boyhood hero Garry Sobers. Side-by-side with the best cricketer in the world. Side-by-side with a new world record holder.

Garry and I were still in our whites. We had left the excited chatter and banter of our respective changing rooms, still trying to take in the events of the last couple of hours. There was a sprinkling of spectators still chatting on the terraces, and a few small boys enjoying their own game on the rugby field, with a rubbish bin providing a helpfully large wicket. From the little gate at the foot of the steps, we headed across the now deserted out-field and pitch, heading for the television camera gantry erected next to the double-decker rugby stand.

Garry paused to light a cigarette. I nervously joked, "Don't forget, you couldn't have done it without me, Garry!" We both laughed, and headed up the scaffold steps for a hastily arranged interview with the BBC's reporter, Brian Hoey.

It had been a strange day – and a quite unexpected conclusion. It's not every day that you are part of a world record and, as world records go, this was a particularly special one. A record that could never be broken.

It would have been the last thing in our minds as we changed into our whites that morning, and it would have been the last thing in the minds of those paying at the turnstiles before the start of the first day's play in what seemed to be just another Championship match towards the end of another long season. There was a good crowd as there almost always was at St. Helen's but, as recordings of the grainy TV coverage confirm, not as many as you might think listening to the number of people who later claimed to have been there that day!

It was our last but one match of the season, and our final home fixture. We went into it knowing that we couldn't win the Championship, but would probably finish second or third. It had been a very successful year under Tony's captaincy and we were proving to be a strong all-round side. Ossie Wheatley, Tony Cordle and I made up a three-man pace attack in this game. As you would expect at St. Helen's, Glamorgan went in with a powerful spin attack, too, with Don Shepherd, Peter Walker and Brian Lewis. Well, actually, we had a fourth spinner available. Me!

At Wilf Wooller's suggestion, I had been practising bowling orthodox left-arm round-the-wicket and was hoping for the chance to bowl a decent spell of it at Swansea. Wilf had, for a while, been attracted to the idea of a side having a bowler or two who could operate in more than one style. I suppose Garry Sobers himself was a great example of this idea in action. He could open the attack or come on first change, bowling his left-arm fast-medium. Then he could come back later in the innings, when the state of the game and wicket dictated, to bowl left-arm slow – either orthodox or his 'chinamen'.

The inspiration behind Wilf's idea had been the impressive bowling figures of Kent and England's Derek Underwood, and his idea was that this faster spin or cutter style might usefully be cultivated as one of the alternatives. So, I'd been busy practising spin bowling – modelling myself (as best I could) on Underwood. Wilf was so enthusiastic about his idea – and my potential part in it – that he had started to make arrangements with Kent for me to go down for a few days to work with Derek, but it was difficult to sort a date during the busy season and, so far, the plan had come to nothing. We were still working on it at our end, though, and I was keen to give it a try. I enjoyed my 'alternative' style, and it had been looking promising whenever I'd used it. Mind you, I bowled significantly slower than Derek Underwood.

I opened the bowling against Nottinghamshire with a six-over spell of my usual left-arm, fast-medium seamers from the Mumbles Road end. Ossie was sharing the new ball, but neither of us was getting much help from the wicket. It was a great strip to bat on. The visiting openers, Brian Bolus and Bob White, must have been rubbing their hands with glee when Garry won the toss! Glamorgan skipper Tony Lewis tried a variety of bowling combinations, with all three spinners having a go before lunch too. It was Brian Lewis who got the only wicket of the morning, Ossie catching White at mid-off ten minutes before the interval.

When Bolus and Graham Frost resumed after lunch, it was still to a spin attack. They looked comfortable and were starting to score more freely. I'd been wanting to try out my spin for a while and this seemed the perfect opportunity. Tony put me on to replace Peter Walker and almost immediately I broke the partnership which had already added 132 in only 86 minutes, with Tony taking the catch to dismiss Frost.

Ossie was off the field from lunchtime, suffering from sore shins so we had to send for Alan Rees, in his final season of first-class cricket, to field as 12th man for the rest of the innings. Alan was widely regarded as one of the best cover fielders in the game, and had fielded as substitute for England in the Third Test against Australia in 1964. While Alan was travelling from his home in Port Talbot, we had the services of a temporary – and unusual – substitute. Trevor Ford, the Welsh international footballer who was at St. Helen's watching the match, had – at lunch – offered to field if we could find him kit. Tony gratefully accepted. Alan hadn't long replaced Trevor when Bolus holed out to him for 140. It was almost 4 o'clock, and Nottinghamshire were a very healthy 289 for 3, but my spin bowling was going well. They weren't scoring too many off me, and I'd got two wickets – and broken two dangerous stands.

After an opening spell with the new ball, I was later brought back to bowl some spin.

The next man in was Deryck Murray, the West Indian Test wicketkeeper/batsman, who had captained the Cambridge University side against Glamorgan in my first first-class game. Now he was facing my new spin offerings, and my tail was up after already taking two wickets in the afternoon session.

Alan Rees fielded as 12th man. Cardiff City's Welsh international Trevor Ford fielded while Alan, himself a Welsh rugby union international, travelled in from Port Talbot.

Soon it was three, and Deryck was kicking himself all the way back to the pavilion having been bowled for a duck. It was easily the worst ball I'd bowled all day. For many days, in fact. A 'chinaman', out of the back of my hand, that was so short that it almost bounced twice and went under the bottom of Deryck's bat when he went back to cart it. It was the last ball of my 13th over.

After Deryck's quick visit to the middle, there was a murmur in the crowd as the new batsman came slowly down the steps. They – and we – had expected to see Garry Sobers come in, but this wasn't Garry. It was John Parkin, a last-minute replacement to the Nottinghamshire team and not a batsman noted for his quick scoring. Where was Garry? We knew that he would be wanting to push on with some quick runs and to be in a position to declare and give us a tricky spell of batting before the close of play. In fact, I had wondered if he might have come in earlier, but knew he tried to stick to his favourite number six spot. Garry always reckoned that this was the ideal position in the order for him to make an assessment of the situation and adapt his innings accordingly. So why on earth had Parkin been promoted ahead of one of the best strikers of a ball the game had ever seen? We weren't complaining, though. A few of the batsmen had already not pushed on as hard as perhaps they could have done, and Mike Smedley certainly wasn't hitting us round the park. Considering the quality of the wicket, we were just about keeping the lid on things.

We discovered at close of play that Garry, always an enthusiast for a wager, had left the dressing-room to place a bet on a horse he fancied. Rather than brief a junior member of the side or the '12th', he had chosen to hot-foot it to the local book-makers himself. He thought that, with things going so well and with such a good batting track, he wouldn't be needed for quite a while – if at all. So when Murray's – and then Smedley's – wicket fell, Garry had only just returned and wasn't changed. Apparently, he only got back into his whites when Parkin came in, just in case some more quick runs were needed.

Parkin and Smedley put on 19 runs in about as many minutes before I got my next wicket – Smedley giving another catch to Tony Lewis. At this point my figures were 16-3-42-4. That's what I stress when people ask me about it. I was bowling well. My figures for the two styles combined were good. I'd got all four of the wickets to have fallen since lunch, and my figures were the best in our bowling attack.

There was now a ripple of spontaneous, excited applause. I glanced behind me. Now, unmistakably, it *was* Garry Sobers skipping down the steps through the bank of spectators in front of the pavilion. Energetic. Athletic. Long sleeves buttoned at the wrist. Bat twirling. I watched as he took guard and looked up at me. I was enjoying the moment. Relishing the challenge.

J.PARKIN
Notts.

John Parkin was standing at the bowler's end.

It had been a successful afternoon with the ball, and now I wanted his wicket, too. I really did want to take the wicket of the best batsman in the world, and I was confident that I could do it.

He started quietly, not scoring off my first three balls, but then you could sense him starting to change gear. The next two balls went for four, and in the ten minutes before tea he and his partner added 25. Garry hit Peter Walker for 15 in the last over before the break, including a six. Nottinghamshire's 335 for 5 at tea was a healthy position to be in, but was still below Garry's high expectations. We could all sense that the push for some extra, quick, pre-declaration runs was on.

When play resumed, Don Shepherd was first in action from the Mumbles Road end. A single to Garry was the only run off the over, with John Parkin struggling to find the fluency he knew was required. Then I bowled to Garry.

Don Bradman said that he 'unhesitatingly rated Garry Sobers as the greatest all-rounder' he ever saw.

Three off the first two balls, and later in the over a boundary from his partner. Shep's next over to an increasingly impatient Sobers was a very tight one – just a single off the last ball. Now I was bowling to Garry again. A single, and then a boundary to Parkin who was starting to find some confidence. Shepherd to Sobers again now – nine off the over, including a single off the last ball to keep the bowling.

Garry Sobers was on 40, John Parkin on 17. My figures at this point were a very respectable 4 for 64 off 20 overs. Nottinghamshire had reached a very commanding 358 for 5. Was it enough?

It was about ten past five. The two batsmen met in the middle of the pitch for a quick word. John Parkin told us later that Garry had said they would give it another ten minutes. I realised I didn't have much longer to get Garry's wicket, and prepared to bowl my 21st over.

This over to Garry Sobers has been written and talked about a lot. Some accounts don't provide the proper context. Others have inaccuracies and mention things that simply didn't happen. For example, that the ball was changed during the course of the over (it wasn't – it just got more battered!). That Garry and I spoke to each other during the course of the over (we didn't!) and that I ignored advice given to me during the course of the over by other players (I didn't – there wasn't any!). In fact, the only conversation I heard, but didn't join in, was the discussion led by the umpires about the finishing point of the fifth ball – and the catcher's bottom!

So this is my chance to put the over into context, and to describe each ball from <u>my</u> perspective. After all, I had probably the best view in the ground!

I knew I needed to keep bowling straight and attacking the wicket. I had to create an error on his part. I had no thoughts of bowling negatively. The ball was coming out well, and my rhythm was good. I was still optimistic about the possibility of a nick to the keeper or slip, a stumping perhaps, or – probably most likely of all – a catch in the deep. I knew that Garry was starting to wind things up. He'd decided the time had come to go for some really quick runs and the declaration which we were all expecting. He later confirmed that his plan was to get us batting for at least an hour at the end of the day, so he made the conscious decision to hit out, come what may. He joked at close of play that he had decided to follow the advice of the great Sir Leary Constantine – if you hit the ball out of the ground, no-one can catch it! He also admitted that he had been quite prepared to sacrifice his wicket. "I wasn't bothered about getting out – I just wanted quick runs," he told me.

I had a quick look round the field I'd set at the beginning of the over. It was essentially what I'd been using in the previous overs with some success – and the one I usually set whenever I used my new 'spin style'. It looked about right. I'd already made a couple of defensive adjustments for someone who seemed to be looking seriously to get on with it. I also had to bear in mind that we were playing a few strips from the middle of the square, making an already short St. Helen's boundary even shorter on the Gorse Lane side of the ground, and tempting to a left-hander. Very tempting.

Accordingly, I had a deep mid-wicket, Brian Lewis, ready for Garry to try hitting with the spin to that boundary. Brian was in front of the old two-faced scoreboard. Then, half-way between deep mid-wicket and long-on, 12th man Alan Rees was on the boundary for a mis-hit, too. I also had a deep long-on, straightish, between the pavilion and the 'The Cricketers'. It was Tony Cordle, who said afterwards that I should have had him up on the pub roof! Alan Jones was at deep backward square-leg, on the fence for one that's maybe dragged down a little bit and, completing the leg-side, was Peter Walker at shortish and squarish mid-wicket to save the little push and run for a single.

Majid at slip and Eifion Jones behind the stumps were the only others close to the bat. Tony Lewis was at cover, Don Shepherd at extra cover and down on the boundary at long-off in front of the steps was Roger Davis, perfectly positioned for a mis-hit over long-off.

I was happy with my field placings, and the thinking behind them. A final quick look round, and I was ready to bowl.

Ball One
Umpire Eddie Phillipson was at my end, standing a couple of paces back from the stumps as I prepared to bowl round the wicket off my five-pace run-up. It wasn't a bad ball. Decent length. Good direction, drifting a little towards off stump, but Garry hit it – very hard – with the spin. I turned to watch it sail way over the head of Tony Cordle at wide long-on and crash into the guttering

at the top of the wall of 'The Cricketers' pub before bouncing down onto the road. The ball passed over the shortest boundary, but that doesn't take anything away from how well it was struck. Garry's power and timing were breath-taking. I waited thoughtfully, focussing on my next delivery, while the ball was retrieved by an enthusiastic spectator who rushed out through the big gate by the gentlemen's toilet.

I turned at the end of my run to see Garry twirling his bat and grinning. He was enjoying the challenge, too. I noticed that Majid had moved across a pace or two from slip and was speaking to Eifion, but I couldn't hear what they were saying. I wasn't daunted by the six. By playing shots like that he was giving me a chance. My purpose as a slow bowler was to get him to hit the ball in the air.

Ball Two

I decided to bowl a similar ball, thinking Garry might be anticipating something different, but he wasn't. He'd guessed right and although this one pitched a little more on leg stump, he played a similar shot. The result was much the same, too. A six in the general direction of deep long-on – towards the toilets and pub – but slightly squarer than the first. Another clean strike but, from my point of view, another decent ball. I still felt my action was good. A high arm and a nice pivot on my front foot.

Ball Three

As I walked back to my mark, I was still optimistic, despite the two big sixes. I honestly felt I was still in with a good chance of getting Garry's wicket. He was clearly intent on hitting out for quick runs, and I was putting the ball just where I intended to. Things were continuing to look promising. It was still a question of him or me! 'There's the great man,' I thought. 'Let's get in there and get him out.' No-one came over for a chat. They were all fielding too far away to have a conversation. Tony Lewis has said since that he was trying to get the message to me that I might want to revert to my fast-medium style for the rest of the over, but I wasn't aware of this at the time and, anyway, I wouldn't have changed. I didn't want to change. I was confident that I could get him out.

Some of the guys – I discovered subsequently – thought that I might have bowled wider, making it more difficult for Garry to reach for and get under the ball, but I had no real thoughts of becoming negative. I didn't want to bowl a yard down the off-side to force him to miss it – that wasn't going to achieve anything. So, I decided to keep going as before. Perhaps this would be the ball that did the trick.

It wasn't. Again, not a bad ball, and again, Sobers went hard, high and straight, this time over deep long-off, the ball scattering spectators as it bounced around on the terracing in front of the pavilion.

Ball Four

As I waited (still in splendid isolation!) for the ball to be returned, I wondered briefly about making a change or two in the field. Should I move Majid out of the slips and strengthen the outfield further? No, I was convinced an edge was still very much on the cards, so I decided to leave him where he was, and to keep attacking the stumps, bowling at the same pace. I was sure I could get Sobers out – and I wanted to so badly!

This ball was flatter and pitched a little shorter. It wasn't such a good ball as the first three. Garry leaned back and pulled it fiercely just backward of square leg. It was a flatter six than the others, but still cleared the low wall surrounding the ground after bouncing on the terracing. I turned and watched a spectator lean over the wall, shouting directions to someone who had gone through another handily-placed gate to retrieve the ball from the street. I watched as the ball was thrown back into the ground, and eventually returned to me. I knew I hadn't bowled this delivery as well as the others in the over but I knew, too, that Garry hadn't hit it as cleanly as he had hit the others. I noticed Eifion speak to Garry, and learned later that he was quietly pointing this out! Still, no-one approached me to offer any words of either consolation or advice. The only person who spoke was umpire Eddie Phillipson. He encouragingly urged, "Keep going!"

Ball Five

I took Eddie's advice and prepared to bowl the fifth ball. 'Keep attacking,' I thought. 'He will really mis-hit one soon.' I did, however, plan on some subtle changes for this delivery. I held the ball back a bit. It was a little slower. Even though I was bowling quite slowly anyway, I decided to give this one more air and drop it slightly shorter. A bit like I'd watched two other left-arm spinners – Ray East of Essex and Norman Gifford of Worcestershire – do so effectively. It was a little wide of off stump, but not much. Garry tried to hit it over mid-off. He got hold of it pretty well, but he didn't middle it. He was slightly off-balance when he hit it, playing off the back foot and leaning back a bit. I think he hit it low on the bat – not toe-ended, by any means, but lower than he would have wished. He certainly didn't middle it, anyway. This was the mistake I'd been waiting for and that I'd been confident would come. My aim of creating a false shot had been achieved.

Roger Davis, one of our best fielders but not someone who was used to being out on the boundary, was under the catch and seemed to take the ball fairly comfortably at chest height, but the catch was made more difficult than it should have been because the ball was spinning as a result of the mis-hit, and because Roger had strayed in slightly from the line. He admitted afterwards that he had been very wary of the drainage ditch that ran around that part of

Garry's fifth six – and almost out!

the ground. He'd watched a teammate disappear into it several weeks earlier in a failed attempt to chase down a boundary. So, mindful of the peril lurking behind him, Roger took the catch a yard or so in from the chalk boundary line, but overbalanced and sat backwards as he did so.

Garry, seeing the catch cleanly taken, immediately tucked his bat under his arm and started to walk off, but some of the crowd were shouting 'six', aware that the fielder's backside had touched the line. Umpire Phillipson went over to talk to Roger. Then the two umpires conferred. All the time, some of the crowd were shouting 'out', while others were shouting for yet another six. I just stood at the bowler's end waiting for it all to be resolved. I remember noticing that Tony Cordle was helpfully signalling a six – and thinking, 'Thanks, Tony'! It seemed to take forever, and I couldn't see how it was to be decided. How would we know exactly where Roger's backside had landed? I knew that the rule relating to catches on the boundary had changed since the end of the previous season, and that – for an experimental year at least – it was no longer permitted for a fielder to touch the boundary line, rope or fence in making a catch. In the end, the umpires erred on the side of caution, as they had to in the circumstances, and ruled 'not out'.

If only I had put a taller fielder at long-off! Peter Walker, for example, would have found it an easier catch to take and would probably have stayed on his feet. Of course, had the catch been taken cleanly, there would have been no world record for Garry. My strategy would have paid off, and I would have had figures of 5 for 88.

Ball Six

I eventually found myself with ball in hand ready to bowl the final delivery. It was a bit more scuffed and dented than it had been at the start of the over, but it was definitely the same ball. I know some people think that

Roger Davis almost changed the course of history!

it was replaced at some point during the over, but the ball in my hand as I prepared to bowl that final delivery was definitely the same Stuart Surridge ball, supplied by Bill Edwards' Sports shop, that I had bowled the first ball of the over with – and the first overs of the match, too. Each time it had gone out of the ground, it had come straight back – though that would soon change!

Having made only minor changes to my style and strategy over the first five balls, I decided on a much more fundamental change for the last ball. Obviously I didn't want Sobers to hit another six, and it didn't take a genius to realise that this would be very much in his mind. He admitted later that the thought of trying for an over of sixes had come into his head after the fourth ball, and then had become a firm intention after the fifth.

So I prepared to bowl a significantly quicker ball, a cutter, more resembling my other style. Foolishly, however, I didn't alter my run up, and tried to bowl my usual eight-pace ball off the same five paces. It didn't work. It was by far my worst ball, too short and dispatched accordingly! The ball soared over the double-faced scoreboard at mid-wicket, over the boundary wall, and up St. Helen's Avenue towards the town. As Wilf Wooller announced excitedly in his TV commentary: "He's done it, and my goodness, it's gone way down to Swansea."

I stood watching, for a moment, in disbelief as Garry – for the second time in the over – tucked his bat under his arm and started to leave the square. Garry Sobers had moved on to 76 not out, Nottinghamshire to 394 for 5 declared. My analysis had quickly become 21-3-100-4.

I'd stayed positive throughout the over. With each ball I'd thought I could get his wicket and I still think to this day that if there had been a seventh ball I'd have got him out.

Should I have done anything differently? Well, hindsight is a wonderful thing, of course, and I've had the opportunity to look back at film of this over more than once. What strikes me now is how Garry went back to each ball, and played every one off his back foot with his feet in the same position. It's his feet that I notice now! All the weight was off his back foot. It was all bottom-hand. He didn't come forward to meet any of them. So, if I bowled that over again, I'd bowl slightly quicker, right from the start, and slightly fuller. I would try to upset his rhythm and his timing.

I don't remember much about following the Nottinghamshire batsmen off the field and up the steep St. Helen's steps, although I was aware of the excitement in the crowd. Back in the changing room, with the door shut, there was also an air of excitement. Our openers and number three were padding-up, of course, but some of the other guys were quick to remind me that something very special had just happened. Tony Cordle suggested that one day I should write a book about it. He came up with a title, too: *Gone with the Wind*. A couple of people were asking me why I hadn't bowled something negative at the end, to ensure that the six sixes were impossible. I explained why, but it was too late for that debate.

Tony Lewis had more practical advice to offer. "They'll be asking for interviews," he pointed out. "Make sure you get a decent fee!"

He was right. The first interview came soon after, at close of play – when Garry and I met with the BBC's Brian Hoey – and we did get a fee, eventually. I can't remember how much it was, but I know Garry got double. Fair enough. After all, it was Garry that had broken the world record!

I tried to explain, on camera, how I felt. No, I wasn't demoralised. No, I didn't think I'd bowled at all badly, and yes, I'd known for a long time that Garry was an exceptional player, capable of doing exceptional things. In short, I realised that it was a special moment, and that my name was now in the record books alongside Garry's.

I bowled to Garry again on a number of occasions and I did get him out, too! When he batted against me next, in Glamorgan's first Championship game of the 1971 season against Nottinghamshire at Trent Bridge, I got his wicket twice – clean bowled in the first innings and caught behind in the second. I remember not only bowling him out, but also the little smile of acknowledgement in my direction that immediately followed.

An interview with BBC Wales' Brian Hoey was hastily arranged.

Whenever we came across each other, Garry and I would always enjoy a beer together and the chance to put the cricketing world to rights. He was always a very knowledgeable and helpful person to talk to, very supportive and full of sound advice and good ideas. We became good friends and, on April 29th, 1975, found ourselves on TV again. We weren't in our whites on this occasion, but we were still talking about 'the Swansea over'.

I'd been chauffeur-driven from Swansea to the London Weekend Television studios in central London. After a briefing from the producer, I found myself waiting with other guests backstage as Eamon Andrews introduced the 157th edition of *This Is Your Life* – a programme which, although then in its sixth season, continued to command huge

Nash gets revenge

SWEET revenge for former Abergavenny cricketer Malcolm Nash. Hit for six sixes in a world record over by Gary Sobers at Swansea two years ago, the Glamorgan bowler had the satisfaction of dismissing the Nottinghamshire and West Indies captain twice at Nottingham last week.

He bowled Sobers in the first innings, then had him caught behind the wicket by Eifion Jones in the second.

Revenge was sweet!

viewing figures. The subject of the evening's honour? The recently knighted Sir Garfield Sobers, in the view of many people (including me) the greatest all-round cricketer that has graced the game.

I was called on stage when Garry's world record was highlighted in Eamon's big red book. We talked a bit about the events of the last day of August 1968 at St. Helen's, and enjoyed a joke or two and some friendly banter. It was a very enjoyable occasion. As well as celebrating some cricketing highlights, the programme included a number of lovely family moments, too. I remember how shocked Garry was when his mother walked on to the stage. She had never been off the island of Barbados before, and had certainly never flown. What an adventure it must all have been for her, and LWT researchers had also managed to get Garry's merchant seaman brother taken off his ship in Los Angeles and flown over for the family get-together, too.

It was good to see Garry again, although we had met up on the cricket field a number of times since '68, of course, playing for our respective counties. We'd come across each other in Australia, too, when Garry was skippering a World XI. We managed to have another chat after the programme, which had been recorded for transmission the following week. All of us taking part were sworn to secrecy before I was taken up to Trent Bridge in readiness for the Championship match starting the next morning. I don't know what the guys made of my arrival at the hotel in a large and very expensive chauffeur-driven car, and I can't remember what yarn I told them, but I couldn't tell them the truth until a week later.

The TV spin-offs didn't end there! Soon after I'd finished playing, Garry and I were in the Shepperton television studios in Surrey being interviewed by Terry Wogan on his early-evening *Wogan* programme. At the time, this very popular live 'chat' programme also achieved huge viewing figures. Again, I was very well looked after, with more chauffeured transport from and back to my home in Swansea.

These days I enjoy watching a lot of cricket on television, and when looking through the listings I still smile to myself when a profile of Garry is being shown and I know that our exploits at St. Helen's will be receiving another airing! What a pity that we don't get royalties!

Of course, I still get asked about the record-breaking over – and the ball. There has been a lot of publicity – and a book – about the ball, and particularly about the fact that a ball supposed to be the one we used at St. Helen's was sold through a London auction house to a collector in India for a large sum of money. I know that it couldn't have been the ball, because the ball we used was a Surridge ball, and the ball that was auctioned was a Duke. What do I make of the controversy? What do I think really happened?

We'll never know for sure, but my guess falls into the category of 'honest mistake'! I think Garry, who was never much for records or fuss or personal glory, dropped the ball into his bag before leaving St. Helen's. It would have found itself in the company of several other balls, as well as numerous other bits of kit – especially at the end of a busy season. When Garry was back in Nottingham, and someone reminded him, he simply pulled out the wrong ball. Don't forget, in all his home games at Trent Bridge he would have been handling a Duke ball.

It's amazing that the ball itself, and my over to Garry at St. Helen's 50 years ago, is still the subject of so much interest and discussion, but I can still enjoy watching an interview with Garry or a re-run of the black and white film, and my memories of that historic day at St. Helen's are all positive ones. As I remarked to a newspaper reporter at the time: "It's an honour just to be playing against him." After all, he was the cricketer that for many years I had admired most in the game – and still do.

So, I'll leave the last word on 'the over' to Garry. In one of the more recent television interviews, he mentions people all over the world always wanting to talk about this record, and comments wryly that "… it seems as if it's the only thing I've done in my cricketing career."

I know that feeling!

7

Champions!

'It was a very good team, make no mistake about that. Possibly the best Glamorgan team of all time, the 1969 side.'
Don Shepherd

Some games you go into knowing they are critical. Some you realise have special significance during the course of the games themselves. In others, at their conclusion.

Our game versus Yorkshire at Swansea in the first week of May 1969 fitted none of these categories. In fact, it was a further four months before we realised just how crucial it had been to the way our Championship season would be recorded in cricketing history.

Yorkshire's captain, Brian Close, won the toss and decided to bat. I guess he was thinking that they would benefit from bowling last on what promised to be a typical St. Helen's wicket offering some assistance to his talented spinners – Don Wilson and Geoff Cope – as it dried out. Wilson, left-arm orthodox, was the more experienced of the two, having already toured India with England in 1963-64 and played in all five Tests. Cope was a young right-arm off-spinner, new to the Yorkshire side but who would also go on to play for England – against Pakistan in 1977-78 – in a long career clouded by questions over his action.

Boycott top-scored with 68 runs, but none of the formidable Yorkshire batting line-up got away from us, and they were all out for 265. I got some good wickets – Sharpe, Padgett, Hampshire and Binks – and their batsmen found it difficult to score off me. I was pleased with 4 for 43 in 26 overs. Don Shepherd got four wickets, too.

Nobody managed a big score in our first innings, either, and we declared 40 runs adrift on 225 for 9. This declaration was a sign of our attacking cricket policy in action. In our pre-season meeting we had all agreed, as a squad and to a man, to attack whenever we could – and, in particular, to score as quickly as we could in our first innings. Here was the plan in action. While Yorkshire had taken 130.5 overs to get their first-innings score (and because of rain delays on the first day had wasted about half of the three days), we batted for only 83.4 overs and scored freely against a strong attack of Nicholson, Old, Hutton, Wilson and Cope.

Everyone had bought in, wholeheartedly, to this positive approach. It was a logical development of the way we had started to play the season before. As well as scoring quickly, our discussions had also included the strategy of declaring behind if necessary, and then being confident that we could bowl the opposition out second-time round and go for – and get – any target they set.

Yorkshire declared, too, setting us the target of 168 to get our season off to a winning start. Despite the fact that time wasn't on our side, we thought we had a decent chance, but disaster struck! The top three got 'starts' with 20-odds, but succumbed in the quest for quick runs. Soon I found myself coming down the long St. Helen's steps at 85 for 6. We were going for it, for sure, but the plan wasn't working!

Things didn't improve, and in no time I had lost partners Tony Cordle, David Lewis and Lawrence Williams (on his Championship debut), with Yorkshire's spinning attack of Wilson and Cope making the most of the turn offered by the Swansea wicket.

We had sunk to a very precarious 91 for 9 when Don Shepherd strode out to join me at the crease, with around 40 minutes left before umpires Buller and Crapp would call it a day. It didn't look as if we were going to enjoy the start to the season that we had planned and hoped for. Our positive approach wasn't paying off, it seemed. Our intention to play positive cricket in order to create a winning position had backfired.

Actually, I wasn't too downhearted when I saw Don stride out. When not in full attacking mode, he could defend pretty well against spin – especially if he was able to kick it away! I think being a spinner himself helped. Of course, I don't know how confident he was to see me at the other end, but we had a very positive mid-wicket chat before he took guard. We decided that he'd take Copey and I'd take Don Wilson. Right hand for right arm, left hand for left arm. The ball leaving you is always more difficult to play than the ball coming in to you.

So, that's what we did. We turned singles down. We concentrated hard and encouraged each other as the Yorkshire side got increasingly frustrated. We heard Tony Nicholson pleading with Closey: "Let me bowl! Give me a bowl,

Don Shepherd (pictured here with Tom Graveney) was a useful tail-end batsman. He and I shared an unbroken – and ultimately crucial – last wicket stand against Yorkshire.

skip." His medium pace had got him 3 for 21 when Yorkshire had heavily defeated us a couple of days earlier in a John Player League game at Neath and he fancied his chances again. Why Brian Close didn't bowl someone a bit quicker, I'm not sure, but he stuck with the spin of Wilson and Cope. Perhaps he wanted to get as many overs as possible in the limited time available – don't forget, it was time rather than overs in those days. Perhaps he just assumed that one of us would lose our patience or technique and do something wild. There was certainly plenty of 'chat', offering advice and encouraging us to play a rash shot, but we didn't. We just offered a dead bat or kicked it away as the increasingly tense overs ticked past until, eventually, the clock showed close of play and 'time' was called.

When we shook hands and headed back to the pavilion, Don had scored a single and I had reached 19 – most of them scored with earlier partners. We had survived for nine overs. Four points each side, including three batting points for us. Although not the winning start we had wanted – and certainly it would be hard to claim that the stand Shep and I shared was part of our intention to play 'positive cricket' – we were all pretty pleased with the outcome. Because we had got ourselves into such a bad position, a draw seemed like a victory of sorts.

How important that stand was to prove at the end of the season – and to cricketing history. Champions – unbeaten! A feat achieved only once before in the history of the Championship, and that was 65 years earlier!

We didn't come as close again to losing for the rest of the season, and at the end our proud record was: Played 24, Won 11, Drawn 13, Lost 0.

As well as our undefeated tag, there was another remarkable aspect to our 1969 Championship success. The team went through the whole campaign almost unchanged. Everyone kept fit or managed to play through injury, and only 13 players were used: skipper Tony Lewis, Don Shepherd, Eifion Jones, Alan Jones, Lawrence Williams, Roger Davis, Majid Khan, Tony Cordle, Bryan Davis, Peter Walker, Malcolm Nash, Ossie Wheatley and David Wyndham Lewis. It was actually a playing group drawn from 12 for much of the time, because David figured in only a couple of games.

The bond and team spirit in the side, under the captaincy of Tony Lewis, was strong – the strongest I experienced over all my Glamorgan years. We were a group of players who enjoyed playing, travelling and spending 'time-off' with each other. We had confidence not only in our own individual

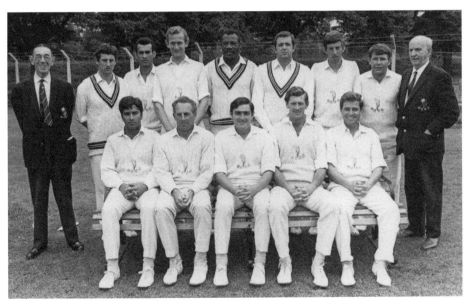

Our 1969 side. This picture was taken at Sophia Gardens, and includes our 12ᵗʰ man Kevin Lyons (standing far left), also our physiotherapist John Evans and scorer Hugh Jeffries.

abilities, but also in those of our teammates. It was an extremely positive dressing-room.

We also enjoyed the fact that, as well as representing the proud traditions of Glamorgan, we were at the same time representing Wales in the County Championship. Our Welshness, and pride in being Welsh, was another significant factor in our strength as a playing unit. We were proud to be playing for Wales as well as Glamorgan.

Another very special feature of our season was that every member of the small first-team squad of 12 regulars contributed and, as Tony later acknowledged, everyone put in some significant individual match-winning or match-saving performances. We carried no passengers!

From a personal point of view, I was pleased with my performances with both bat and ball. I had a good season, and made some important contributions in several memorable games – though these were not always the games that drew most attention at the time. I thoroughly enjoyed playing in some very exciting games – and being part of some excellent team performances.

Although we had started the season full of confidence after a third place finish the summer before, in all honesty the 1969 Championship season got off to a pretty low-key start. You wouldn't have fancied our chances, particularly after the first few rounds of matches. You would probably not even have put money on us finishing in the top half of the table. At the end of May we looked anything but Championship contenders, languishing in last place, still without a win, with only four draws to show for our efforts, and without a batsman having a century to his name.

The key, however, was that we knew we were playing some good cricket. We were a happy and confident group and we were enjoying our cricket. Also, very importantly, we felt that our plans were working despite the results – in particular, our agreed policy to play attacking cricket when we could, and to go for first-innings runs as quickly as possible.

The points system operating in the 1969 Championship gave ten points for a win (five for a tie), with one batting bonus point awarded for every 25 runs over 150 in the first 85 overs of the first-innings, and one bowling bonus point for every two wickets in the first 85 overs of the first innings.

We knew, too, that we had been unlucky with the weather, and that our early-season results would probably have been better but for a few rain-affected matches. We were sure that a change in fortunes was just around the corner: and it was!

Most of the guys would agree that the turning point – the matches that really set up the season for its dramatic conclusion and our emergence as genuine Championship contenders – was the pair of fixtures against high-flying Gloucestershire. When the two sides met in the first game at Cardiff in mid-July, Gloucestershire were leading the Championship table and, to many people, they looked likely candidates for the title.

Between our hard-fought draw against Yorkshire and the first game against Gloucestershire at Sophia Gardens, however, a lot had happened – on and off the field! We'd played seven more drawn matches, though in the last two of these – against Somerset at Glastonbury and Lancashire at Old Trafford – we ended very much in control. In both cases, more time would almost certainly have seen us to victory. We might also have done better if there had been less rain around, and if Tony hadn't kept losing the toss! In a run of remarkable consistency, he lost the first six in a row.

We'd also had four really good wins. The first two were at Sophia Gardens, against Somerset (by ten wickets in two days) and Sussex (by an innings). The other two victories had been against Worcestershire at New Road and, in the game finishing the day before Gloucestershire's visit to Cardiff, the second part of the 'double' against Sussex at Hastings.

One of our draws was against Leicestershire at Colwyn Bay. Tony Cordle's analysis was amazing, not just because he took a career-best 9 for 49, but because he didn't come on until fifth change. Interestingly, I wasn't in the side at Colwyn Bay, and neither was Lawrence Williams in the winning side at Glastonbury. We had each been dropped for one game. Why? Well, it was a long story!

At that time Lawrence and I were in digs together in Cardiff. The Tonna-born right-arm fast-medium bowler was in his first season and, like me, had come into the Glamorgan team straight from club cricket. We shared a one-room bedsitter opposite St. David's Hospital on Cowbridge Road. At the end of the first day's play of the game against Sussex at Sophia Gardens, we'd gone for a couple of steaks in the Model Inn in Quay Street,

Lawrence Williams made his Glamorgan Championship debut in the first game of the season. We shared digs in Cardiff.

91

just opposite the Arms Park. It was a favourite stop in those days, especially after a hard day in the field! We had a couple of beers to wash supper down, and then walked home. We had nothing else to drink, and were in bed by 10.30pm.

The next thing either of us knew was being woken by an agitated Tony Cordle hammering on the front door! It was now 10.30am and the game was re-starting in an hour. When we hadn't reported to the ground, he'd borrowed the club kit van and come to find us. Thanks to 'Speedy', we just made it for the start of the second day's play.

Well, we didn't exactly sneak in through the back gate – there was only one entrance anyway! – but once in the ground, Lawrence went one way and I went the other – which, unfortunately, took me past the caravan which acted as our secretary's office at the ground. Wilf Wooller missed nothing. He shot out. "Hey, where are you going?"

"I'm going to the dressing room."

"Are you just arriving? You're late."

"Well," I said, "I overslept."

"Oh, out on the tiles last night, were you?"

"No, actually I was in bed at 10.30."

Wilf looked unconvinced, as only Wilf could. To make my case even more strongly – but without thinking – I added, "My roommate can vouch for that."

"Oh, he's late too, is he?" said Wilf. It was getting worse. Now I'd dropped Lawrence in it as well.

"Look," I said. "Don't worry about it Mr Wooller. I know you're a busy man with all the letters to get out and everything. You carry on with that and I'll go and make my apologies to the captain."

"Don't you talk to me like that young man. You'll probably not play in the next game," came his terse reply.

I kept digging! "Look, I'll explain to the captain and he can decide that."

At this point, Wilf made his position perfectly clear. "I decide, not the captain. The captain does as I tell him."

The first day's play had seen Sussex rolled over for only 79 on a wicket with little moisture in it, Lawrence taking 4-23 and me getting 4-22. Sadly, our success with the ball made no difference to Wilf's decision and, sure as eggs were eggs, I missed the next game against Leicestershire at Colwyn Bay, and a week later Lawrence was left out of the side against Somerset.

We had a laugh about it in the dressing room when I told the lads, but it was an important lesson about the ex-skipper's continuing sphere of influence and power. Thankfully, however, the good thing about Wilf was that once it was done, it was done. He didn't mention it again, and he didn't hold it against you.

There was another game I missed in that Championship season, but not for disciplinary reasons this time! It was the match at Hastings. Between our games at Glastonbury and Old Trafford, our busy Championship schedule had been interrupted by a meeting with the mighty West Indian touring side at St. Helen's. Going in as night-watchman, I got hit on the back of the hand protecting my face from a very unpleasant bouncer from Vanburn Holder. A visit to nearby Singleton Hospital showed that several small bones were broken, but I was given what seemed at the time to be an extremely large – and painful – cortisone injection in the hope of getting me back in action as quickly as possible! I took no further part in the tourist match, but declared myself fit for the next game against Lancashire at Old Trafford.

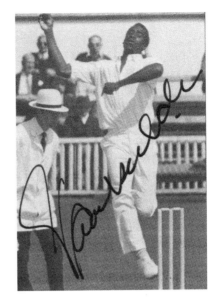

I was injured playing a Vanburn Holder bouncer.

I bowled 17 overs in this game, but my hand was far from being right. I really didn't want to, but it was probably a good idea to take the following game off and, as it happened, it suited Tony's plans, too.

Tony Lewis was keen to include David Wyndham Lewis in the game against Sussex at Hastings – a ground that had a reputation for taking spin and where the skipper felt David's leg-breaks and occasional googlies would be an asset alongside the more conventional spin of Don and Peter. Wilf, on the other hand, was less enthusiastic and wanted to stick with the same side. He told Tony that, if he insisted that David played, he would have to book the additional accommodation himself – and pay for it! In the end, our leg-spinner did travel to Hastings – and he did play. I'm not sure how the hotel bill was settled, though.

As things turned out, from my perspective, Sussex at Hastings wasn't a bad match to miss! It was a spinners' wicket, and we played four of them. Shep bowled a staggering total of 65.2 overs in the game, and Peter Walker wasn't too far behind with 45.4 overs. Roger Davis chipped in with five second innings overs of his right-arm off-breaks, and David Wyndham Lewis enjoyed a decent stint of 18 overs. Tony's team selection was justified as our spinning quartet accounted for 18 of the Sussex wickets to fall in an excellent win – and one of the two they didn't get was a run out!

Gloucestershire's opener David Green.

After a tough few days for the spinners against Sussex, and a long evening drive back from Hastings to Cardiff to play Gloucestershire, they were not sorry to see Tony win the toss and elect to bat. My hand injury had benefitted from the time out, and I was cleared for the game. We knew we were in for a battle.

Against a strong Gloucestershire attack, we got a large – and, again, quick – first-innings total of 337. It included several useful contributions. A stand between Majid and Tony, who both got stylish half-centuries, added 91 and gave us a solid foundation to build on. I enjoyed myself with the bat again. Tony Cordle and I both got 50s, too, and put on 87 quick runs for the eighth wicket.

Gloucestershire, who were having such a good season, never really got going, and we made their life difficult by bowling well. I got their Welsh-born opener, David Green, who would go on to be named as one of *Wisden's* 'Cricketers of the Year' for the 1969 season, and his partner Ron Nicholls. Then Shep chipped in with two wickets in a typically tight spell – 26-11-38-2 – but 'Speedy' starred for us with the ball, taking 6 for 21 in only 12.2 excellent overs as the Championship leaders collapsed to 117 all out, and Tony Cordle hadn't got the ball in his hand until they were already 78 for 2.

We decided not to enforce the follow-on. Tony Lewis got another half-century in our second knock, and we declared with six wickets down leaving Gloucestershire to score 364 in the same number of minutes to win the match. It never looked likely and they lost wickets steadily, with only a fighting last-ditch tenth-wicket partnership between John Mortimore and Barrie Meyer delaying our victory. A very significant victory it was, too, giving us 19 points against top-of-the table Gloucestershire's three, and moving us further up the table, which, of course, helped our self-belief considerably.

A very good July ended with a draw against Warwickshire in a match which saw the whole of the second day lost to rain, and a very convincing away win against Derbyshire, with centuries by Alan Jones and Roger Davis – in an opening stand of 224 – putting us in a strong position after we had been put in to bat. My match figures of 9 for 88 – and a few lusty blows to get us a fifth batting point – won me the *Sunday Telegraph* 'Cricketer of the Week Award' and a very welcome case of champagne!

Our excellent run of form continued into August with an away win and another exciting finish against Northamptonshire. Set 140 minutes to get 218 runs, a superb stand of 132 in 77 minutes by Tony and Majid saw us home. We should have followed this with another win in the return against Derbyshire at Cardiff but, once again, poor weather cost us important points. Time was lost to rain on all three days but, even so, Derbyshire were tottering on 56 for 7 in their second innings – still 21 runs short of wiping out the first innings deficit – when the game finished. We were so close!

So, three weeks after our very significant home victory over Championship-leaders Gloucestershire we met them again, this time as part of the annual Cheltenham Festival. Although they were still enjoying top spot, this wasn't a happy experience for the Gloucestershire faithful packed into the marquees and temporary seating at the picturesque old school ground. In *Wisden*'s words, Glamorgan 'dominated the game'.

The home side batted first after winning the toss. It turned out not to be a great decision, and none of the Gloucestershire side reached 20 as they collapsed to a disastrous 73 all out. I had a particularly good day, getting 6 for 37 – including David Green, Arthur Milton and Tony Brown – in 15.2 enjoyable overs. My fellow bowlers and I were supported by excellent fielding and catching, by this stage an almost routine feature of our season.

We got 283, our two overseas players Majid and Bryan Davis leading the reply with scores of 69 and 67 respectively, and Majid hitting three 6s and eight 4s – a half-century of boundaries.

A demoralised Gloucestershire got off to a terrible start when they batted again, losing both openers without a run on the board and then sliding to 17 for 4. They couldn't recover, and only a defiant half-century from off-spinner David Allen, supported by Mike Bissex, held us up. We claimed the extra half-hour and needed only ten minutes of it to wrap up another convincing victory by an innings and 50 runs in two days.

We took 20 points and moved into second place, only eight behind Gloucestershire and breathing down their necks – hard!

For the first time in the season, press reports started to acknowledge that Glamorgan were serious contenders for the Championship and, as we drove to Trent Bridge for our match with Nottinghamshire – and another encounter with Garry Sobers – we felt on fire!

Our good form continued. Garry put us in, but an undefeated century by Alan, and solid half-centuries (or close to) by Bryan, Majid and Tony, together with a speedy 22 from me (I was pushed up the order to get quick runs), saw us to a healthy 320-4 declared off only 101 overs in less than five and a half hours.

I got opener Mike Harris (not for the only time in our careers – the guys used to call him my 'rabbit') leg

I got Mike Harris out more than once in our careers!

before, for a duck. We were well placed. Unfortunately, though, rain washed out the whole of play on the Monday and Tuesday, and I didn't get the chance to bowl at Garry again on this occasion.

Thankfully, every cloud has a silver lining, and our two-day win at Cheltenham followed by two days with our feet up at Trent Bridge meant that we were not too tired when we travelled back to Swansea to meet Middlesex in an absolutely crucial game for us. We needed to continue our run of top form. This was the first of three successive home fixtures – our final home matches of the season – which together turned out to have such a significant and decisive bearing on our Championship fortunes. It was another incredible game to be part of, and another nail-biting finish.

England international Peter Parfitt, captaining a strong Middlesex side, won the toss and decided to bat on what looked like a decent St. Helen's wicket – though one which might well turn out to be trickier to bat on towards the end of the game. We got off to the perfect start when I quickly removed another England international, Scottish-born opener Eric Russell, leg before, and then had Parfitt himself caught by Alan Jones. Both were back in the pavilion before Middlesex had a run on the board!

Middlesex then clawed their way back, thanks largely to a patient hundred from Clive Radley with valuable support from wicketkeeper John Murray – two more England players. These two put on over 100 after we'd reduced Middlesex to 77 for 4. In the end, their first innings total of 301 towards the end of the first day was quite a formidable one.

We didn't get off to a great start, either. Early on the second morning we lost the overnight, makeshift opening partnership of Lawrence Williams and Roger Davis with only 26 on the board, but if Clive Radley batting at number four had inspired a Middlesex revival, our own number four, Majid Khan, played even better and led us out of trouble. In compiling his 122, he shared in important stands with Alan Jones, Tony Lewis and Bryan Davis – the century stand with the skipper being crucial in shaping the Glamorgan recovery. Our runs came more quickly than the oppositions' had, and we were able to declare at 310 for 6 off only 86 overs – and with some useful batting points. The team plan of quick runs in the first innings was again paying off, and we had them batting again with plenty of time still left on the second day. At close of play they'd reached 96 for 2 with Smith (47) and Radley (10) the not-out batsmen. It was going well, but we knew a tough final day lay ahead.

Tony Cordle got Mike Smith's wicket first thing next morning for his overnight score, and Radley was soon back in the pavilion too, their wickets falling at 100 and 101. Then 'Speedy' dismissed Mike Brearley for the second time in the match, and I had John Murray caught behind for a duck: 102 for 5, 104 for 6. Four wickets had gone down in only 28 balls and for only eight runs. Now we knew we were in with a real chance. Norman Featherstone and Fred Titmus rallied Middlesex with a useful stand – and took some valuable time out of the game – but I got Titmus and Ron Hooker, and the obstinate Featherstone was run out. Game on! A second-innings total of 196 would see us to an important win, but there were only two hours and 50 minutes left in the day's play.

A superb 71 from Tony Lewis, supported by contributions from Alan and then Majid, kept us up with the clock. Then, dramatically and crucially, we lost a cluster of wickets at 122, 124 and 126, and I found myself walking down the long St. Helen's steps to – once again – join Eifion. We still needed 38 to win and I confess that, as I approached the crease, it seemed a lot, especially after the run of dismissals. We were now seven wickets down, with time running out, but Eifion batted beautifully, finishing the match in style with two lovely, cleanly-hit sixes in the last over – the second, which sailed over long-on, when we required only one for victory!

Our attacking approach and quick-scoring strategy had again paid off handsomely, putting us in the position to force a vital win over a very strong side. The win moved us to the top of the table for the first time, ten points ahead of Gloucestershire (who had played one game more) and 17 points ahead of Surrey. We were making the headlines! We were on a roll, and feeling good!

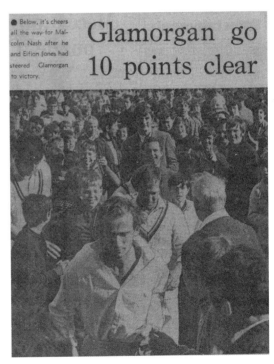

● Below, it's cheers all the way for Malcolm Nash after he and Eifion Jones had steered Glamorgan to victory.

Glamorgan go 10 points clear

Whichever route you choose, it's a long way by car from Swansea to Chelmsford! Well over 250 miles by any of the roads available to us in those days – probably nearer to 300 miles – but that was the journey that faced us as we showered and changed at the end of that exciting victory at St. Helen's. There was no celebratory drink or a chance to rest our tired feet. Just a long evening of driving and an early-hours arrival at our Essex hotel ready for the start of another championship game the next morning.

Perhaps this tough schedule accounted, in part, for our poor start as we found ourselves 18 for 3 before

Making the headlines! Front page of the Western Mail.

we knew it. Only a consolidating stand of 61 between Tony Lewis and Bryan Davis for the fourth wicket, a breezy 47 from Tony Cordle, and a hard-hitting but unexpected last wicket stand between bowlers Lawrence Williams and Don Shepherd kept us in the game with a first-innings total of 225.

Quick-scoring centuries from Keith Fletcher and Keith Boyce, who together put on 156 in just an hour and three-quarters, rescued Essex from a similarly poor start to ours – 32 for 3. Boyce was particularly ruthless on our attack, his hundred including three sixes and ten fours, and the home side declared with six wickets down and a useful lead of 51 runs.

Alan Jones was unlucky to miss out on a well-deserved century of his own when we batted again, falling to a catch off David Acfield for 98. Supported by useful runs from Majid and then Tony, Alan's innings enabled us, in turn, to declare at 249 for 6 and try to force another seemingly unlikely win.

Essex were left needing 199 at just over 70 runs an hour for a victory of their

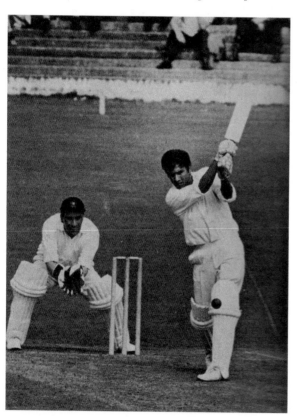

Essex's determined skipper and wicketkeeper Brian 'Tonker' Taylor would always give you a hard but enjoyable game. Majid Khan is the batsman.

own. Both teams had a chance of getting something out of the match and both sides enjoyed a contest. We liked playing against each other and everyone was up for a hard scrap. Importantly, of course, we also needed as many points as possible to keep us at the top of the table, but the weather was against us all!

An experimental ruling from Lord's meant that the decision to come off for rain no longer rested with the umpires, but was handed to the captains. When the rain started falling – light at first – it was clear that neither captain was interested in leaving the field. Soon it was raining harder. Then it was chucking it down. We stayed on, plugging away, but to no avail. We had no success, except for the retirement with a muscle injury of opening batsman Ian Ward. That only served to bring to the crease Brian 'Tonker' Taylor, the opposing wicketkeeper and very determined captain. He had promoted himself to number three. It seemed that Essex were the only possible winners now – and still it rained.

None of us had played in such poor conditions before. I stayed on at one end, but it was far from easy to keep a foothold or to hold the ball. However, both captains seemed doggedly determined to see things through – come hell or, literally, high water. In a forlorn effort to keep dry – or, more accurately, less wet – 'Speedy' had resorted to borrowing an umbrella from a spectator to field on the boundary. Peter, elsewhere on the boundary, kept nipping into the press tent between balls and overs.

So it went on. For more than an hour, and for 17 long overs, Glamorgan bowled and fielded in rain that seemed to be getting heavier by the minute! To make matters worse, Essex had reached 75 without loss.

'Tonker' was a good opponent and we always enjoyed matches against him and the Essex boys. He always played hard, but fair, and he called a spade a spade! I was too far away to hear his comments before he suddenly tucked his bat under his arm and marched off in the direction of the dressing-rooms, followed by his batting partner, two bedraggled but grateful umpires, and a relieved Glamorgan team. I'm told that the Essex skipper's loud observation was along the lines of: "Chaps, this is getting very silly. I don't think there is much point in us continuing." Or something far blunter, and very much more to the point. He was certainly not quoted in the next day's cricket pages! The match was drawn, we'd only gained two points, and the top-of-the-table positions were still too close to call.

The record books show that it was our penultimate match of the season, against Worcestershire at Cardiff, that officially secured the Championship for Glamorgan, but the key match in terms of clinching the Championship-winning position was the previous one against Essex at St. Helen's. With three matches left to play, we were now top of the table, 13 points ahead of Surrey, but Surrey, at The Oval, would be our final fixture. To remain favourites for the title, we needed to win against Essex.

Everything was set up for a great game. Our supporters, only too aware of its significance, packed noisily and excitedly into St. Helen's on all three days. The second day attendance of 12,000, boosted by schoolboys in the last throes of their summer holiday, was a record post-war crowd for a Championship match at St. Helen's – and an amazing one for a Monday in September!

The teams were very aware of the significance of the game too, of course, and the two skippers, Tony Lewis and Brian Taylor, agreed before the toss that whoever batted first would leave a challenging but gettable target for the opposition. We were two sets of players who enjoyed their cricket, and were looking forward to this contest.

We won the toss and batted, but soon slumped to 65 for 3. Things weren't looking so good until Alan Jones was joined by Bryan Davis and they added 91 to steady the ship, but another poor session after tea saw 210 for 5 quickly become 241 all out. Then, just when it seemed as if we had thrown away the advantage of the toss, Ossie Wheatley – back in the starting XI – got two late wickets to keep us in the game as Essex closed on 68 for 3. It was proving to be the tight contest we had expected.

It was also one of the three-day Championship games punctuated by a John Player League match – our last of the season – against Essex, again, and at St. Helen's, again! It was mighty close again too, with Essex winning by one run after we just failed to chase down their 40-over total of 180 with our last two men in the middle. After the game, as had become a popular tradition at Swansea, the two teams retired to The Fountain at Pontarddulais for a few well-earned beers and some lusty singing!

The Championship game resumed on Monday morning and saw the visitors continue their interrupted first innings. Big contributions by the hard-hitting South African Lee Irvine – with his first century for Essex – and 'Tonker' Taylor, who put on almost 130 together, allowed Essex to declare on 336 for 7, a comfortable and potentially match-winning lead of 95.

The game seemed to be slipping away from us, especially when, at the end of the second day, our second innings had slid to 123 for 4, with key batsmen Roger, Majid, Tony and Bryan all back in the pavilion and our lead only 28. Alan Jones was still there, however, with a fighting half-century to his name.

The third day – again with an excellent but, by now, less optimistic crowd – started with Alan and Peter Walker, the other over-night batsman, continuing to fight hard. After Alan was out to Lever, the resistance continued, with Peter Walker anchoring the innings with a dogged 50 in three and three-quarter hours, supported by contributions from Eifion (28), Tony Cordle (30) and me. Like Peter, I played an uncharacteristically restrained knock as we tried to occupy the crease for as long as possible and salvage a draw. I was on 36 not-out when Tony declared, with Don, once again, at the other end in defensive mode.

It was a bold and imaginative declaration. *Wisden* described it later as 'an inspired piece of captaincy', and it was. It probably owed something, too, to Tony's pre-match agreement with 'Tonker' that whoever batted first would try to make a game of it and to strive for a positive result by setting a challenging – achievable though not easy – target.

Our challenge to Essex was to get the required 190 runs for a win in just under two hours. The challenge was accepted! It looked as if, following Sunday's thrilling last ball and one run result, this was going to be another very exciting ending.

Ossie and I shared the new ball as the Essex batsmen enthusiastically set about their task. The openers fell to Ossie, but Essex were up with the clock. When umpires Constant and Pope signalled the start of the last hour, and its mandatory 20 overs, Essex were on 89 for 3 with Keith Fletcher looking in ominously good form. They were still only three down when the 100-mark was reached, and still up with the clock. Then, out of the blue, Fletcher fell to a brilliant diving catch by Bryan Davis off the spin of Roger Davis – 109 for 4.

We were back in with an outside chance. Three more wickets fell in quick succession as Essex continued to go for the win they knew was still well within their reach – 123- 4 became 123-5, then 125-6, and 131-7. Now it was more than an outside chance. Gordon Barker and Robin Hobbs continued to chase runs and, with four overs left, the Essex score had moved on to 163-7. They were still looking good for a win with just 27 runs needed.

With only two overs left, 16 were now required. Don Shepherd and Roger Davis were bowling. The excitement on the field and in the crowd was mounting. It couldn't be tighter.

At the start of the last over, to be bowled by Roger Davis, seven runs were needed with two wickets in hand. Singles were scored off the first two balls, then Barker was brilliantly stumped by Eifion. Lever joined East. Two more singles were scored. Now Essex needed 3 to win off the last ball. The two batsmen met for a mid-wicket conference.

In came Roger Davis. John Lever flashed outside the off stump and the ball squirted down towards the third-man boundary. He saw Ossie, never our most agile fielder and someone who had already bowled 36 tiring overs in the game, set off to intercept the ball. As the batsmen turned, it looked certain to be a safe second run which would see the scores tied, but Ossie surprised us all! He set off, running to his right, swooped to pick up the ball in his right hand and in almost the same movement returned it the keeper. It was an excellent piece of fielding. Although the throw came in just wide of the wicket, some great glove work by Eifion collected it cleanly and broke the wicket with a surprised Lever still a yard short of the crease. I was fielding at deepish mid-off, saving two and ready to cut off the boundary, and had a great view of Ossie's pick-up and throw, and of Eifion's speedy glove-work and typical agility behind the stumps. It was magic to watch. Cricket theatre.

It had been an amazing end to an amazing game, and an thrilling conclusion to great four days of cricket against excellent opponents. It was the closest result of the season – even closer, I suppose, than the first match draw with Yorkshire. St. Helen's had got our season off to a dramatic and nail-biting start, and now the old ground had done us proud again. *Wisden* noted that 'the thrilling last over wins against Middlesex and Essex at Swansea will long be remembered as one of the most wonderful weeks in Glamorgan's history'.

A great pick-up and throw by Ossie Wheatley, and some typically smart glove-work from Eifion Jones, gave us a vital victory.

As the crowd flooded on to the field and gathered in front of the pavilion, we quietly congratulated each other, knowing that the Championship was now almost in our grasp. We were all but home and dry as we set off confidently down the road to Cardiff for our last home fixture of the season against Worcestershire.

Going into the match we all knew that victory would ensure that we'd be flying the Championship pennant in 1970. It was set up perfectly. A big crowd. BBC Wales showing live television coverage. More press reporters than usual. Strong opponents who had themselves won the Championship twice only a few years before and, very understandably, a definite buzz in the changing room.

We'd already beaten Worcestershire a couple of months earlier at their New Road headquarters, but we knew they were a dangerous side with some individuals who could easily and quickly turn a match. With batsmen like Ron Headley, Alan Ormrod, Basil D'Oliveira and Tom Graveney, and bowlers like Jim Standen, Vanburn Holder, Brian Brain, Norman Gifford and the often underestimated but very talented Doug Slade, we knew this wasn't going to be easy.

As things turned out, it was less of a thriller than the close home encounters with Middlesex and Essex, but it had enough excitement all the same, and some good cricket.

The skipper won the toss and we batted first on a wicket that was always going to give bowlers a chance, with the bounce on the Sophia Gardens strip being variable and unpredictable. It wasn't the easiest to bat on, but Majid's quality showed through, and he very quickly put us in a commanding position with a stunning 156 out of the 214 scored while he was in the middle. His runs came quickly, too – in only three hours and 20 minutes – and badly dented Worcestershire's chances of getting anything from the game. What a time to get his top score for us!

Despite a battling 71 from West Indian international Ron Headley, with support from the always reliable Tom Graveney, Worcestershire were never really in the hunt and ended their first innings 82 behind. I got 4 for 43, including the prize wicket of Basil D'Oliveira, and Ossie and Don were in the wickets too.

Don reached a remarkable personal milestone when he took his first wicket, Jim Yardley pushing at a ball and providing Peter Walker with yet another catch. It was Don's 2,000th first-class wicket, and he became only the 30th bowler in the history of cricket to reach this incredible figure. Play stopped for a few minutes while Phil Clift came on to the field with a glass of champagne and we all gathered round as Don celebrated his incredible achievement – reached in his 20th season of first-team cricket. It was a great occasion to be part of.

Peter Walker pushed on in our second innings with 63 not out, backed up again by Majid and – until he had to retire injured after being struck just under the eye by a sharply-rising ball from Holder – by Eifion Jones. So it was fairly comfortable for us, extending our lead to 255 before declaring in the knowledge that batting last on the wearing Cardiff wicket would be challenging.

So it proved. Only Rodney Cass, opening the batting for Worcestershire as well as keeping, got a score of any note – 30, before becoming one of Tony Cordle's five victims. Only two other batsmen got into double figures as our visitors slid to what had by then become an inevitable defeat. Shep got important wickets, too, finishing with 4 for 20, and Majid's huge contribution to the

Don Shepherd's 2,000th first-class wicket.

The one bad moment for Glamorgan—Eifion Jones is felled by a ball from Holder and has to go to hospital. But Walker again steadied the side for a reasonable declaration to be made

Eifion Jones falls victim to a Vanburn Holder delivery at Sophia Gardens.

game was rounded off when he kept wicket for the injured Eifion and took a couple of important catches.

There were, predictably, very excitable and quite emotional scenes at the end as we all congratulated each other and received the generous congratulations of the Worcestershire players – themselves double-Championship winners only a few years earlier. Stumps were grabbed as souvenirs – I got one, though I don't know where it is now. Bryan Davis, who had taken the catch to end the match, stuck the ball in his pocket – producing it 20 years later at an anniversary lunch! Inevitably, the crowd invaded the pitch, and there was plenty of joyous singing that even St. Helen's would have been proud of.

We celebrated in the changing rooms before all making our various ways home, Peter Walker accompanied by the Glamorgan flag which he had managed to quietly free from its flagpole. He must have slipped out unnoticed at some point. The flag was proudly produced at the same anniversary lunch as the ball, much to everyone's amusement.

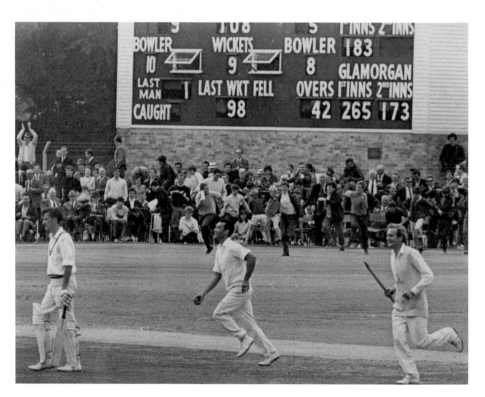

I grabbed a souvenir stump as the last Worcestershire wicket fell.

We'd done it. We were top of the table – and couldn't be caught! Strangely, though, the idea of being Champions took some getting used to. Don Shepherd said later that he bought lots of different newspapers the following day just to make sure it was true!

Fortunately, we had a week to recover – and come back down to earth – before our final game of the season at The Oval. I don't think we did much between the two games – just a couple of nets – before setting off for London, but we certainly weren't intending to sit back and take things easy. We were determined not to let Surrey spoil our unbeaten record at the final hurdle.

We needn't have worried. We played like Champions, and again put ourselves into a commanding position at the end of the first innings. John Edrich scored 92 – almost half his side's

Leaving the Sophia Gardens outfield through a sea of excited spectators.

runs – but Surrey found the spin of Don Shepherd (4 for 47 off 36 overs, 14 of them maidens) supported by Roger Davis (3 for 33 off 23) very difficult to deal with. Graham Roope was caught behind off Roger's bowling to give Eifion his 74th victim of the summer – 68 caught and six stumped – and leave him in top place in the national wicket-keeping table.

Poor weather took time out of the game, and by the end of the second day we had almost matched Surrey's total of 212, with only six wickets down and Bryan Davis still going strong. He carried on next morning to get his first century for us and make our record safe. We were 120 ahead on first innings and time was running out fast. Another classy innings from Edrich of 111 not out, who with fellow opener Mike Edwards put on 150 in just two and a quarter hours, saw the match to a draw (and us to another six points).

Now, with the season's fixtures completed, we really could call ourselves Champions!

'A Great Day for Welsh Cricket' proclaimed The Guardian. Glamorgan were making the front-pages – and I was holding the champagne!

Glamorgan v. Surrey at the Oval
Eifion Jones, Bryan Davis, Malcolm Nash, Lawrence Williams, Roger Davis, Majid Jahangir,
Tony Cordle, Peter Walker, Tony Lewis, Don Shepherd, Alan Jones

Champions! A team photo taken during the Surrey match at The Oval.

		P	W	L	D	Pts
1.	Glamorgan	24	11	0	13	250
2.	Gloucestershire	24	10	6	8	219
3.	Surrey	24	7	1	16	210

It was a great feeling. The first Glamorgan Champions since Wilf Wooller's legendary side of 1948, and unbeaten – the first unbeaten Champions since Lancashire in 1930.

In the celebrations that followed I couldn't help thinking back to St. Helen's and that third afternoon of our first game of the season against Yorkshire when Eifion and I had hung on for what proved, in the end, to have been such a vital draw.

Bryan Davis scored his first century for us in the final game to help preserve our unbeaten status.

8

Sunshine and Celebrations

*'I had the idea that we should try to get some warmth
into our winter bones rather than freeze to death
in the April pre-season nets at the Neath Indoor
Cricket School.'*
Peter Walker

So, the final game of the 1969 season petered out in a draw. There wasn't much of a celebration back in the dressing room. A couple of the Surrey boys came in – Pat Pocock and 'Inty' Alam, I think – and there were a few beers around, but essentially it was a quick shower, change and pack. We did have some messages of congratulation, including one from Harry Secombe who was working in London at the time. Swansea-born Harry liked his cricket and always kept in touch with Glamorgan's progress. Even more welcome than his cheery message was the case of very good champagne that accompanied it!

There was no time for cork-popping in The Oval dressing room, though. Not even time to catch a word with the guys or supporters. We had a train to catch! Our '12th', Kevin Lyons was busy getting all our bags ready and stacked, and had already summoned a fleet of taxis to get them – and us – to Paddington Station. "Don't worry," said Tony reassuringly. "We'll have a proper drink on the train. Plenty of time before Cardiff General."

Kevin Lyons was on 12th man duty in our final game at The Oval.

It was a mad dash to get changed, loaded up and through the heavy rush hour traffic in our taxi convoy, but we made it. Of course, it was a tough job for Kevin, paying off the taxis, rustling up some porters to help and, at the same time, keeping the boys together and getting them and the kit all safely aboard the right train within a very limited time frame. He did it, though, without anything or anybody going missing in the chaos of a crowded London railway platform, and with a couple of minutes to spare. It was an organisational triumph. You could see the relief on his face. We were all in our allocated seats. The bags were all safely stowed in the guard's van and the case of champagne was …

The terrible truth dawned on the hapless Kevin as the train started to gather speed out of Paddington. The colour drained from his face. He nervously confided to a couple of us sitting with him that although our kit was safely stored in the guard's van, the case of champagne wasn't. In getting everything and everyone from taxi to train, the champagne had been overlooked and was, in all likelihood, still going round the capital in the back of a black cab.

It wasn't long before Don and a couple of the other guys suggested that it was a good time for a glass of Harry's bubbly. Kevin broke the bad news. Of course, they thought it was a leg-pull at first, but the penny slowly dropped. As did jaws.

We still celebrated, though, and got through a significant proportion of the bottled beer carried in the buffet coach – and a large number of bags of crisps. It had been a very successful few days in the capital, and we had achieved our main goal of performing like table-leaders and remaining unbeaten. So it was a very contented – and very united – group that crossed back into Wales through the Severn Tunnel.

We never did discover what happened to the case of champagne. It wasn't handed in at Paddington Station, or to the police. Thankfully there was no shortage of celebratory alcoholic beverages in the days and weeks following our return to Wales! Far from it.

Towards the end of September we were entertained by the Lord Mayor of Cardiff to a dinner at City Hall. It was a fairly formal occasion, with speeches, but very enjoyable, and a welcome acknowledgement of the importance of our success to the whole community – and to Wales. Glamorgan County Council, the Western Mail and Echo, and Cardiff Cricket Club also hosted formal celebratory functions in the capital later in 1969, though I was out of the country by then.

Before I left, we were also invited – as a team – to less grand but certainly no less welcoming and generous evenings of celebration at a number of local cricket clubs. It was very significant to us that Welsh cricket followers, many themselves club cricketers or ex-club players, wanted to celebrate our achievement with us and to share in the occasion. To be part of the history

Glamorgan County Council invited the team to a celebratory dinner at the City Hall, Cardiff.

of cricket in Wales. One epic evening in Pontarddulais still stands out in my memory. Having been short of something to drink after the final match, now there was always plenty!

The media also played a part in our celebrations. Most of the side – I think only a couple had other commitments by then – were invited to the BBC Wales studios in Cardiff for a half-hour *Champions Special* hosted by Alun Williams. He went through the season, showing clips of exciting moments from some of the key matches, and getting individual reactions from us. Great fun! We looked very smart in club blazers and ties, and I thought we acquitted ourselves very well. Of course, BBC Wales had shown parts of a number of the home matches live, and so we as players – and our exploits on the field – were already well known to a wider audience than just Glamorgan members and those paying at the turnstiles.

I saw this programme again recently and was struck by the power of some of the things said. They really brought home the enormity and significance of our achievement. Wilf Wooller was one of the studio guests, and said that he felt our 1969 team was "a stronger all-round side" than his 1948 Championship winners. He also felt we were "a well-balanced bowling side", and "easily the best batting side we've ever had". High praise! I was also delighted to hear Wilf suggest that "Nash at nine – he would bat six in most county sides"!

Peter Walker was one of several team members to emphasise the great spirit in the group, noting that, "it's the best *team* I've ever played in", and skipper Tony Lewis spoke for all of us when he said, "it was a great dressing-room to go into every day of the week".

As well as the television interest, there were also various newspaper and other media interviews in the weeks following the end of the season – not as many as there would be today, but a significant number. There was also the exciting news that a Champions Tour to the West Indies was being organised for the weeks before the start of the 1970 season. That was something for the whole team to really look forward to.

I also had exciting plans of my own to look forward to, because in October 1969 I set off for South Africa for the first of two amazing winters spent coaching and playing in the African sunshine. My destination was Springs, about 40 miles or so east of Johannesburg and 50-plus miles south-east of the capital city, Pretoria.

My Glamorgan teammate Alan Jones – and before him Don Shepherd – had been the very successful professional at Springs, and when he was offered the opportunity to spend the winter of 1969-70 playing for Western Australia in Perth, Alan asked me if I'd like to replace him in South Africa. It didn't take me long to say "Yes, please".

Glamorgan's link to this small South African city was our ex-all-rounder, Jim Pressdee, who had emigrated to North East Transvaal – working for a sports outfitters – after leaving Glamorgan in 1965. Jim had quickly become involved in both local and provincial cricket, captaining the Springs High School Old Boys team and becoming a valued and highly-regarded member of the North East Transvaal side.

My role as resident professional at Springs High School Old Boys' Cricket Club involved working, through the club and the Springs Cricket Association, with their ten member schools. As well

It was an incredible opportunity to be able to play in Springs with Jim Pressdee, one of my schoolboy heroes in the Glamorgan side. I remember getting his autograph!

as coaching in schools most days – sometimes two or three schools in a day – I was also working in the nets with the club's players, and playing in the club side at weekends. Back then, a weekend match was usually a two-day, two innings affair, often involving a lot of travelling. We'd think nothing of making a 50 or 60 mile each way trip on a Saturday – to Pretoria, for example – and then doing it all again the next day. So it was very much wall-to-wall cricket for me – and I loved it!

The standard of club cricket was very high – higher than I had anticipated, and far stronger than league cricket here. Players involved in provincial cricket, in what was then the Currie Cup, would play a programme of only eight, or so, four-day matches in a season. There was no other professional cricket, so the Currie Cup players, and all the top international players, played club cricket too. Week in, week out.

For example, South Africa's very talented wicketkeeper Denis Lindsay was playing just down the road for his home-town side Benoni as well as turning out for North East Transvaal in provincial cricket and for the national side. Denis had toured England in 1965 and played in all three Tests, and had been in outstanding form in the 1966-67 series against the Australians.

At this time, overseas players were not allowed to play at the provincial level, so I wasn't able to play any Currie Cup cricket, which from my point of view was a shame. It would have been a great experience. Yet I was able to coach at schoolboy level within the Currie Cup set-up – Nuffield Schools Cricket – and I looked after the North East Transvaal under-13s and under-11s. Working with these talented youngsters was really rewarding – and enjoyable, too. Also, from their point of view, playing provincial cricket as schoolboys was a superb platform for them to develop their game.

As well as the invaluable experience of playing some very good cricket with some excellent players, and playing on different wickets and in different conditions to those in county cricket, I found that I also benefitted a lot from my coaching roles. Through coaching, I learned a great deal about my own game and about cricket itself. It was an important learning experience for me.

Playing with, and under, Jim Pressdee was also an important learning experience. I hadn't played with Jim in Wales – he left just before I started – but he had been one of the players in the Glamorgan side that, as a schoolboy follower of the team, I'd admired most. I can still remember getting his autograph at Abergavenny!

Jim was a hard task-master on the field, but a very generous host. During a six-week break from cricket over Christmas and the New Year, when Jim and his wife went back to Wales for a holiday, I was left with instructions to use his car as much as I wanted and make sure it wasn't stolen. He said he wasn't bothered if my Beetle was stolen as long as no harm came to his much-prized

The South Wales hockey side, season 1965-66, with a smiling M. Nash, front row, far left.

Mercedes! So, my girlfriend Sue – who would later become my wife and who had come out to join me for an extended break – and I did as we were told and travelled all over South Africa in Jim's car. It's such a lovely country, and our travelling was a memorable experience with so many incredible – and very different – places to see.

The only downside to my South African adventure was that, for the second winter, I had to forgo the hockey which had become such a significant part of my sporting year. I'd been involved in different levels of representative hockey for a while, and in Welsh trials which took the form of a triangular tournament between the South Wales, North Wales, and London Welsh teams – my South Wales team used to win the tournament nearly every year. I'd also been selected for Wales under-23, and captained them to a 2-1 win against Ireland at Lansdowne Road, Dublin.

Welsh hockey had a very peculiar set-up at that time. The national side contained a lot of Anglo-Welsh, people playing with London Welsh, for example, and we also had what was called a 'Home Welsh XI' – the team I represented – that was made up of players from Welsh-based clubs.

Sophia Gardens was an important centre for hockey at that time, with a brand new hockey pitch to the side of the cricket field. It was one of the first artificial pitches in the country and a fabulous facility. It was used for the

I had the honour of captaining the Welsh under-23 side against Ireland in 1966 ...

Olympic trials, and national training weekends. The GB squad used to come down to Cardiff for their training, and play against a South Wales XI. I used to feature fairly well in those games, and my name was in the mix for consideration as a member of the side to go to the Mexico Olympics. As it turned out, I wasn't eligible for selection anyway. The Olympic Games were strictly for amateurs, and I was earning my living from sport – even though it was a completely different game! I was a professional athlete and that was that.

I loved my hockey, but when I got back from Springs – having already missed a second

Malcolm Nash to captain Wales Under 23 side

Nash led Wales to victory

... and the local paper reported our success.

Nash decides: Hockey must take a back seat

COUNTY'S MR. MODESTY PUTS CRICKET FIRST

As the Evening Post reported, I found myself faced with a difficult decision.

winter – I had some serious thinking to do. I'd put off making a decision up until this point, but now it really needed to be made. Was I able to continue playing serious hockey, or should I put hockey on the back-burner and focus on cricket?

My hockey team in Swansea were really keen that I should continue so I started to play again, but they wanted me to play in the European hockey cup, which meant training three days a week and playing on Saturdays – and I was playing county hockey on Sundays, too. Decision made! It was impossible to keep up such an intense commitment in two sports. I suggested that I'd be quite happy to drop down and play with the 2nd XI, and perhaps doing a bit of coaching with them at the same time. So, I didn't give up hockey altogether, but I did give up serious hockey and any international ambitions. It was still a good way of keeping fit, though, and it was great for hand-eye co-ordination.

The idyllic six months coaching and playing in South Africa wasn't the full extent of my exciting winter of cricket and travel – and sunshine. I'd only been back in Wales about three days – just long enough to get some washing done and repack – and I was off to catch a plane again, this time for Glamorgan's tour to Bermuda and the West Indies.

This was an important post-script to our Championship success. Although it took place at the beginning of the 1970 season, it was officially linked to our 1969 triumph, and also doubled as pre-season training in readiness for another busy cricketing summer.

The 'brains' behind the organization of the tour was Peter Walker, with his travel-agency background and contacts. He had the help of a friend in advertising, journalist Peter Corrigan, and Bill Edwards, a member of the Glamorgan committee who had West Indian contacts and also – very importantly – ran his sports shop business on King Edward's Road, Swansea. As well as supplying much of the Glamorgan kit, Bill also supplied equipment to the West Indies team – and seemed to know everybody in the Caribbean who had a cricketing link. Our teammate Bryan Davis was another important

Anthony Lewis, Prince Bartholomew, Willie Rodriguez, Inshan Ali, Harry Ramoutar and Dudnath Ramkissoon.

SEAMERS

Glamorgan skipper Tony Lewis said yesterday that his players – Ossie Wheatley apart – are all fit.

But the leader of the English champion team was not breathing any fire as he watched his men go through a practice session at the Queen's

'MR. 36' HIMSELF!

MALCOLM NASH is the name ... does it ring a bell?

Well that's the man (See picture below) who West Indies Test skipper Gary Sobers thumped for six sixes in a six-ball over in 1968, playing for Nottingham against last season's English county cricket champions Glamorgan at Swansea.

And that will remain as a world record, since 36 runs is the highest that could be scored in a six-ball over.

Nash will be in action today against Trinidad, the Shell Shield champs, at the Queen's Park Oval.

Peters' big date

THE DATE for Edwin Peters' international boxing card is Friday, May 8.

The South promoter made this announcement yesterday despite the fact that he hasn't signed up his card for the big night as yet.

But the South promoter said he had already decided on the fights and hoped to get the boxers to initial their contracts today.

He had hoped to finalise plans with Circle S manager and H.A. Clarke today.

The main bout will be between Ramon Guzman, top Venezuelan lightweight and the new Trinidad champion, Trevor Glasgow.

HOCKEY SCORES

(NTHA 2nd Div.)
Carib (3)   Malvern (1)
Wilcox   G. Harris
Cowie
A. Bain
(TTWHA "A" Div.)
Casuals (2)   Jets (0)
A. Davis 2
("B" Division)
Checkers (1) Blue Streaks (0)
V. Payne

I discovered I was already well-known to Caribbean cricket fans. This article had been published in Trinidad.

part of the planning and, by the time we left, he was back home in Trinidad waiting to join up with us.

Interestingly, our tour wasn't paid for by the club, nor was it sponsored – as it might be today – by a large insurance company or bank. The two Peters managed to get sponsorship from Rizla, a company well-known to roll-your-own exponents as makers of probably the best cigarette papers in the world. How fashions and the social climate have changed in the intervening years!

For me, the West Indies turned out to be the ideal touring destination. Not only because of the wonderful climate, silver beaches and generous hospitality, but because – as I discovered – I was quite well-known on the islands we visited. In fact, throughout the Caribbean! It seemed that my link with Garry Sobers the previous season had given me heroic status – and if not heroic, at least curiosity! Their celebration of the achievement of their national hero had somehow rubbed off on me!

We met up at Cardiff's Rhoose Airport for a short flight to London Heathrow where we boarded our flight – in a VC10, I think – to Bermuda. In the photograph taken on the tarmac at Rhoose I am the only one wearing a sweater under my club blazer! It was cold being back in Wales after the warmth of South Africa.

One of the touring group was our 19-year-old, right-arm medium pacer Graham Kingston who had shown such promise in making his Championship debut, aged only 16, against Worcestershire at Colwyn Bay. In 1969 he'd got 6 for 36 in a John Player League match against Derbyshire but, perhaps, his main claim to fame – and one that he probably dined out on for many years

The Glamorgan squad at Cardiff's Rhoose Airport en route to the West Indies for their Rizla-sponsored 1971 Champions' Tour – left to right: Roger Davis, Alan Jones, Graham Kingston, Kevin Lyons, Eifion Jones, Peter Walker, Malcolm Nash, Ossie Wheatley, Don Shepherd, Tony Lewis, Lawrence Williams and Jeff Jones.

– was that he got Garry Sobers out in a John Player Sunday League game at Ebbw Vale in 1970! He was a good lad, but sadly he didn't make a go of it in the first-class game and left the staff soon after.

We'd only been in the air ten minutes when young 'Kingers' ordered a scotch and settled back into his seat with a large cigar. I liked his style! Looking back, that set the tone for the tour. We were royally entertained by our Bermudan and West Indian hosts, with wonderful and memorable welcomes wherever we went. It was a nightly whirlwind of receptions, dinners, parties and entertainments. We made a lot of friends – and were also treated to some incredible sightseeing and swimming but, as well as partying hard, we played some good, competitive cricket.

As I'd had a lot of winter cricket in South Africa, and wasn't so in need of a warm-up in the middle as most of the other guys, it had been decided that I'd sit out some of the games. As a result I didn't play in the first two-day, single-innings warm-up game against the local side in St. George's, Bermuda, which we somehow managed to lose. Perhaps the flights had caught up with us – and some careless run-outs didn't help. I'm sure the excellent evening of entertainment put on by the local Cambrian Society wasn't a factor in our collapse on the second day!

Our schedule took us from Bermuda to our first West Indian destination via New York, so we had a day exploring some of the sights of the Big Apple,

Ready for the first match of the tour at Hamilton, Bermuda.

Ossie Wheatley bowling in the game against Bermuda.

including a trip to the top of the Empire State Building – an unforgettable experience! That evening we were back on a plane to Antigua, for one night, before a flight to St. Kitts early the next morning for a fixture against the island's team. We touched down around breakfast time for a three-day match starting at 11 o'clock!

Mercifully, we batted first. Alan Jones, Roger Davis, Bryan Davis and I got the bulk of our 279. I was pleased with my own form with the bat, getting 48 before being run out. The game saw the first of a number of exciting finishes on the tour, ending in a draw with St. Kitts nine wickets down and still 37 short of their winning target. It was an enjoyable game, and a moral victory in physically demanding conditions – cocktail receptions each night (including one at the Governor's residence), a lot of singing (much of it in Welsh), and searing heat! Then more flights, and more hair-raising taxi rides.

I wasn't too sorry to sit out the next match on Dominica. It was another draw, and a lovely end to the game with a very large and enthusiastic crowd gathered with the Governor and teams in front of the pavilion for the inevitable speeches and farewells.

The travel arrangements continued to be challenging, even for county cricketers used to driving the length and breadth of the country for back-to-back Championship and John Player League games. We were up at 5am – after another reception with entertainment from a local band and dancers – for a long drive to the airport and an island-hopping flight to Grenada. Another lengthy drive saw us arrive at the ground at around 2.15pm – and we were in the field 30 minutes later!

I played again in this two-day game at the old Queen's Park ground in St. Georges. By the close we'd got a respectable 153-5 off 50 overs, and declared overnight. The next day Grenada matched us with 152-7 off the same number of overs. I put in a tight opening spell, with only 14 runs (and a couple of wickets) coming off my ten overs. Second time round, Alan and Roger put on 76 for the first wicket, and we declared on 103-1, setting our hosts 105 to win. They were on a precarious 88 for 8 when time ran out. It was another super game of cricket.

We saw so many beautiful places on our tour, but Grenada was one of the most spectacular. We stayed in some chalets right on the beach at Grand Anse. On the second morning of the game we were all swimming in the beautiful clear, blue-green water before breakfast. Not a bad way to warm up for a day's cricket, though Ossie may have had a different view after cutting his foot on some coral. Grenada was also memorable for an amazing Grand Ball – with over a thousand guests – at the Governor's residence. These were all not-to-be-forgotten experiences.

We had a rare day off from cricket, with more swimming and some socialising with a small group of enthusiastic Glamorgan supporters who had caught up with us and were staying at a nearby hotel. Then came the inevitable plane journey, this time to Trinidad and an unbelievable welcome from a steel band and local dignitaries – political and sporting! We felt like visiting royalty. It was very different from playing at an almost deserted Oval on a cool Tuesday evening in September!

We played two matches in Trinidad. The first was a 40-over game against Trinidad Colts, and we got a decent 157 for 7. I enjoyed my knock of 33 off only three overs. Don, 'Speedy' and Roger bowled well, restricting them to 132 all out. After a free day, with shopping and sight-seeing in Port of Spain and lunch at the Hilton, we managed a net before another swim and another cocktail party. I was really starting to feel that it was a lifestyle I could happily get used to!

The final match of our tour, a three-day encounter against a strong Trinidad and Tobago side that had just won the domestic Shell Shield competition, was one we had all been particularly looking forward to. It was to be played at the historic, and very picturesque, Queen's Park Oval – a Test venue since 1930 when England were the opposition, but a ground that had hosted international matches since the visit of Lord Hawke's tourists of 1897. Only two years before our match there, the ground had hit the cricketing headlines when a generous – and controversial – declaration by Garry Sobers had led to an unexpected England win. Playing there proved to be an amazing experience, every bit as exciting as we had expected and a fitting climax to our tour.

In very warm conditions indeed, we batted first and were off to a good start, reaching 102 for 2 at lunch. A decent afternoon followed and although we lost some quick wickets through chasing runs, we posted a competitive 279 – Alan Jones top-scoring with an excellent and exhausting 114 in intense heat. Then, in a challenging session for the home side before close of play, Lawrence Williams bowled beautifully and took two wickets. We had them on 20 for 2 overnight, and we were very much in the box seat.

The temperatures were much the same the next day, nudging 45 degrees Centigrade. Lawrence, Shep and Peter Walker were probably the most effective of our attack, but we bowled well as a unit and our efforts were – as usual – backed up by excellent fielding. At lunch we had reduced them to 134 for 9 and were still well on top.

We then experienced one of those turn-arounds that crop up in cricket every so often. Trinidad and Tobago's last pair, Inshan Ali and Harry Ramoutar, neither renowned for their batting, thwarted us. We tried everything but simply couldn't get the final wicket – despite some very close umpiring calls! They put on 108 together before number 11 Ali was at last bowled by Bryan Davis for 55. At 242 all out, our hosts were only 30 behind and very much back in the game.

Worse was soon to follow as the change of fortunes continued. When Peter joined Eifion in the middle, our first five batsmen were already back in the pavilion with only 17 on the board. Day 2 ended with the home side now very much on top, and us tottering on 33 for 5.

Despite Eifion (36) and Peter (24) continuing to fight next morning – the only two Glamorgan players to get into double figures – we were soon all out for a paltry and embarrassing 96, leaving them to get only 127 to win and lots of time to do it. We continued to try hard, of course, and there was some panic in the home dressing-room when the fifth wicket went down at only 76, but that was the extent of it. Trinidad and Tobago won another very enjoyable game by five wickets.

There was, for me, an interesting post-script to our visit to the Queen's Park Oval in Port of Spain. I came across Wes Hall again. Wes was approaching what would be his final season as a player in domestic competition, and the previous year had played the last of his 48 Tests for the West Indies. After many years playing for his native Barbados, he had accepted a coaching role that included leading a scheme to develop youth cricket – a passion of his – in Trinidad, and at the same time to play for Trinidad and Tobago in the Shell Shield. A number of the youngsters he had helped to develop were playing in the match against us.

I'd met him at St. Helen's in 1966 on his final tour to the UK. He was not then the force he had been three years previously (when he'd blown Glamorgan away with 7 for 51 off 20 fearsome overs), but was still a very formidable bowler. I wasn't officially 12th man at Swansea, but was changed and managed to get on to the field – only briefly, but long enough to drop Basil Butcher at mid-wicket.

At the end of the day's play I chatted to Wes in the bar about fast bowling. He was, like a lot of hostile fast bowlers, a very gentle and thoughtful character off the field. He was also an excellent coach. So when I met him again, in Port of Spain, I reminded him of our conversation in Swansea and asked him if he would be good enough to watch me bowl in the nets and give my action the 'once over'. He was only too happy to help, and his advice was very similar to that given to me several years earlier

Wes Hall's observations on my bowling were very helpful – and reassuring.

by Bill Voce – don't change anything and definitely don't spoil things that are working well, including lateral movement, by searching for additional pace.

Incidentally, this conversation with Wes Hall was one that I would recall some six years later when the Chairman of Selectors, Alec Bedser, suggested that I needed to bowl quicker in order to get into the England side.

It was reassuring to get the views of one of the all-time bowling greats. That time I spent in the nets with Wes was a memorable end to a memorable tour, rounded off the next day with a final swim and farewell party at the very smart Hilton, followed by a fairly hurried departure for the airport and our Heathrow-bound flight with 'Black Power' rioting spreading across the island. Excitement to the end! Peter Walker and his co-organisers, and tour manager Phil Clift, had done us proud. It had been a very fitting celebration of a great achievement the previous season. It was a collection of experiences that none of us would ever forget.

As a team, and as a group of individuals, we continued to gel well. We were in good spirits. We were basking in the glory of our Championship win, and had benefitted from basking in the warmth of the West Indian sun – perfect for muscles recovering from a season of almost daily cricket. We all returned suitably refreshed, looking forward to the demands and challenges of the new domestic campaign, and hoping for more success, but first there was one more piece of the Championship celebrations to be put into place.

From the West Indies tour we went almost straight into the new season, and what was, I suppose, the final stage of our celebrations. It was the traditional season-opening fixture between Marylebone Cricket Club and the Champion county. This historic fixture, which for a few years had featured a Rest of England side, was always played at the end of the season but 1970 saw the first such game scheduled to mark the start of the new season. It also reverted to a MCC rather than Rest of England fixture.

So, here we were at Lord's, as Champion county and proudly flying our Championship pennant at the 'Home of Cricket', and preparing to meet a strong MCC side captained by Ray Illingworth, the current England captain.

We acquitted ourselves well. After electing to bat, Alan Jones and Roger Davis got us off to a great start, putting on 92 for the first wicket, and although wickets fell fairly regularly once they were dismissed by Illingworth for 47 and 53 respectively, Tony was able to declare at our close of play score of 212 for 7. It hadn't been thrilling cricket, but it was a slow wicket and the batting practice back on a home strip after the Caribbean pitches was very useful.

The next morning saw us get off to a cracking start! In my first over I got Gloucestershire's north Walian opener David Green, and Kent's Brian Luckhurst (who would make his Test debut against Australia the following winter). We had them 1 for 1, then 4 for 2. In his first over, Lawrence got Harry Pilling of

Lancashire – 4 for 3. We were very much on top, and before too long I bowled Hampshire's Richard Gilliat – 21 for 4. We were playing like champions! These were good wickets to be getting.

A stand of 212 by Keith Fletcher (74) and Tony Greig (65), both England internationals, then stopped the rot and Illingworth declared at 191 for 9, still 21 behind but leaving us with a difficult spell before close of play. His plan worked and we lost Alan Jones quickly to the pace of Alan Ward – Derbyshire's fast bowler who also went with Illingworth's England side to play in the 1970-71 Ashes series. Roger Davis and Kevin Lyons safely saw out the rest of the second day, though, and we finished on 27 for 1 – 48 ahead – and the match seemingly evenly poised.

That soon changed, and only Kevin and Eifion got any runs as we collapsed to a very disappointing 113 all out. At one

Skipper Alan Jones got our season as reigning champions off to a great start. He is pictured on his way to a century against Jamaica at Swansea later that summer.

stage we lost six wickets while adding only one run with 80-2 soon becoming 81-8, and there was no way back. On a pitch that we had known from the start would become more helpful to the spinners, the Yorkshire and England duo of Ray Illingworth and Don Wilson tied us up in knots. Our spinners were effective, too, with Roger Davis and Peter Walker bowling the majority of the overs in MCC's second innings and getting a couple of wickets each, but a powerful 74 by David Green saw them easily to victory.

It was a disappointing end to the game but, as a team, we had played some good cricket and there had been encouraging individual performances against strong opponents. My own bowling had been pretty decent and I was pleased with my performance. The winter of South African cricket and the pre-season tour were paying dividends, and my first-innings figures of 5 for 32

I was starting to be mentioned for a place in the winter's Ashes tour – and Fred Trueman was one of those backing me.

off 14 overs, including the wicket of the England captain, clean bowled for 15, helped to keep my name mentioned on some of the sports pages as a possible selection for the winter tour of Australia.

From Lord's, we travelled straight to Swansea for the first match of the new Championship season – the first of 24! The relentless schedule was starting all over again, but this time with our Championship pennant flying proudly at every ground we played at, and with every side more determined than ever to beat us and take the scalp of the Champions!

Our first opponents, on a slow St. Helen's wicket, were Kent – a very powerful line-up led by the ex-England captain Colin Cowdrey. I didn't get Colin out this time, but I did get the wicket of a future England skipper – Mike Denness had already won his first England cap and in 1973 would take over the captaincy from Ray Illingworth.

It was a super game of cricket to open the season. Bryan Davis top-scored for us in both innings, his 83 not out in the second, against the formidable international pairing of England's Derek Underwood and the West Indies' medium-pacer John Shepherd, enabling Tony to declare and leave Kent a difficult total to chase. In Kent's first innings, Don Shepherd and Roger Davis did the bulk of the bowling and got nine wickets between them, Shep finishing with 6 for 43 off 28 overs as the visitors were dismissed for only 103. Their second innings saw Don again spearhead the bowling attack and get through 39 overs (18 of them maidens) for only 57 runs. The pressure he put on the Kent batsmen was relentless. His main support in this innings came from Peter Walker, who got through 34.5 overs and took 5 for 86. This was a good win for us, and an excellent start to the new campaign.

In the end, we didn't quite repeat our success of the previous season, but we came very close, finishing as runners-up and only 17 points behind the eventual champions – Kent! One more win might have brought us back-to-back championships.

We each won nine games, and Glamorgan had the satisfaction of beating the eventual champions, fairly convincingly, in our only encounter of the season. It was another great year for us, the third in a row with a hat-trick of top-three finishes – third, first and second. Those three seasons had been a hell of a ride, and with an outstanding set of guys. It was a great side to be in.

However, the triumphs of those years – and of that side – would start to fade sooner than any of us would have imagined. Key players, including Peter Walker, Don Shepherd and Tony Lewis, would soon not feature again for the club. There would be some questionable decisions over releases and appointments and, before we knew it, we would find ourselves in a new and less-rewarding era of mid-table and lower finishes.

In fact, unimaginable as it would have seemed to me as we pursued the exciting and very successful 1970 season, Glamorgan would not finish in the top half of the Championship table again for the rest of my time with the club. In fact, worse than that, it would be another 20 years, in 1990, before Glamorgan would manage to reach the top half.

That didn't mean, of course, that we didn't still have some talented guys in the side, or that we didn't on many occasions play some good cricket, both collectively and individually.

There was still plenty of excitement to come.

9

Rules – and Changing Them

'I feel no shame in being in the vanguard which helped to bring about changes in what had been a feudal system of master and servant for over a hundred years.'
Peter Walker

Sometimes people set out quite deliberately to change rules and regulations. Aspects of my involvement with the Professional Cricketers' Association would certainly fall into this category. Sometimes people cause change by chance. I did both!

A lot of people across the cricketing world know my name – and so know of my part in cricketing history – because of the 'Sobers over'. The events at St. Helen's have become part of cricketing folklore and I suspect that my name will always be linked with that August afternoon in 1968, but there were two other, less well-publicised, cricketing incidents in my career that resulted in changes in the rules and regulations of the game – and continue to influence practice – and for that reason also have a place in cricketing history.

Both involved change caused by accident – quite literally. Both were days I would prefer to forget but which, for different reasons, it is important to remember.

It was a ball I'd bowled hundreds of times before – perhaps thousands of times – but its horrific outcome was something I had never experienced before. Nor, thank goodness, did I ever experience it again, but once was more than enough for all of us involved.

Glamorgan were at Sophia Gardens, Cardiff. It was Saturday May 29th, 1971. Just after tea on the opening day of our Championship match against Warwickshire. For us, it was a routine day at the office. A greyish day, but dry and, with the cricket reflecting the weather, unremarkable and greyish.

We hadn't performed at our best or according to plan and, after winning the toss and deciding to bat, found ourselves all out for 191 before an early tea.

Only Peter Walker (57) and Tony Cordle (43) had done anything of significance with the bat. Mike Llewellyn had not been the first player in cricketing history to get a duck in his first Championship innings! I'd weighed in with 25, but overall it was a disappointing team performance. On the other hand, on an unpredictable Sophia Gardens track, it might turn out to be better than it looked. Time would tell.

Neal Abberley was opening the batting for the visitors. I had the new ball and knew I had a chance to get him cheaply. The pitch was damp in places after rain the day before, and the Cardiff wicket in

Warwickshire left-handed batsman Neal Abberley.

those days often gave you a chance anyway. I remember being pleased at the amount of movement I was getting in to the right-hander bowling my left-arm over the wicket. Perhaps our score had not been too bad after all.

I knew that Neal, although a very good right-handed batsman, tended to be vulnerable early on in an innings – yet it was a different story once he was set. So I had hopes of a bowled or leg before, but in particular had thoughts of the ball swinging to get a nick, perhaps a little bat and pad, to one of our close fielders.

We had developed a deserved reputation for being a strong fielding side, and this owed much to our close-fielding skills, with our close fielders at that time each having their own specialist position. They were the engine-room of a field that largely set itself. Bryan Davis was first slip, Majid second. Peter Walker, after a number of years at short square-leg, had taken over the backward short-leg/leg-slip berth and, finally, Roger Davis was short square-leg. All were brave and superbly athletic fielders. Great anticipators, and with wonderful, safe pairs of hands. A great group to have backing you up as a fast bowler.

I could sense that the guys round the bat were registering the amount of movement I was getting, and were on their toes for a catch. I bowled a couple more balls to Neal that almost had him in trouble. It was a good contest, and I could sense his frustration. He wanted to get on with it. The next ball was another in-swinger. Decent line and length. Full, and moving into Neal fairly sharply and late. With very little back-lift and a lot of wrist he whipped it round with an almost straight bat. It wasn't a pull or a hook. Certainly not a sweep. It was a very quick movement, a real whip, beautifully timed, and difficult for a close fielder to anticipate.

Roger was close. He always fielded close to the batsman. Perhaps that day, because of the slow and unresponsive pitch, he was a touch closer still. The

Bryan Davis, Majid Khan, Peter Walker and Roger Davis – the best set of close fielders you could wish to bowl to. Australia's John Gleeson is the batsman.

ball flew off the full face of the bat and hit him behind his left ear as he instinctively turned away. The noise of ball hitting skull was horrific. Playing professional cricket you got used to seeing the occasional injury on the field – perhaps a broken bone or nose or tooth, or a torn muscle – but this was different. We all knew instinctively and immediately that this was as serious as it could possibly get. Fielders, batsmen and umpires rushed to help but, confronted with Roger's unconscious body, didn't really know what help to give. We were terrified. Out of our depth.

As steps were taken to summon an ambulance and medical help, a doctor ran out to the middle from his seat in the Members' Enclosure. He announced to the huddle that Roger had swallowed his tongue and stopped breathing. We could see that his colour was changing as we watched. Blue became purple. A second doctor appeared from the crowd and began mouth-to-mouth resuscitation. Thank goodness it was a Saturday or these two medical men, who saved Roger's life, might well have been in their surgeries miles away.

Suddenly, and thankfully, Roger was sick. His colour started to recover. He was breathing again, thank God. After what seemed an age but was probably only another 15 minutes or so, the decision was made to move him to the now waiting ambulance.

As you can imagine, nobody was interested in continuing with the game. We felt ill. Useless. I suppose we were all in shock, poor Neal Abberley more than most, but as if taking pity on us and with wonderful timing, right out of the blue – well, grey – came a small dark cloud which hovered over Sophia Gardens and managed a little light drizzle. We all, umpires included, needed no second invitation and headed for the sanctuary of the dressing-rooms and a 45 minute break in which to start to pull ourselves together. When play resumed for the last part of the day, skipper Tony Lewis took the decision to put himself at forward short-leg, but after a while Peter Walker moved from backward short-leg to relieve him – and so to temporarily resume the position he had taken up with such distinction for so many seasons.

Next day, with overnight news of Roger from the hospital continuing to cause concern with anxieties over possible brain damage, we found ourselves with a new close catcher. Tony Cordle donned a white motor-cycle helmet and proudly announced to the skipper – in fact, the whole dressing room – that he was our new forward short-leg fielder. Umpires Bill Alley and David Evans didn't raise an eyebrow. Indeed, when 'Speedy' wasn't positioned close to the bat, they willingly held his new improvised headgear.

We lost the game by eight wickets, scoring a feeble 90 in the second innings. Warwickshire's West Indian spinner, Lance Gibbs, bowled beautifully taking 7 for 28 in just over 20 overs, ten of them maidens, but our minds were not properly focussed on events in the middle. Our hearts weren't in the battle. We were thinking of Roger lying in a hospital bed, fighting a battle of his own.

Thankfully, Roger started to slowly improve as the weeks passed. The signs gradually started to be more positive until eventually, and amazingly, he made a comeback in August, but

Tony Cordle took over the forward short-leg position for Glamorgan.

no longer opened the batting, nor fielded again at short-leg. He did, though, deal beautifully with some hostile short-pitched bowling.

Inevitably, the accident sparked discussion about safety on the field, and on how close was too close. It provoked debate – with views strongly put forward on both sides – about whether the wearing of helmets by close fielders was a positive or negative step. Did a helmet give the fielder an unfair advantage? Did it encourage reckless or less skilful fielding? Or was it a sensible and timely precaution, and really only a logical extension of the forward short-leg's box?

Roger's accident changed the appearance of the cricket field for ever. When Tony Cordle emerged from the dressing-rooms at Cardiff on May 31st, 1971 it was, as far as we know, the first time that a helmet-wearing fielder had been seen in a first-class game.

Following the events at Sophia Gardens, several other teams started to employ modified helmets of some sort for their close-to-the-wicket fielders. More followed suit, and gradually the practice spread. Later, players in the vulnerable forward short-leg position abandoned protective headgear converted from other sports or pastimes and were wearing helmets designed specifically for cricket. As time has passed, we have seen MCC regulations relating to both fielding and batting helmets, their construction, and their involvement in dismissals – regulations and designs which continue to change and which have recently undergone further intense scrutiny following another sickening accident and the death of poor Phil Hughes on the field at Sydney.

It was another accident – though thankfully not nearly as bad – that saw another cricket regulation under scrutiny – and a new ruling. On this occasion I had the bat in my hand, not the ball and, ironically, a helmet was involved too.

In June 1978, Glamorgan went to the historic and very pretty tree-ringed Queen's Park ground in Chesterfield, tucked in the shadow of the famous twisted spire of All Saints, to meet a strong Derbyshire side captained by the formidable South African international Eddie Barlow. It was one of my favourite grounds, and its shortish boundaries were ideal for some quick scoring. When we arrived, the pitch looked good and so it proved to be, with decent bounce and pace.

We lost the toss, and before too long had almost lost the match, too! Batting at number three, Peter Kirsten, Derbyshire's other South African who had recently arrived on Barlow's recommendation, scored a magnificent and rapid double-hundred. He took us apart, scoring five sixes and 21 fours in his 206 not out. This was his highest first-class score to date, though he went on to score two further double-hundreds in his four years with Derbyshire. Two years later at Derby, when I was the Glamorgan captain in the firing line, he scored 213 not out – including a century between lunch and tea.

Kirsten's Queen's Park knock dwarfed the contributions of his teammates, and he took his side to 341 for 6 declared in very good time. There was no way back for us. I top-scored with 41, but we ended up all out – and, unusually, all caught – for 140, a daunting 201 behind and following-on. Colin Tunnicliffe and England's Mike Hendrick did the bulk of the damage with four wickets each.

To be honest, our second innings performance was equally ordinary. Alan Jones, captaining the side, and John Hopkins raised a flicker of hope by getting us off to a better start, the first wicket falling at 50, but quick wickets followed and I found myself strapping pads on again and joining Eifion Jones at a

Derbyshire's hard-hitting Peter Kirsten.

disappointing 133 for 7. A crushing defeat was staring us in the face.

There was no *Roy of the Rovers* ending, but my modest second innings of 21 was significant for two reasons. The first was personal, as it saw me pass the milestone of 5,000 Championship runs. The second was because I became, again quite literally by accident, involved in a change in the rules of cricket!

I had enjoyed my first innings knock, and the ball was coming off my bat well in the second innings, too. My timing was good, and the Chesterfield boundaries looked invitingly close. Eifion had not lasted long, so my new partner Barry Lloyd and I, faced with the inevitable, decided to simply make the best of things and give the ball a good crack when we could.

So when Colin Tunnicliffe, left-arm medium-pace, bowling over the wicket, sent down a ball that pitched somewhere around leg or middle-and-leg, just slightly short of a length and very much in my arc, right in the pick-up zone for a left-hander, I hit it powerfully in the direction of mid-wicket. It was one of my favourite shots, and I connected well. Too well for poor Phil Russell, the right-arm medium pacer, fielding at short-leg. The ball caught him full in the face. Fortunately, he was wearing a helmet with face-grill. Unfortunately, the ball penetrated, and lodged in, the wire grill.

We all knew immediately that this was a nasty injury. Umpire Dickie Bird wrote later that 'there was blood all over the place, as well as the odd bit of bone'. With his cheek-bone shattered, a dazed Phil staggered and then crumpled to his knees like a sack of potatoes, but the ball remained firmly lodged in his helmet grill. Captain Eddie Barlow, showing great presence of mind if not huge sympathy, shouted to one of his fielders to run over and remove the ball, at the same time appealing enthusiastically for the catch!

Phil Russell sustained nasty facial injuries despite wearing a helmet.

Dickie, of course, standing at the bowler's end, was in his element! He went whiter than the coat he was wearing! What should he signal? The weight of the decision rested heavily on his shoulders as he nervously transferred his weight from one foot to the other before calling 'dead ball' and making the appropriate signal to the scorers in their box. I was out soon after, and we lost by an innings and 20 runs in two days.

Was it the right decision? Should I have still been in, or was it technically a catch? As we had all stood anxiously around worrying about Phil, no-one had been sure. None of the players had seen anything like it before. It was an unusual incident, and one that had given Dickie Bird and fellow-umpire Eddie Phillipson plenty to think about and discuss while the stricken fielder received lengthy medical treatment on the field before being carried off and taken to hospital – a discussion that had continued on their return to their changing room.

Soon after close of play, as we got news from the hospital that Phil would be OK, a still agitated Umpire Bird telephoned Lord's to tell them what had happened. Had he made the correct decision? Yes. The 'Powers That Be' agreed, and later the rules were changed by the TCCB to address a possible repeat of 'the Russell question'. The next edition of *Wisden* confirmed that 'dead ball' was now 'the official ruling from Lord's in the event of a similar incident'.

Not for the first (or last!) time, I found myself involved in cricketing controversy – and inadvertently influencing future regulation and practice. Happily, Phil Russell recovered from his injury and continued for a while as a player with Derbyshire before turning his hand to coaching, first with his old county and then with KwaZulu-Natal. He also had a career as head groundsman at the Kingsmead Stadium in Durban. Years later, when I was living in Canada, I had a couple of weeks in South Africa playing 'golden oldies' cricket and came across Phil again when we played a match on one of his immaculately prepared strips.

The acceptance of the helmet on the cricket field – and subsequent improvements in its design – has developed quickly. I sometimes wonder if it has brought with it some negative consequences in terms of impact on skills and technique of batsmen, but in general terms anything that improves the professional cricketer's safety is to be welcomed.

I had, albeit inadvertently, played a part in two incidents that shaped change. Two examples of change by accident, but what about setting out deliberately to challenge and change things?

I've always been quick to speak out and to challenge unfairness. Perhaps, on reflection, sometimes a bit too quick for my own good. That tendency was in evidence from very early in my career when I reacted to what I saw as a basic injustice over pay – and a club 'rule' that simply didn't make sense!

I was genuinely very proud to be awarded my Glamorgan cap in 1969. It was during a League game against Warwickshire at St.

Caps for Davis and Nash

ROGER D A V I S and Malcolm Nash, two of the pacesetters in Glamorgan's assault on the county cricket championship, have been awarded their county caps by captain Tony Lewis.

Each played prominent roles in Glamorgan's most recent victory, the innings triumph over Derbyshire.

In this match opener Davis hit a maiden hundred and seamer Nash had a nine-wicket haul.

News of my County Cap award.

Helen's. There was no great presentation or fuss in those days. It wasn't like you see now with Test caps! Skipper Tony Lewis just called for quiet in the changing room and told the guys that Roger Davis and I were being awarded our caps. Everyone clapped and said, "Well played". Then it was announced over the tannoy system and we got a good ovation from the crowd when we took the field. It was a nice moment. I had a few drinks that night to celebrate.

What rankled with me, and to be honest took the shine off it a bit, was that there was no immediate pay rise. Although I was now officially a capped player, I would not be paid as much as other capped players until the next season. That seemed a very obvious injustice – and quite illogical. Equal pay for equal work and equal status! My argument wasn't so much about money as principle – and self-esteem. It was about how you saw yourself and, at the same time, how the club regarded and valued you, too.

So I sent a message to the cricket committee, via the captain, thanking them for awarding my cap and saying how pleased I was, but asking for a meeting and an opportunity for me to explain my concerns about the increase in pay – or lack of it! Wilf said 'no' at first, arguing that there was no precedent for a meeting, and that the increase in pay had always been deferred – that was the way it worked. In the end, however, they did let me meet with the cricket committee, at that time consisting of Wilf, Jim Pleass, Phil Clift and Tony as skipper. After I'd put my argument and they had discussed it, I was called in to be told I would, after all, be getting the pay rise to match the capped status, and that they would back-date it to the beginning of the season.

I guess I've always been a black and white guy. It was never about shades of grey. Right or wrong. I didn't sit on the fence. That's part of my nature, I suppose, and sometimes it is accompanied by being a bit attacking – and aggressive – in my approach. So it was probably no surprise to my friends when I was elected by my Glamorgan teammates to take over from Don Shepherd as the club's Professional Cricketers' Association (PCA) representative at the beginning of the 1969 season – big shoes to fill. Don had been the first to hold this post, after the formation of the Association a year earlier. Each club had its own representative, and it was a position I relished and continued in until I stopped playing.

When I came back from the Caribbean in 1970, or it may have been South Africa in 1971, I attended the PCA's AGM at Edgbaston and was elected to its executive. There were players from about a dozen counties in this group, and we worked as a network of sub-committees. For a number of the 15 or so years I sat on the executive – again, until I stopped playing – I was part of a group focussing on issues of players' conditions and salaries.

We met two or three times each winter, usually at the Liberal Club in London. John Arlott was our first president, and his active involvement and encouragement was hugely important to the success of the venture, especially in the early days. His international status as a journalist and broadcaster – together with his knowledge of cricket and cricketers, and the fact that he was very respected in cricketing circles – was so useful to us. John was a lovely man, and always generous with his time and energy. He was also extremely talented in choosing excellent food – and even better wine – to make our meetings doubly memorable.

In developing the work and structure of the PCA, John was also able to gather around him some other very shrewd and distinguished people, bringing with them expertise in legal, financial and medical matters. With the additional support and energy of our first chairmen, Roger Prideaux of Northamptonshire and then Jack Bannister of Warwickshire, John Arlott was instrumental in getting the association off the ground. I look back on those early days with great affection. It was the start of an organisation that has gone on to prove so important and so influential in the game, reaching the central position it holds today. I suppose, in its formation, it mirrored some of the then recent developments in soccer, particularly relating to wages. At the time, the lot of the professional cricketer – and particularly youngsters coming into the game – was difficult. Even if you had a 12-month contract, you were paid for only six months. It was up to you to sort out some suitable winter employment, and for many this would be outside the game.

John Arlott was a huge influence on the PCA's successful formation and development.

The upheavals of the Packer and post-Packer days in the second half of the 1970s were particularly difficult, with some counties trying to ban Packer-players from domestic cricket. The PCA fought for players to have the right to work when and where they pleased, but it was an issue that brought us into conflict with cricketing authorities, both nationally and at county level, and there were some difficult times.

I know that at Glamorgan Wilf Wooller had always been very much against the idea of the Professional Cricketers' Association – as far as Wilf was concerned, a cricketers' union –

J. D. BANNISTER

THE WORLD'S BEST CRICKETERS

J. D. BANNISTER
Warwickshire
Right-arm, fast-medium bowler and right-hand batsman. Born at Wolverhampton, 1930. He first played for Warwick in 1950 and gained his County "Cap" in 1954. He was in the Minor Counties side v. West Indies in 1950. Among his best performances are eight wickets for 54 runs for Warwick v. Yorkshire in 1954 and 100 wickets, average 22.72 in season 1955.

PRESENTED WITH
The ROVER
THE PAPER FOR BOYS

Warwickshire's Jack Bannister was a very significant force in the PCA for many years.

from the start, even though he had huge respect for John Arlott and they remained good friends. Wilf was especially unhappy when, on the back of the Packer debate and PCA enquiries into the range of wage structures in operation, a minimum wage was agreed and enforced. His argument, shared by many fellow administrators, was that county staffs would have to be reduced to offset the increased salary bills. His immediate response was, "You're all fired"!

It was disruptive for a year or two, and unpleasant. It was particularly difficult for some of the younger players, several of whom left the game in the atmosphere of uncertainty about their futures. Yet it was something that needed to be done to make contracts fairer, to reward players better, and to create a more secure future for young cricketers coming into the professional ranks. When our PCA sub-committee had reviewed pay structures in the mid-1970s, we found that no two counties had the same structure. There were wide variations in pay, as well as in bonuses and expenses, and there were some very unwelcome and unfair practices, too.

Of course, the efforts of the PCA in the years leading up to, and immediately following, the introduction of the minimum wage were not universally welcomed by the cricketing establishment. *Wisden* suggested that the decade saw 'the biggest financial revolution in the history of the game', and revolution is not always popular, of course. At some of our meetings with the cricketing authorities, it felt very much a case of 'them and us', and I sometimes felt we were being treated as second-class citizens. Trouble-makers. Plotters, even, but I'm really proud of the work of the PCA and of the effort we put into those formative years. It wasn't always easy, but it was never dull! We had a real sense of being pioneers, and I am so glad that I had the opportunity to be part of it – right at the heart of the action – and helping to change the system (and some of the rules).

On a more light-hearted note, I discovered that you can also sometimes change rules simply by being bloody awkward!

Majid wasn't enthusiastic about travelling by car. He didn't enjoy it. So, during his captaincy, he decided that we should all travel together by coach. It was compulsory. No cars. A new rule. However, the arrangement wasn't entirely successful. Everyone wanted to stop at different places or at different times and for different lengths of time, and we found we were by-passing some of our favourite eating spots! There were rumblings in the ranks.

We were playing a three-day game down in London – it was at The Oval, I think – which had started on a Saturday. After breakfast on the Sunday morning, we travelled up to the Midlands for a John Player League game in the afternoon. The coach stopped at the first service station on the M1 to fill up with fuel, and we all took the opportunity to stretch our legs and grab a coffee. The driver filled up and then tracked us down. The good news was that we now had a full tank – just under £100 worth of diesel. The bad news was that his credit card wouldn't work and he was unable to pay for it. Worse still, the manager of the service station wouldn't let him move the coach until the bill was settled! Bill Edwards, who was on the Glamorgan Committee, was travelling on the bus with us. He and Majid and the driver deliberated and then Bill suggested a solution. Perhaps we'd all like to chip in! We said – very politely, of course – that we didn't think this was a great idea, and ordered another coffee, pointing out at the same time that we hadn't wanted to be on a coach in the first place. Meanwhile, the empty coach stayed parked by the pumps.

Eventually, Bill pleaded our cause with the management of the service station and made phone calls to Wales. Wales made calls back. It was sorted. We were on our way, and got to our afternoon game in time. Not long afterwards the experiment of coach travel was abandoned, and we were back in cars!

10

A Tale of Two Hat-tricks

'Malcolm Nash was, pre-eminently, a highly skilled manipulator of medium-pace seam bowling.'
John Arlott

Tourist matches were always special. I thrived on the 'big match' atmosphere, and on testing myself – and my skills – against some of the best batsmen in the world. I always wanted to see my name on the team sheet, especially if the Australians were in town. A match against the Australians was extra special, and the Australians at Swansea was even better still!

During the 1975 season, it had been decided that Glamorgan wouldn't be playing the Australian tourists in our traditional August Bank Holiday slot. The season's fixtures had been arranged to fit around the first ICC Prudential World Cup competition, held in England during June. The Australians had reached the final, losing to the West Indies after winning the toss in an exciting game at Lord's. Australia's response had fallen 17 runs short of the West Indies' 291, and had included five run-outs. Skipper Clive Lloyd had scored a century for the West Indies, and his opposing skipper Ian Chappell had also top-scored with 62. Despite losing, the Australians had continued to play well. They arrived in south Wales in good form.

A four-game Test series had been arranged following the World Cup, and the visit to Swansea was just before the first Test at Edgbaston. Our three-day game started on Saturday, with the Test beginning the following Thursday. The Australians rested their fast-bowling pair of Thomson and Lillee, but otherwise the team to play us was a strong one as they took the opportunity to get as much time in the middle as possible before meeting England – who they had already defeated in the World Cup semi-final. Even without their 'deadly duo', Australia had a more than decent bowling attack. Gary Gilmour, their left-arm fast-medium bowler who could swing

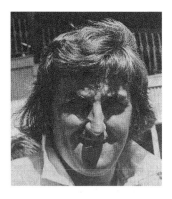

Gary Gilmour arrived at St. Helen's having finished leading wicket taker in the World Cup.

the ball both ways, had enjoyed a particularly successful Word Cup. In the final he had taken five key West Indian wickets – Kallicharran, Kanhai, Lloyd, Richards and Murray – and had finished as top wicket-taker in the whole competition.

The Swansea fixture had received a lot of publicity, sandwiched as it was between the World Cup and the Test series, and because of Glamorgan's history of successes against Australian sides at the ground. Would there be another upset? The local and national press had been full of stories and speculation, and a large and excited crowd packed into St. Helen's for the beginning of the first day's play.

Ian Chappell was the official captain of the touring side, and was down to play at Swansea, but after the demands of the World Cup and with a tough Test series just around the corner, he had asked

Greg Chappell leading the Australian side on to the field at St. Helen's.

his younger brother to deputise so that he could relax and concentrate on his batting in the longer form of the game.

Majid won the toss and elected to bat on what looked like a decent St. Helen's wicket. It was obvious that our visitors would have liked to bat, but tourist fixtures were very much proper matches in those days, and the aim was to win rather than give the visitors some friendly batting practice. So we were very happy to try to get a good first innings score and get in a position to control the game. Things went according to plan, with Alan Jones and his young opening partner, 18-year-old left-hander Alan Lewis Jones, both getting half-centuries and putting on 132 for the first wicket. Roger Davis and Majid Khan then carried on their good work, with Majid batting each side of lunch to get a super century in less than two hours. Although we fell away a bit after that, we were in a position to declare on 302 for 8 and leave our visitors with a tricky little session at the end of the day. Although there were a few close shaves, they reached stumps with 32 on the board and all wickets intact.

I couldn't wait to get the ball in my hand as we took the field on Sunday for the continuation of the Australian innings in front of another large and

Alan Jones (left) and Alan Lewis Jones (right) got us off to a great start against the Australians.

expectant crowd. After all, this was the ground where we had beaten the Aussies twice before, and a lot of the people present had seen one or both of those famous victories.

I usually bowled from the Mumbles Road end, with the sea behind me. The prevailing westerly or south westerly wind blowing in over the pier helped the swing. Perhaps the wind was from a different direction that day – I'm not sure, now – but for some reason I found myself bowling from in front of the packed pavilion.

The two umpires, Messrs. Spencer and Bird, had only a couple of weeks earlier officiated together at the World Cup final. Both were experienced international umpires. Tommy Spencer was at my end. In his playing days with Kent, each side of the Second World War, Tommy had been a batsman. He had also been a decent footballer, playing professionally for Fulham, Lincoln City and Walsall. At the other end was Harold 'Dickie' Bird, another very experienced umpire, and another ex-footballer and ex-batsman, too – with a career best of 181 made for Yorkshire against Glamorgan!

Australia had opened with right-hander Rick McCosker and the less experienced left-hander Alan Turner. The pair played steadily at the beginning of the first session but, with the score on 44, I bowled McCosker with one that dipped into him really late and beat him all ends up. Clean bowled, leg stick. Knocked it out.

Ian Chappell, another right-hander, came in to replace him. As usual, Ian didn't take a big movement, he just shuffled across into line and tried to play it late, but the swing did him. Hit him straight on the toe. Tommy lifted his finger. Leg before, first ball.

Ian had a few comments to make to me on the way past. I just said "Look in the paper tomorrow." Perhaps his irritation bothered Tommy more than me, I don't know, but it shouldn't have, because Ian was absolutely plum – and I think he knew it!

Greg Chappell, again a right-hander, passed his brother on the steps. Arriving in the middle, he took guard from Tommy as I prepared to bowl the hat-trick ball.

I bowled exactly the same ball and, unbelievably, Greg played exactly the same shot as Ian. With exactly the same outcome – it hit him bang on the toes. In front of middle – "Howzat?" Well, the outcome wasn't *exactly* the same because this time Umpire Spencer didn't raise his finger. "Not out," he mumbled, and his face went as red as the new ball. I stared at him. I just couldn't believe it. As I stared, with Greg shuffling around in his crease, Tommy said, "I couldn't give him out as well ... I couldn't give two in a row."

I was dumbfounded. No umpire had ever said anything like that before. I went back to my mark and finished the over without speaking, but I knew it was out. Eifion behind the stumps knew it was out. Greg Chappell knew it was out. Even the umpire seemed to be acknowledging that he knew it was out, too. Yet Chappell was still there and, as it turned out, would be there for a long time.

Tommy called "Over". Then, as we started to change ends and I collected my sweater, he actually apologised to me. "I'm sorry. I couldn't do it," he said. "Not another one. I'm in line for a Test match." In those days, before 'neutral' umpires, the captains of touring teams could nominate (or object to) particular officials for Test duties.

"Tommy," I said. "What can I say? That's just terrible umpiring. Terrible."

I wasn't afraid of telling them if they made a mistake. If I got reported to Lord's, well, I got reported – Arthur Jepson had done that once – but it was a sad moment for me. I felt I'd been cheated of something I'd earned.

Greg Chappell went on to score 144 before falling to Roger's spin and, of course, it is his innings – a good one it was, too – that is headlined in accounts of the game. No mention of his first-ball escape. Greg's innings, supported by tail-end runs from Rod Marsh and Gilmour, took Australia to an 84 run first-innings lead, and despite a battling 87 from Roger Davis when we batted the second time, we could not get back into the game. For the record, Australia won by seven wickets.

Tommy Spencer did go on to umpire the second Test match between England and Australia at Lord's, and also the fourth and last Test in the series at The Oval – this one in partnership with Dickie Bird again – but his questionable decision might well have cost Glamorgan the chance of a third victory against the Australians at Swansea. Who knows?

The hat-trick that wasn't!

Rick McCosker, bowled Nash, 22.

Ian Chappell, lbw Nash, 0. Plum!

Greg Chappell, given not out.

It might also have cost me my own chance of Test involvement later in that summer. I always did well against Australian touring sides. That point had been highlighted in the papers, and in the lead-up to the Swansea game my name had again been mentioned as a possible for inclusion in the Ashes Test series. So, if I'd knocked over three of their key Test batsmen – including the skipper – and with all the publicity a hat-trick would have generated, who can tell what that might have led to? In those days, a very strong performance against the tourists could sometimes tip the balance in terms of Test selection.

At the end of the 1975 season I found myself back in Worcester and in the familiar surroundings of the old wooden pavilion facing the Cathedral. New Road was one of my favourite grounds. I always enjoyed playing there, and catching up with some of the guys from my Worcester City days. The leaves on the famous horse-chestnut trees were taking on their September colours, and it was our last-but-one John Player League match. Two months had passed since my near hat-trick at St. Helen's.

Nash has nervous Aussies reeling

BUT BRIGHT AND KERRY O'KEEFFE HOLD OUT

By JOHN BILLOT

MALCOLM NASH is always the man for the big occasion. And he made it a big one at Swansea yesterday by whipping out the first two Australian batsmen in his first over without a run on the board.

The Aussies, desperate at 39 f. six and chasing a by then impossible target of 184, forced a draw but this was very much a moral victory for Alan Jones and his Glamorgan team in yet another day of drama against the famous Green Caps.

Ray Bright and Kerry O'Keeffe prove resolute if at times harassed blockers in holding their team together to finish a 86-6.

Nash's second innings 5-32 from 12 overs of seam and, later, left-arm spin, gave him a match analysis of 9-103 and may have awakened in Australian breasts a slight stirring that this 1977 tour could

● ONE WHO GOT AWAY . . . Australian Kerry O'Keeffe looks as though he was going to be caught by Tony Cordle off Rodney Ontong, watched by wicket-keeper Eifion Jones and John Hopkins at slip, but the ball struck the ground first. O'Keeffe was unbeaten with 21 at the end of the match with Glamorgan at St Helen's, Swansea, yesterday.

'Malcolm Nash is always the man for the big occasion' wrote John Billot in the Western Mail.

Worcestershire, captained in this fixture by Norman Gifford, batted after winning the toss. Openers Glenn Turner and Alan Ormrod got them off to a decent start. I had Ormrod caught by Alan Wilkins, but then Jim Yardley, John Parker and Basil D'Oliveira all got useful runs too. Glenn was top scorer with 39, but the others weren't far behind. At 165 for 4, a reasonable 40-over score beckoned.

I hadn't opened the bowling at New Road, which was unusual. We'd started with Tony Cordle and the left-arm medium-pace of Alan Wilkins. I'd come on to replace Alan eight overs into the game, and had bowled a spell of six overs before myself taking a break. That was unusual too, and another change from our normal Sunday League bowling pattern. I usually opened and bowled right through my eight overs, the idea being that we'd keep the total down with me making it difficult for the top-order batsmen to score as quickly as they would like.

This ploy was successful over a number of seasons, and I had some excellent figures – especially when compared to modern limited-overs figures. For example, I bowled my 11-over allocation for only 10 runs in a Benson and Hedges Cup game against Lancashire at Cardiff in 1976, and in 1983 I went for only nine runs off an 11 over spell that included seven maidens, against Combined Universities at Fenner's. Also, on three separate occasions in the Sunday League matches, against Surrey and twice against Lancashire, I bowled my full eight-over allocation for just eight runs. I got some wickets in these spells, too! That was the other part of our plan – that I would knock over one or two (and hopefully more!) key wickets at the same time as keeping things tight.

For some reason, however, in this final game, I'd taken a break after an initial six-over spell. Now, with Worcestershire seemingly in charge on 188 for 5 and with Imran Khan and wicketkeeper Rodney Cass in the middle, I came back into the attack and prepared to bowl my final two overs.

Suddenly everything changed. I bowled Cass off the third ball. He was replaced by the skipper, Norman Gifford, who nicked his first ball to Eifion behind the stumps. Enter Paul Pridgeon – another first baller! Clean bowled. The first – and, as it turned out, only – hat-trick of my professional career. It was a great feeling, even if my victims weren't front-line batsmen.

Vanburn Holder survived his first ball – the last in my seventh over. He also survived the first in my eight over – just! – but he went lbw to the second ball. Brian Brain, never famous for his batting exploits, then arrived at the wicket. Out first ball – and caught by Eifion again. I had taken five wickets in seven balls for one run, and Worcestershire were all out for 190, still nine balls short of their full allocation. It may have been unusual for me to be bowling at the end of an innings, but it was a change in strategy that paid off handsomely on this occasion. My innings figures were 7.3-0-29-6.

And the hat-trick that was!

Rodney Cass,
bowled Nash, 6.

Skipper Norman Gifford,
c E. Jones, b Nash, 0.

Paul Pridgeon,
bowled Nash, 0.

Vanburn Holder (left) and last man out Brian Brain (right) gave me five wickets in seven balls – but we still managed to lose the game!

I don't think I was given the match ball. That didn't happen so much in those days. Anyway, we had our batting to think about as we walked off.

We had a good chance, but got off to a poor start and lost both openers with only 13 on the board. Only Len Hill, Mike Llewellyn and Eifion Jones got into the 20s. I couldn't repeat my success with the bat and was bowled by Imran Khan for a duck. We lost the game by 48 runs.

My hat-trick had been in vain – but I did enjoy it! It was a good feeling. Of course, I would have willingly swapped it for seeing Tommy Spencer's finger go up for the third time of asking at Swansea.

11

May's Bounty – in July!

'Tall and lean, Malcolm Nash was a lively seam bowler whose left-arm over the wicket bowling made him one of the best new ball bowlers in county cricket during the 1970s.'
Andrew Hignell

always enjoyed driving to matches. Some of the guys didn't. They'd have welcomed the coach travel available to today's teams, but for me, travelling by car between games on the county circuit was another enjoyable aspect of being a professional cricketer. There was quite a lot of travelling to be done, especially once the Sunday League fixtures were added to the already busy Championship schedule.

We usually travelled three to a car, so that would normally involve four cars plus the kit van, with a couple of the guys in the van sharing loading, driving and navigation duties. Sometimes we'd squeeze into three cars plus the van! The scorer always travelled with the players, but not the physio – we always left him back at base. We'd use the opposition physio if necessary and slip him a few bob for a drink – but we didn't often need one!

I know there must have been tiredness and safety issues involved, but for me there were lots of advantages to the car. You could choose your own route, your own timings and, very importantly, your own stops. Some of these stops were carefully planned! If you were on a long journey in those days, especially if you were travelling with what I'll politely call one of the 'more established' players, you needed to carry a Good Food Guide as well as a road atlas!

We didn't go mad on meals, but if we could find the right establishment with only a modest detour – well, a reasonably modest detour – why would we miss the opportunity? I suppose we tried to have a least one decent social meal per trip. Sometimes, inevitably, this meant journey times between venues being significantly longer than originally planned.

Of course, in those days before mobile phones and SatNav, before emails and texts, planning was at the same time easier and more difficult – depending on how you look at it! At least, linking up with other cars at one of the stops was more difficult. There were things that could go wrong, too – especially for the guys in the van who, because they had to load all the kit we dropped off on our way to the cars, would often set off long after the other vehicles. Invariably, this was a role for the younger and fitter members of the team. Well, younger, anyway! Journeys could also, sometimes, take a lot longer than anticipated – especially if not planned thoroughly enough.

The perils of van duty – and the need to research the route carefully – had been well illustrated several years earlier when Kevin Lyons and his co-driver Lawrence Williams had set off from Edgbaston one sunny evening after close of play to make their way to Middlesbrough in readiness for the next day's fixture against Yorkshire. Who will ever know how their route – which apparently was planned as 'head north and turn right' – came to take them through the by-ways of the Pennines? Who will ever know if the van's breakdown would have occurred on a less mountainous and demanding route? What we do know is that they became both hopelessly lost and hopelessly broken-down in uninhabited and inhospitable countryside, and that in desperation they accepted the generous offer of a tow from a passing lorry – which a short time later they watched disappear into the distance after the tow-rope snapped. We know, too, that they eventually arrived at the Acklam Park ground, in their semi-stricken van containing the whole team's kit, less than half-an-hour before the start of play – having had not a wink of sleep. In a final unkind twist of fate, skipper Tony Lewis lost the toss, we fielded, and the unfortunate Lawrence found himself sharing the new ball with me – and bowling to no less formidable an opening pair than Boycott and Padgett. As it happened, we reduced them to 24 for 4 before a thunderstorm gave Lawrence and Kevin a chance to have a well-deserved rest in the pavilion! Also, an early opportunity to double-check their route in readiness for the drive back from Middlesbrough to Cardiff at the conclusion of the Yorkshire game (a hard-fought victory for us, by the way) for another Championship match starting the next morning. It could certainly be a tough schedule at times. The cautionary tale of Kevin and Lawrence has gone down in the annals of Glamorgan cricket!

Happily, no such navigational misfortune had hampered our trip to Hampshire in July 1975. Indeed, the journey was much more relaxed than usual because on this occasion we'd used a rare day off – a non-cricket playing day sandwiched between a tourist match and a Championship fixture – to get ourselves and our kit safely and uneventfully from Cardiff to Basingstoke.

I'd driven with my two passengers, including my usual 'roomy' and great friend Eifion Jones. We'd had a good meal and a couple of drinks before turning-in, and had enjoyed a leisurely start to the first day. It would not have come as a surprise to my teammates when I did not appear for a hearty breakfast. A slice of toast and a cigarette, washed down with a few coffees, usually saw me right for the day.

May's Bounty was a lovely ground. Awesome! It was where John Arlott had watched his first cricket. I'd played there the previous season in a Sunday League game. Unfortunately, our cricket that day was not as pretty as the ground and we got thrashed by 137 runs! Barry Richards, Hampshire's South African opening batsman, scored a majestic 123 and I got 0-52 in my eight overs.

Despite painful memories of that particular setback, I was pleased to be back for what proved to be the only first-class game I would play at the headquarters of the Basingstoke and North Hants Cricket Club. It was my sort of ground. I always much preferred the smaller, more intimate grounds to the larger and less personal 'city grounds' – though there were exceptions, like Lord's, which was always a thrill to play at. Generally I liked to be close to the crowd and to feel the atmosphere, so I especially enjoyed playing on

Hampshire's Andy Roberts bowling to Alan Jones in 1978. Two seasons later Alan scored 204 not out at May's Bounty, the only first-class double-hundred ever scored at the ground.

out-grounds and at festival venues. Of course, there were far more of those used for county cricket than there are today.

So, we arrived at the picturesque May's Bounty ground in Basingstoke in the best of spirits. The ground looked even more picturesque than I had remembered and we had come straight from acquitting ourselves well against the Australian tourists – as had become something of a Glamorgan tradition – and knew we were performing well as a unit.

At a personal level, I felt particularly positive. Just three days before, I'd had the satisfaction of removing Australia's captain, Ian Chappell, first ball with a real beauty, a real toe-crusher – and nearly getting his brother first-ball too. Added to that, this was the return Championship fixture against Hampshire, and I had enjoyed one of my best days with the ball when we'd played them at Swansea only a couple of months before. In that game I'd improved on my career-best figures with a very pleasing 8-56.

To cap it all, I always enjoyed playing against Hampshire. It was invariably a good contest, and it gave me the chance to have a crack at one of the best opening partnerships in cricket anywhere in the world – Barry Richards and Gordon Greenidge.

Hampshire's captain, Richard Gilliat, won the toss and put us in. It wasn't a surprise. On arriving at the ground, we'd been delighted to hear that the local consensus was that conditions were fairly helpful, with 'a bit in the wicket'. We were also aware that the opposition line-up included the formidable pace of West Indian international opening bowler Andy Roberts, who only the previous season had won his first cap against England. Not really someone you'd want to be facing on a bowler-friendly wicket. So, I wasn't at all surprised to find us batting – and anyway, Richard's decision meant that I had a quiet morning to myself.

I was never much for pre-match routines, and my warm-up usually consisted of a few gentle bowls to one of the guys, just to get my arm turning over. As far as I was concerned, when you were facing the prospect of a day in the field and perhaps 20 or 30 tough overs, the last thing you wanted to do was waste a lot of energy before play started!

My pre-match preparation didn't even include marking out my run-up. Nor having it marked out for me. No sign of these modern conventions of tape-measure and sprayed initials in those days! Like other bowlers, I'd just pace out my run when the time came to bowl. Then I'd scratch a mark with my boot and was ready to go. However, making my bowling mark did involve one unusual feature, and I think it's a significant one in terms of the habit today for bowlers to 'press' the line – and all too frequently bowl no-balls. I'd mark a line with my studs eight inches behind the bowling crease, and then I'd pace my run-up from my own line rather than from the crease. I did the same when bowling in the nets, too, to avoid getting into bad habits. Not surprisingly, I bowled very few no-balls. I don't think it could have been more than a couple of dozen in my whole career.

My most demanding task earlier that day had probably been selecting the ball with which my fellow fast bowlers and I would eventually open Glamorgan's attack. Before play started, the umpires would give us a box of six to choose from. It was an important job! I was ball-chooser-in-chief from 1969, usually in tandem with Tony Cordle. We'd look for a nice dark ball – the darker the better. Or one with a prominent seam. Or, preferably, one that was both dark and had a prominent seam. You'd think a box of six brand-new balls would all feel the same, wouldn't you? But

I very rarely over-stepped for a no-ball.

choosing wasn't always as straightforward as you might think, and it became an important ritual that we took very seriously indeed. You needed to hold the ball in your hand. Sometimes a ball just didn't feel right – it would feel like a pineapple. And Tony reckoned smell was important, too – he reckoned he could sniff out a good ball.

Once we were underway and despite the misgivings of the locals, the wicket played well enough as openers Alan Jones and Alan Lewis Jones got us off to a steady start, the first wicket not falling until there were 49 runs on the board. When skipper Majid Khan joined Alan Jones at the fall of the third wicket, a reasonable Glamorgan total looked comfortably within reach, but only Alan managed to pass the half-century landmark as wickets continued to fall regularly. The Hampshire attack looked confident, and now their tails were up. I found myself batting with wicketkeeper Eifion Jones, a favourite batting partner and great fun to be at the wicket with, and managed to score a typically quick-fire 32 to take our total past the 200 mark. We knew, though, that our tea-time first-innings total of 207 all out was disappointing with so many batsmen having got starts. I remember thinking over a cup of tea that, having batted on it and seen it from close quarters, my initial view that the pitch probably had something to offer was correct. There was definitely some movement through the air and off the wicket, but it was nothing out of the ordinary, and there had certainly been no hint of the excitement that was soon to follow.

'Speedy' was my fellow-new ball chooser!

So, straight after the tea interval, with the ball I'd chosen fitting snugly in my hand, and with my eight-pace run marked with a stud-scuff, I was ready to open the bowling to Hampshire's experienced international opening pair of Barry Richards and Gordon Greenidge. They and I knew we were probably in for a good contest! We always enjoyed pitting our wits against each other and they were two quite different propositions to bowl to.

Hampshire's Barry Richards (pictured driving in a match against Glamorgan) and Gordon Greenidge – one of the best opening partnerships in the world, and two very competitive batsmen.

Barry Richards could be very patient. He was the best opening batsman I ever bowled to. Technically, he was so sound. He could destroy you. I'll never forget that Barry once confided in Don Shepherd how highly he rated me as an opening bowler. I was delighted to hear it, of course. It was a significant and welcome compliment from someone that talented with a bat in his hand.

Unlike Barry, Gordon would always give you a chance because you could frustrate him and he'd lose patience. You just needed to keep putting the ball in the right place. Of course, he was also very talented and could punish you if you weren't on your game. It was a world-class pairing.

As things turned out, Gordon didn't have time to get frustrated in this innings. I got him lbw without a run on the board! I also got their second wicket – Richard Lewis – for a duck before the home team was in double figures. It was the perfect start for us, but then Trevor Jesty and Barry Richards steadied the ship and took the score to 64 without further mishap.

My opening bowling partner was Gregory Armstrong, a Barbadian, like our other pace-bowler Tony Cordle, and someone who could bowl very quickly and with hostility – though, unfortunately, not always accuracy. He also had a habit of overstepping and would rarely have a nought next to his name in the no-balls column! Sometime after we signed Greg in 1974 there was a rumour that a scout with links to Glamorgan had been watching a Shell Shield game between Barbados and Jamaica, involving two young, promising, and very fast bowlers playing on opposite sides. The names Greg Armstrong and Michael Holding went into his notebook as worthy of attention, and in his later confusion he thought it was Holding that he was suggesting should be signed.

Greg was no mean performer, but this wasn't his day. After getting through only six overs he pulled up with a foot injury and left the field. It was clear from his conversation with Majid that he wouldn't be coming back, and it dawned on me that 'Speedy' and I were going to have a lot more work to do than usual, with no opportunity to rotate our three-pronged pace attack. The usual pattern at the beginning of an innings at that time was me opening with Armstrong the other end, then Tony Cordle coming on, usually replacing Greg. On that day, Greg had been on the field long enough to bowl some very lively balls, including an unplayable bouncer that flicked Barry Richards' cap clean off and got us all very excited indeed!

Perhaps seeing that one ball inspired me, I don't know, but towards the end of the day I had one of those spells every bowler dreams about. I got another four wickets, including the prize wicket of Richards, while their total moved on by only nine runs. At the end of the first day, 25 overs into their innings, Hampshire were in deep trouble at 76-6, with captain Richard Gilliat and night-watchman (and wicketkeeper) Bob Stephenson at the wicket. Bowling unchanged through the evening session, I had taken all six wickets to fall.

Greg Armstrong's injury provided me with some extra bowling – which I made the most of!

After a few beers and an early night – bed before 11 – I remember arriving at the ground on the second morning raring to go. I knew the wicket was talking and I couldn't wait to get the ball in my hands again.

I was bowling a good line and had the ability to keep the ball on or around off-stump. With marginal movement, it was a problem for batsmen. Soon our depleted bowling attack was continuing where it had left off the previous evening. Gilliat and Stephenson were both given leg before – two of five lbw decisions to go my way in this innings. I got a lot of lbw victims over the years – 261, I think, out of a total of 991 wickets (and I reckon I'd get even more these days with the influence of 'Hawkeye' and television replays on the decision-making of umpires).

With Hampshire now nine wickets down for only 106 – still 100 behind – it dawned on me that a rare ten wicket haul was a distinct possibility. I'd got all ten wickets for only 29 runs playing for Abergavenny against Lydney on Whitsun Bank Holiday Monday 1965, and I could remember just how exciting that had been. A great feeling. Of course, I knew that in first-class cricket it was a very rare occurrence indeed, but here staring me in the face was a real opportunity.

Andy Roberts had joined Andy Murtagh at the crease. Both were always likely to give you a chance. Suddenly Murtagh called for a crazy single – right out of the blue - and was run out by a good throw (I can't remember who fielded it) and some typically nifty glove-work from Eifion behind the stumps. I still don't know to this day what on earth prompted the Hampshire all-rounder to run after hitting it straight to cover – he was out by a mile! – but things like that happen in the game, and I was happy enough to finish with figures of 9-56. My first '9-for' for Glamorgan, and a new career-best – the second of the season, the second against Hampshire. It was a good couple of days' work.

The events of the second innings of both teams were less notable, though the start of our knock saw another dramatic fall of wickets as we were quickly reduced to 89-6 – and suddenly Hampshire were back in with a real chance of winning a match they had already all but lost. However, Majid, ably supported by Eifion, rescued the situation with an important stand of 72 – a significant total in terms of the match. Tony Cordle also contributed some useful runs batting at number nine – 34 not out – as we reached 227 just before the end of the second day. For the record, I was bowled by Bob Herman for the second time in the match!

People assume that we had a big celebration that evening to mark my '9-for', but we didn't. It wasn't the Glamorgan way. As a team, we weren't particularly struck by individual performances. We talked about it for a bit, back in the dressing-room, and of course the guys said "Well bowled, Nashy", but we just got on with things as usual. There was more hard work waiting for us the next day!

Starting the final day on six without loss, and chasing 303 to win, Hampshire progressed confidently as the match continued to see-saw. Richards and Greenidge both reached half-centuries and were looking dangerous. Then, with the score on 105, I got Barry Richards for the second time in the game – bowled with a beauty! Pitching off, swinging in to hit middle. I think he played the wrong line. I can still see it now. As their score passed 150 with still only two wickets down an unlikely Hampshire 'double' again seemed a

Receiving the St. Helen's Balconiers Man of the Match award from founder member Gerry Munday, in the company of iconic Welsh entertainer Ryan Davies (fifth left).

distinct possibility, and nagging doubts started to set in. You could see the guys starting to wonder if we were letting it slip.

Fortunately, in the nick of time I managed to produce another good spell that one of the journalists present was generous enough to write 'ripped the heart out of their middle order' – Jesty, Gilliat, Murtagh and Rice, the last with a caught and bowled. Predictably, there was some more long-handle hitting by Andy Roberts (at number 11, their third top-scorer on both his visits to the middle) before the Hampshire innings closed 67 runs short of their victory target.

I was delighted with my second innings figures of 5-81 in 25 overs (with six maidens). Added to the first innings career-best 9-56, I came away from May's Bounty with my best ever match figures of 14-137. Bounty indeed!

These figures kept me in the top five in the national averages – and still in the selectors' minds for the 1976 home Test series against the formidable West Indies. Unfortunately, there was no 1975-76 England winter tour, only a short MCC tour to West Africa. International recognition hadn't come my way yet, but at least I was being talked about in those terms.

By the way, there is a salutary postscript to the Basingstoke game, and it is proof – if needed – that cricket can be both a cruel game and a great leveller! We played Hampshire away again the very next week, this time in their more familiar surroundings of the County Ground in Southampton. It was a 60-over Gillette Cup game, and was the third time we had met them in that same 1975 season.

Well, Richards and Greenidge took revenge for their defeat at Basingstoke with a devastating opening stand of 210 as Hampshire posted 371-6 declared – a very significant one-day score in those days. Gordon, who I'd sent back for a duck only the week before in the first innings of the Championship match, top-scored with a memorable 177 and was made Man of the Match. I did get him in the end – but that was scant consolation! My figures of 2-84 off my 12 overs didn't make pretty reading. In cricket there are good days and not such good days – and this was definitely one of the latter.

12

England Expects

'Nash is a fine all-rounder who has been remarkably consistent through his career. I rate him better than some of the players England have picked lately ... He has always been a good front-line bowler, accurate and aggressive and with an angle of attack which England have not had for some time.'
Wilf Wooller

I suppose it was the biggest stage of my career to date – I'd been called up for an England trial.

It was the last week of May, 1976, and cricket was making its annual comeback after the long winter of football and rugby. Earlier in the month, Southampton – then in the Second Division of the Football League – had surprisingly beaten the mighty Manchester United in the FA Cup final at Wembley Stadium and, following on from their success in winning the First Division title, Liverpool had achieved their second success of the season by beating Bruges to win the UEFA Cup for the second time.

In cricket, all attention was focussed on the arrival of the powerful West Indies squad, managed by Clive Walcott, and the forthcoming five-Test series against England. Clive Lloyd, Lawrence Rowe, Viv Richards, Gordon Greenidge and my old teammate and Glamorgan favourite Roy Fredericks formed the backbone of the powerful West Indies batting line-up, and all eyes were already on the potentially devastating pace attack of Michael Holding, Andy Roberts, Vanburn Holder and Wayne Daniel.

The first Test at Trent Bridge was only eight days away, and here I was at the County Ground in Bristol playing for 'The Rest', captained by Mike Brearley, against an England XI led by Tony Greig, in the official trial, performances in which would shape the final 12- or 13-man squad.

Mike Brearley, skipper of 'The Rest'.

Tony Greig, captain of the England XI.

In the England side were fellow fast-bowlers John Lever and Mike Hendrick, and alongside me in 'The Rest' were Alan Ward and Chris Old. John Snow, already with ten years of international cricket under his belt, wasn't playing in the trial but would be available for selection. So it was stiff competition for quick bowling places, and I knew that in terms of pace I was the slowest of the group. I did, however, have the advantage of being able to move the ball both ways, and had taken 85 wickets for Glamorgan the previous season at an average of 23.55, including my new career-best.

I knew, too, that I was handier with the bat than most of the others. Earlier in the month I'd made my maiden one-day hundred in the Benson and Hedges Cup, and a week before that my first Championship century. I thought my batting form might help in what was obviously a very competitive selection call.

I was also heartened by Mike Brearley's faith in my bowling, even on a Bristol pitch that was as unresponsive as usual! The evening before the game started he'd got Chris Old, Alan Ward and me together to talk about the new ball. He told us that he had decided that I would open the bowling, with Alan the other end. You didn't have to be a great detective to know that Chris wasn't entirely happy with the plan, anticipating, I think, that he and Alan

John Lever (left) and Mike Hendrick (right), fast bowlers in the England XI.

would have been taking the new ball, but the skipper explained that he felt I would get some significant movement early on.

Sure enough, in the first over I got one to swing late into Dennis Amiss, and Phil Edmonds snapped up a bat-pad catch at short square-leg. Mike Brearley, in his usual position at first slip, turned to fellow-slipper Chris Old, standing next to him, and smiled! They were 0 for 1 with a key batsman back in the pavilion, and Mike's hunch had paid off. Of course, I felt ten feet tall. What a start! Mind you, Amiss would get 124 not out second time round!

I also got the wicket of David Steele batting at number three – caught behind by Somerset's Derek Taylor for 50. In between my successes, Chris Old had got a couple more early wickets and we had them in some trouble at 27 for 3, but Steele, Woolmer and Greig – the skipper

I justified Mike Brearley's confidence in opening the bowling with me, by getting the prize wicket of Dennis Amiss in the first over of the England XI's innings.

top-scoring with 64 – helped them to recover and be in a position to declare on 216 for 8 and leave us with a potentially awkward spell of batting before the close of the first day. Happily, Lumb and Brearley survived, and we were feeling fairly pleased with ourselves at the end of the first day. We hadn't let ourselves down.

Back in the team hotel, chairman of selectors Alec Bedser and England captain Tony Greig had a few words with me over a beer before dinner. "Well bowled today," Tony said. I was delighted, but it wasn't all good news. Bedser was also complimentary, and said that I had a real opportunity to play for England – if I could bowl a yard or two quicker. I told him that I thought I could, but that my initial reaction to the suggestion was that I risked losing the effectiveness that came with swing. I realised that I needed to think about this carefully.

Next day we took 'The Rest' on to 266 for 7 before declaring with a useful lead of 50. Then came a tricky period for them to bat through before the end of the day. Unfortunately, with the wicket losing the little life it had started with, we were unable to repeat our breakthrough of the first day. The bounce on the Bristol strip was getting lower and lower, and they pushed on in the final morning session, declaring on 225 for the loss of only two wickets.

Our bowling in the second innings was largely down to our spinners, Phil Edmonds and Geoff Miller. My figures were 9-1-32-0, but taken with my first innings 28-6-65-2, I felt I'd had a decent enough game. I was also feeling positive as my two wickets were both top three batsmen! In the same innings, Chris Old's figures were 26-10-54-3, and Alan Ward's 17.1-2-48-2. Like me, they didn't get much of a bowl in the second innings as the pitch was fast becoming a spinner's dream.

It certainly wasn't the sort of deck you'd want to face Derek Underwood and Geoff Cope on, but that was our fate, unfortunately. We just folded, Underwood getting 4 for 10 in 15 overs, 11 of them maidens. Cope's figures were 14-7-27-5 – and to his great delight David Steele got our last man out with his fifth ball to return 1 for 0! All out 48, with only Richard Lumb creeping into double figures and me being joint fifth top-scorer with four. We left the field disappointed and knowing we hadn't done ourselves justice on the final day.

At the end of the game, my personal feedback from Alec Bedser was still positive. Yet, at the same time, he was still asking me about finding an extra yard or so of pace. I said again that I was confident that I could, but that in doing so I risked losing a significant element of control and, importantly, would probably sacrifice my ability to move the ball both ways – my main weapon. I reassured him that all the advice I had received over the years had been not to strive for additional pace. In fact, not to change my action at all. I pointed out – politely – that it was season after season of consistently bowling long, tight and accurate spells, and getting wickets by moving the ball both ways, that had got me to the Test trial in the first place! That this was who I was as a cricketer. I didn't want to change, and at the same time almost certainly spoil, what I was good at.

Derbyshire spinner Geoff Miller and I roomed together at the Test Trial in Bristol.

To Alec, however, it was all about pace. I suspect that, mindful of the West Indies' fearsome reputation for hostile fast bowling, the England selectors had decided to try to match them, like-for-like, in a battle of speed!

It was strange playing in another environment, away from the familiar Glamorgan faces – and also experiencing the feeling of being 'on trial', of course. My 'roomie' at the hotel in Bristol was Derbyshire's young right-arm off-break bowler, Geoff 'Dusty' Miller. Like me, Geoff was hoping to win his first international cap as a result of his performance in this match. In the end, neither of us was named in the side for the first Test, but we were both assured that we were still in the selectors' minds. Later, Geoff was called up

If I'd been selected for England I'd have had the daunting task of bowling to on-form Viv Richards, later to play for Glamorgan, who scored 291 in the final Test of the summer.

for the final Test of the summer at The Oval where he and his fellow bowlers had a couple of tough days as the West Indies racked up a daunting 687 for 8 declared. Viv Richards, who had already scored a double-hundred in the opening Test and a century in the third, got 291 in their first innings – and England tried nine bowlers! This challenging debut gave 'Dusty' the first of his 34 caps.

As we chatted in our hotel in Bristol, speculating on our chances of selection and comparing notes on the peculiarities of the selection system, I never imagined for a moment that my roommate would go on to become an England selector himself – and later the national selector – and in these posts to have a significant influence on making changes in the organisation behind the selection of the national team. I'm pretty sure that Geoff didn't, either!

One of the things that has changed in recent years – influenced by Geoff Miller – has been the structure behind the selection process. I realise that selection is always likely to be, to some extent, contentious, but in 1976 it was a less professional process, managing to be at the same time both more straightforward and more complex. In those days, before central contracts were dreamed up, if you were excelling at county level, in theory you had as good a chance of selection for England as the next man. Having said that, stories abounded about 'unfashionable' teams that the selectors saw less of,

Don Shepherd - probably the greatest uncapped bowler.

and some of us would still argue that Glamorgan was one of them. Looking back at England teams of that era it is still difficult to explain how, for example, Don Shepherd, Alan Jones and Eifion Jones did not get a cap between them. There are many other examples of players who did not get the chance they deserved to perform at international level.

One of the criticisms we used to make at the time was that, as far as we knew, a selector was seldom seen at one of our games! We knew that Peter May had famously travelled down to Swansea in 1965 to cast a selectorial eye over Glamorgan's Jeff Jones, only to find on arriving at the ground from his hotel for the start of play that the young left-arm opening bowler had been left out of the side because the wicket was likely to be spinner-friendly. We joked that Peter's unhappy experience might have put off his colleagues and successors. I've been asked who watched me, and how often my progress was assessed. The answer is that, as far as I'm aware, none of the selectors ever came to see me bowl. I think a lot of it was simply done informally by word of mouth, often by telephone. People like Wilf Wooller, Ossie Wheatley and Tony Lewis might well have been contacted to offer a view on how I was doing and whether I should be under consideration. It was at best a haphazard process, and one that was unsatisfactory to most of the players on the county circuit.

The news that I had been selected for the England Trial was given to me by the secretary, Wilf Wooller, following a phone call to the club by the selectors. To some extent, it was out of the blue. Having said that, neither was it a total surprise. I knew 1975 had been my best season since turning professional, with some impressive figures including two new personal bests – an '8-for' and a '9-for', both against Hampshire, and my name had been mentioned as an England possible in the press, and by the odd commentator, for several seasons.

In fact, as far back as autumn 1969, following our successful Championship season and my part in it, Fred Trueman had argued in his popular weekly newspaper column that I should be considered for inclusion in the MCC party to tour Australia, and to contest the Ashes, the following winter. They were lengthy tours in those days, months away and with a lot of cricket – not just a couple of warm-ups and the Tests themselves. Fred knew that I could bowl long spells and long overs – I could bowl all day if necessary. He felt that my pace and action would suit some of the Australian wickets perfectly.

In putting my name in the frame, Fred also made the point that I always bowled well against the Australians. He thought that the Aussies were susceptible to sideways movement. He was right. They were!

I'd continued to get mentions in the national press from time to time after that – by Fred and others. Now, in 1976, it was *Daily Express* cricket writer Jim Hill who was arguing my case, highlighting recent successes with the bat as well as the ball.

Garry Sobers, too, had suggested that I was on the fringes of the England squad. In an interview he gave to Peter Walker, he included me in a group of Test hopefuls who, having seen play on the county circuit for several years, he 'rated' and who should be regarded as knocking on England's door, but whose quality he felt was 'undervalued' by the cricketing press and public alike.

If the cap fits let all-rounder Nash wear it

By Jim Hill

GLAMORGAN all-rounder Malcolm Nash who was 31 last Monday, has been so busy redressing the balance between the extremes of his cricketing life that he could win an England cap before he realises it.

At one end of a wide scale of ability Nash, of left-arm and medium pace, is known as the bowler who was hit for a world record six 6's an over by that one-man cricket team called Garfield Sobers.

At the other he is growing a rapidly rising reputation as the fastest bat in the West.

The happy swing to a less painful notoriety has been achieved in just 10 days of his tenth season in the first-class game.

It began with a maiden century scored in 76 minutes of a county championship game against Surrey at the Oval.

Then it accelerated to a Benson and Hedges 100 hammered off Hampshire in 52 minutes at Swansea.

Though he bats late in the order neither innings was in any way agricultural, and the second one was a Glamorgan record.

It beat the previous fastest centuries by former England opener Gilbert Parkhouse and present skipper, Pakistani Test star Majid Khan, by eight minutes.

Patriarch

County secretary Wilfred Wooller, 62-year-old Welsh cricket patriarch who skippered Glamorgan to their first championship win in 1948, rates the latter innings among the best he has seen.

That covers quite a lot of cricket, because as player and Test selector Wooller was concerned with such useful performers as Peter May, Colin Cowdrey, Cyril Washbrook, Tom Graveney, Peter Richardson, and David Sheppard.

As a Test selector, Wooller also helped England produce teams which won six out of seven series, a run of success which somewhat overshadows the efforts of more recent seasons.

Malcolm Nash
... rising reputation

'The fastest bat in the West', wrote Jim Hill in the Daily Express.

Having the support of players of the stature of Fred and Garry meant a lot to me. I know Wilf Wooller and Tony Lewis put in a few words of support, too, and another person who more than once offered words of encouragement, and who was someone else I admired and respected greatly, was John Arlott. Unusually for a 'stranger', John was a familiar and always welcome face in the Glamorgan dressing-room. We appreciated the fact that he knew his cricket, that he would always try to be positive in his observations, and that any criticism would be fair and well-intentioned. He was a great supporter of the county game, and of county cricketers. Over the years, on more than one occasion he, too, publicly linked my name to the national side.

Another reason for me thinking that I was being picked-up on the England radar around that time was that, together with my Glamorgan teammate Alan Jones, I played three matches for D.H. Robins' XI. These were wins in consecutive games against Oxford University and Cambridge University in 1975, and a loss against Sussex at The Saffrons, Eastbourne, the following season.

I took a total of 20 wickets in those three games which, unfortunately, were not counted as first-class – though some Robins' XI fixtures were. This was a great pity because, as things turned out, those wickets would have taken my career first-class total well past the elusive 1,000 mark!

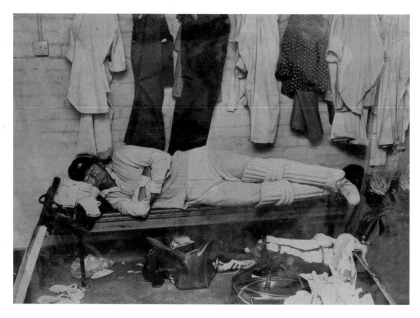

Preparing for action with the bat for Glamorgan at Sophia Gardens (wearing my D.H. Robins' XI cap).

The D.H. Robins' matches had an additional significance for me because they presented the chance to bat up the order and show my usefulness as an all-rounder. Against Oxford, I came in first-wicket down in the first innings and got a very satisfying 45 – followed up by 40 in the second innings against an attack that included Imran Khan. Against Cambridge, I made 34 not out at number four (after Alan and Harry Pilling had got centuries), and I also had a decent knock against Middlesex, scoring 36 batting at number six.

Unsurprisingly, in the light of my conversations with Alec Bedser and Tony Greig at Bristol, I didn't get called up for any of the 1976 Test series. I was disappointed, of course, but I felt a sense of achievement too. I'd taken part in the trial, and had bowled well and received positive comments. It was a strange mix of satisfaction and disappointment. Bearing in mind the 3-0 mauling of England by the West Indies – and it could easily have been worse – omission from the team might be regarded by some as a blessing in disguise! It was a tough summer for England's batsmen and bowlers alike, but I would have loved to have had the chance.

Interestingly, Arlott later picked up on the issue of my pace. Commenting that I was 'at my most puzzlingly dangerous with the new ball', he confirmed that it was my unwillingness to make the change that eventually ruled me out of the England thinking. However disappointing that was, I still think Alec Bedser made the wrong call about pace, and I have no regrets about not trying to adapt my action and become something that I wasn't!

Even if I didn't walk away with a cap, playing in a Test trial was a memorable experience and a significant honour. I took a lot away from that match in Bristol, including the experience of having played under Mike Brearley. I still regard Mike and Tony Lewis, my skipper in the early years at Glamorgan, to be the two most impressive captains I came across as a player.

I didn't ever play under Garry Sobers – except in my 'Owzat!' World XI team as a child, of course! Perhaps if I had, his name would join those of Mike and Tony, but I still smile to myself when I recall how close I came to playing in a team he captained, and appearing in a real World XI.

When the South African cricket authorities withdrew their invitation to Australia to tour in the 1971-72 season, the Australian Cricket Board organised a Rest of the World squad to play five games against a full Australian side – effectively, five pseudo 'Tests'– as 11 other games against State sides. It was essentially a full tour, with the Rest of the World squad made up of internationals from six Test playing countries.

The England representatives were Tony Greig, Norman Gifford, Richard Hutton and Bob Taylor. There is little doubt that Peter Lever and John Snow would have been certainties for places, but neither was available to tour. So the quartet of fast bowlers available to Don Bradman, Neil Harvey and their fellow Rest of the World selectors was all-rounder Richard Hutton, New Zealand's Bob Cunis, South Africa's Peter Pollock, and Pakistan's Asif Masood – supported by skipper Garry Sobers, of course. Garry could be surprisingly quick for a few overs with the new ball – quicker than people would imagine, and up there with the best of the West Indian 'quicks'. By all accounts, there were some disappointing performances by the Rest of the World side. Masood, in particular, was not at his best and did not play in a number of the bigger games. To make matters worse, Sobers was unable to play for part of the tour because of an eye infection.

Garry's return to fitness improved things for the World XI. In the third New Year 'Test' at Melbourne, after the shock of a first innings duck, Garry scored a majestic 254 in the second innings to give his side a victory by 96 runs to level the series. His innings was described by Sir Don Bradman as 'probably the greatest exhibition of batting ever seen in Australia'.

I was in Sydney on business when the fourth representative game was about to start, and after completing all I needed to do a bit quicker than expected, decided to watch some cricket and at the same time get in touch with Garry again. Perhaps he could find time to have a drink together, I hoped. I rang him at the SCG and explained that I was in town. He said to come over to the ground, and arranged to leave a ticket for me at the gate.

It was great to see Garry again and to chat about cricket, including the World XI tour, over a few 'cool ones'. Garry was unhappy about the lack of effectiveness of some of his fast bowlers against the strong Australian batting line-up. A couple were already struggling with niggles, and Bob Cunis was due to leave the side to join up with New Zealand for their tour of the West Indies. Garry himself had opened the bowling in the first three 'Tests', and also in this current game at Sydney. Suddenly, he asked, "Hey, Nashy, have you got any kit with you? If you aren't in a hurry to go back to the UK, you could turn out for us."

I assured him that, as long as I made a couple of phone calls, I was in no rush to leave Australia. I also checked that he was serious about his suggestion – and he was. He knew I could bowl long spells, and keep things tight. Also, that I had a reputation for getting top-order batsmen out – and some very good batsmen, too. After all, I'd got Garry himself out a couple of times in the previous County Championship season. I could see that he really wanted me to join up with the squad for what was left of the tour – four or five games, including the final 'Test' at Adelaide – and he could not have pressed my case harder.

He arranged for me to borrow some kit, and before I knew it I found myself in the nets bowling to some of the Rest of the World batsmen, with their manager Bill Jacobs and a couple of selectors looking on. At the end of the session they were all very positive, agreeing with Garry's feeling that my style would suit

Do I know Garry Sobers?

Garry Sobers struck a Napoleon - like pose in the World XI dressing room yesterday, but Malcolm Nash remembers only too well when the champion West Indian struck at Swansea (UK), batting for Nottinghamshire.

The luckless Nash got a kink in his neck as Sobers thrashed his 32nd over to set a world record — a maximum six sixes in an over.

The Glamorgan leftie said he felt "quite sick" when the first four balls disappeared over the fence.

"I reckoned I had him next ball when Roger Davis caught him on the boundary, but he fell over the fence to make it five in a row.

"I remember looking hopefully towards my skipper, Tony Lewis and all he could say was "keep it up, son."

"That's exactly what I did and Sobers made no mistake.

Garry and I met up again in Sydney.

the Australian wickets and that I would be difficult to handle. I knew the net session had gone well, despite my lack of recent practice and being in borrowed boots. I was pleased with the way I had bowled, and that I had justified Garry's faith in putting me forward as a possible addition to the squad.

The management team checked again on my availability, and on the possibility of me quickly getting some of my own kit together. I said I could get what I needed sent out – or even fly back for it myself. Then there was one more box to tick. A box I didn't realise existed – how many times had I played for England?

Of course, I had to explain that I hadn't. They, in turn, explained that a condition agreed with the tour sponsors was that every member of the World XI squad would be a full international. I joked that I'd played hockey for Wales, but we agreed that this didn't count!

So that was the end of Garry's plan. How cool would that have been, though. Just imagine, suddenly finding yourself playing in a World XI side, captained by Garry Sobers, against Australia! Awesome! My childhood games of 'Owzat!' almost brought to reality!

13

Millionaire Cricket

'I think people like to see attacking cricket. They don't really enjoy watching the ball being blocked all the time. They want batsmen to hit the ball ...'
Garry Sobers

I f 1975 had been a season of personal achievement with the ball, then 1976 got off to a spectacular start with the bat! We'd gone up to London for the first game of the season, against Surrey. The Oval had never rated as one of my favourite grounds. It seemed so huge and impersonal, and not that pretty, either, with a drab yellow brick wall all the way round.

Surrey won the toss and batted. Considering that they had got off to a strong start, with John Edrich, Geoff Howarth and Ahmed Younis getting them to 170 for 3, we felt we'd done reasonably well to have them all out for 338. It was still a decent total, though. Opener Alan Butcher – who would years later join Glamorgan – was my first wicket of the new season, and I also got Robin Jackman later in the innings. It was a long and tiring day in the field, especially as it was the first bowl of the season! I got through 24 overs for 82, and I think we were pretty glad to see them all out.

Alan Butcher (who later played for Glamorgan) was my first wicket of the 1976 season.

A useful right-hand batsman, Len Hill's career as a professional footballer with Newport County and later Swansea City meant that his cricketing appearances were limited.

The relief was short-lived. Surrey's domination of the opening day continued in the tricky session we had batting before close of play. We lost Majid Khan, Alan Jones and Roger Davis early, then worse was to follow as the day ended with Len Hill joining the procession. Mike Llewellyn was still there on 16 not out, but we were in trouble on 47 for 4.

Although the final session had not gone according to plan, my fellow bowlers and I felt we'd worked hard and had a reasonable day. We looked forward to having a drink and relaxing, while the batters – or what were left of them – got ready to carry on the fight in the middle next morning.

That night, a couple of my teammates (who shall remain nameless!) and I decided we'd make the most of being in the capital and, after our first hard day in the field at The Oval, have a little celebration. Nothing too extravagant, but in the end we had a pretty good night.

There were unwritten rules amongst the players in those days. Things you could do and things you couldn't do. If you stayed up late, you didn't drink, and if you did have more than a couple of drinks, you went to bed early – well, early-ish, anyway. You couldn't do both! The other understanding we had was that if the bowlers – and the 'keeper – had done their job and got the opposition out, it was our night out. The batsman's responsibility was to get to bed and have a good night's sleep but, if we'd been batting all day and it was the bowlers who were needed to carry the brunt of the action next day, then they turned in early. That's the way it was!

So, after the hard first day in the field a few of us went out for the evening. A long evening! We weren't drinking. Just a couple of beers – that was fine. We ended up in the Knightsbridge Sporting Club, quite a posh venue in those days. I didn't often go to a casino. I'd learnt my lesson about gambling – and the unpredictability of the roulette wheel – when we'd toured in Zambia at the end of the 1972 season, but I did enjoy the casino atmosphere and the opportunity for some people-watching. It was a fascinating environment. I must admit we were there longer than planned and it was a late night. When we eventually got back to the hotel, I was ready for my bed. My head had hardly hit the pillow when it seemed to be time to go back down to The Oval.

On reflection, and with the added wisdom that I'm told comes with age, my expedition to Knightsbridge was probably not the best way to prepare for the second day of the opening game of a new season, and not the course of action I'd recommend to young players coming into the game. It did seem like a good idea at the time, though, and in my defence, when I was putting the plan together I was anticipating a gentle day in the calm of the pavilion.

Arriving at the ground I was tired, of course, but my plan was to do the pre-match warm-ups and then, a quarter of an hour or so before start of play, to treat myself to a nice cup of tea and cigarette in the pavilion before getting my head down for a sleep until lunch time. As Mike Llewellyn and John Solanky were just getting ready to set off for the middle, and Eifion was strapping pads on just in case, I found a quiet corner of the dressing room, stretched out on the bench, and was quickly in a wonderful, contented sleep.

"Nashy. Nashy, wake up. Get the pads on."

"What? What's happening? What's the time?" I must have overslept.

"Nashy, pads on. We're in trouble. We're five down. You're batting next. Eifion's just gone in."

I couldn't believe it. I'd only been asleep for about half an hour, and it seemed to have

Hitting out against Surrey in an earlier innings at Cardiff.

done more harm than good. I felt worse than I had before! I needed to splash cold water on my face, but there wasn't time. Next in. I tried to concentrate. Not easy, though. It was a muddled scramble. Find my box. Strap my pads on.

While this was happening, there was a loud appeal from outside, followed by a groan from inside our dressing room. Eifion had become Jackman's fifth victim – for a rare duck. I still hadn't finished fiddling with my kit when someone stuck my bat in my hand and I was ushered towards the door. It was still only 11.40 or so, with the scoreboard displaying a very sad 65 for 6.

I took guard at the Vauxhall end with the huge gasometer behind me. Mike Llewellyn was the other end. But Eifion's wicket had fallen to the first ball of the over, so Robin Jackman – who was on fire with five of the six wickets to his name (Roger had been run out) – had the rest of the over at me unless I could nick a single.

Well, I played millionaire cricket and started off as if there was no tomorrow. A shot a ball at all five. Two shots at some of them! A miss every time. At the end of the over, after Robin Jackman had shared a few thoughts with me, Mike Llewelyn came down the pitch. "What's going on?" he asked. "What are you doing?"

"It's fine," I said. "I just got some sighters. I'm OK now."

"OK? You're joking! We're lucky not to be seven down."

"No, really, I'm OK now. No problem. We'll go from here."

I think Mike played a maiden, or he may have got a two. Anyway, much to his relief I stayed at the other end, but that meant I was back in the firing line when Jackman got the ball back in his hand again. Steaming in. On a roll.

I did connect with the first ball of that over – and hit him back over his head for six! That did it. 'I really am fine now,' I thought. 'Here we go.' I saw it like a melon, and I took them apart! It felt great. I got to a hundred in 76 minutes. I blasted it to all parts. I can't tell you how much I enjoyed that knock! I loved it.

I was still there, 119 not out, at lunch (which was at 1.15, I think). I should have turned it into a really big hundred, but on 130 I cut one to backward point and set off for a run. It was a case of 'Yes', 'No', 'Oh dear!'

I couldn't get back, and was run out. How crazy was that! Mike and I had put on 171 together, which turned out to be Glamorgan's biggest seventh wicket partnership of the season. It was also a new club record seventh wicket partnership against Surrey. If I hadn't got out, we might have gone on to beat the record seventh wicket stand against any county – 195 set by no less than Wilf Wooller and Willie Jones back in 1947! What an achievement that would have been, but we were still happy with what we'd achieved. Mike went on to get 73, and we were all out for 271 – a lot more than it had looked as if it might have been when I had stumbled out on to the field, still rubbing my eyes, earlier in the day.

Mike Llewellyn was my batting partner in a memorable morning at The Oval!

I was thrilled, of course, to get my maiden first-class century, and I'd got half the Glamorgan run total, but there were certainly no celebrations that night. I needed to catch up on sleep and be ready to bowl again in the morning. Surrey had finished the second day on 133 for 4. We were still in this game – just!

Younis was 93 not out when Surrey declared leaving us 327 to get for an improbable victory. We were never really in the hunt for that, but tried to make a go of things – and, as the day wore on, save the game. Mike Llewelyn and John Solanky got scores in the 40s, and Geoff Ellis, in what would be his last season with Glamorgan, weighed in with a valuable 31. I managed 15 before becoming one of four victims for England's Welsh-born off-break bowler Pat 'Percy' Pocock as the pitch increasingly responded to spin.

In an exciting finish, our last pair of Tony Cordle and Greg Armstrong hung on to frustrate the Surrey attack with an unbeaten stand of 17 to earn us a draw that, because it had at times seemed so improbable, felt almost like a victory. When umpires Lloyd Budd (who would officiate in the Old Trafford

Test later in the season) and Peter Rochford at last called time, we were 234 for 9 – Glamorgan seven points, Surrey eight points.

My good form with the bat continued into our next game at Cardiff, the second Championship fixture of the season, against a formidable Somerset bowling attack spearheaded by Ian Botham and Hallam Moseley who picked up 17 wickets between them across the two Glamorgan innings. I top-scored again, first time round, with 40 in an innings-saving stand of 66 with Eifion Jones after I'd gone in at 35 for 7, with only one of my dismissed teammates having managed to get into double figures.

I got another 39 in the second innings, and this time Eifion top-scored with a hard-fought 70, though our efforts weren't quite enough to prevent a last-gasp Somerset victory orchestrated by opener Brian Rose and skipper Brian Close. This was after I'd got the other opener, wicketkeeper Derek Taylor, and number three, Peter 'Dasher' Denning, for ducks and we seemed to suddenly hold the advantage with Somerset at 6 for 2 chasing 244.

The next day we were at Swansea to face our old adversaries Hampshire in a one-day Benson and Hedges Cup match. Once again, I'm afraid, it was a familiar story! After winning the toss and batting we were soon in trouble again.

The Glamorgan score at lunch was a depressing 85 for 6, with 36 of our allotted 55 overs already bowled. Eifion on six, and me still not off the mark, were the not-out batsmen with the task of trying once again to mount a rescue operation. Even a good St. Helen's picnic lunch or a game of cricket on the outfield with a tennis ball couldn't cheer up even the most optimistic of our supporters. There was little evidence of the usual excitement in the ground and even the always loyal Balconiers in Fred's Bar were subdued as Eifion and I walked out to resume the innings to a faint ripple of polite applause. As far as most of the spectators were concerned, the match seemed already to be lost.

We didn't think so and, suddenly, everything changed. In the next 19 overs I hit an undefeated 103. My century included seven sixes and seven fours, and was later generously described by Wilf Wooller as 'the most remarkable piece of scientific hitting seen for Glamorgan in a limited overs contest'. High praise, of which I am still proud. With stands of 102 with Eifion, and then 58 (unbroken) with Tony Cordle, we were able to take the score to a respectable 245 for 7.

It was my first limited-overs hundred. It was also the fastest hundred in the Benson and Hedges Cup – and remained so until the competition ended after 30 years in 2002. So it is a record I shall always hold!

I remember thinking that it was a bit like London buses: You wait for ages – I'd been playing professional cricket for ten seasons without scoring a century – and then two come along together! There was only just over a week between my two century knocks at The Oval and St. Helen's.

It really was a match-turning – and, in the end, match-winning – innings, too. We bowled well as a unit, Lawrence Williams, Greg Armstrong and me sharing the wickets, well supported by Tony Cordle and John Solanky. When Lawrence had Bob Herman caught by Alan Jones, the final wicket had fallen off the second ball of the 55th and final over, with Hampshire still three runs short.

What had, earlier in the day, seemed like a lost cause had, by mid-afternoon, turned into a nail-biter. As the remaining overs ticked by and Hampshire wickets continued to fall, a now very vocal and involved crowd was treated to one of the most exciting finishes ever seen at the Swansea ground.

Barry Richards – always difficult to get out.

There is an important footnote to this victory – quite literally! – and it relates to the very ample foot of my fellow fast-bowler Lawrence Williams.

A very significant momentum swing occurred when Hampshire's opener Barry Richards, who would have been capable of single-handedly taking the game away from us, was brilliantly run out by Lawrence for a comparatively modest 30. As he hit the ball, Barry advanced down the wicket hoping for a sharp single. Realising it wasn't there he turned, but was still struggling to regain his ground when Lawrence, half-way down the pitch in his follow-through, kicked the ball on to middle pole! It was a brilliant piece of footballing skill.

St. Helen's was always a popular venue with us. By no means the smallest we played on, it certainly wasn't the largest, either. I guess the adjoining rugby pitch on one side makes it seem bigger than it is. Over the years it has figured in a number of spectacular batting displays. I've been on the wrong end of some of them – Garry Sobers, Clive Lloyd and Frank Hayes all instantly spring to mind, for example – but it's a ground I've always enjoyed batting on myself, too, and my Benson and Hedges century wasn't the only batting record I managed to set in Swansea.

In May 1970, in a League game against Kent, I reached 50 off only 33 balls and secured the award for the fastest televised half-century of the season.

Some poor weather around lunchtime meant that each side's allocation of overs was reduced from the usual 40 to 38. I was caught by England 'keeper, Alan Knott, off Norman Graham's bowling from the final ball of our innings. We had been 57 for 7 when I'd gone in to join Bryan Davis, and together we'd taken the Glamorgan score to 145 for 8. Not a massive total, but a lot better than it had looked like it was going to be! Yet it proved to be too good for a strong Kent XI skippered by Colin Cowdrey and including Brian Luckhurst, Mike Denness, Bob Woolmer, Asif Iqbal and Derek Underwood. They ended

Opener Roy Fredericks – an exciting batsman.

up all out for 130 – a good win for us against a very useful side.

The following two seasons saw me get tantalisingly close to what would have then been my first first-class century. At Sophia Gardens, in the penultimate Championship fixture of 1972, I scored 82 against a Middlesex attack that included Titmus, Edmonds, Price and Selvey – before being run out. In the same game, our popular Guyanan opener Roy Fredericks, in the second of his three seasons with us, scored a typically exciting century, having the previous season established a record opening-stand of 330 with Alan Jones against Northants at Swansea.

The Middlesex match also had a particular significance in that, as well as being Peter Parfitt's final match, it was also the last Championship appearance by Peter Walker. I was at the wicket with Peter when the game ended, and it was a sad moment – doubly so because, two games earlier at The Oval, Don Shepherd had made his final first-class appearance, too. Peter and Don were leaving massive boots to fill.

Then, in August 1973, in the first innings of an amazing game at Swansea against Gloucestershire, I managed two other records with a bat in my hands – and in doing so got even closer to that elusive first hundred! Although I fell short on 89, I set what was at the time a club record of nine sixes in a Championship innings. It was a record that was to stand for 42 years until Graham Wagg, batting at number eight against Surrey at Guildford in 2015, hit 11 sixes as he compiled a memorable double-hundred.

Most of my sixes, in an innings lasting 98 minutes, were scored batting at the Mumbles Road end, off the right-arm off-spin bowling of John Mortimore – and ended up in the same areas that Garry Sobers had famously favoured off my bowling almost exactly five years earlier! Anywhere in that arc from deep

One of my favourite shots!

mid-wicket to long on to straight back over the bowler's head. Aiming roughly for 'The Cricketers' pub just over the road from the ground! Eventually, as I continued to be aggressive, I was caught by Gloucestershire's new young wicketkeeper/batsman Andy Stovold off the medium-pace of Roger Knight, and soon afterwards Majid declared with Eifion on 96 and us 69 behind Gloucestershire's mammoth first-innings total of 444 for 7.

I always enjoyed batting with Eifion. He was a great guy to have the other end, and we had some memorable knocks together over the years. This was one of them! We put on 142, beating the previous Glamorgan record seventh wicket stand against Gloucestershire. Our record also stood for a good length of time, beaten in 2010 by Jim Allenby and Robert Croft who put on 153 at the SWALEC Stadium.

Eifion was a very useful batsman. We rescued things together more than once.

The game had started well for us when I'd bowled opener Stovold for a duck, but Knight (ending on 101) and Mike Proctor (getting the better of us that day with 152, his fourth century in 11 days, and including six sixes and 17 fours in his two-and-a-half hours at the crease) had put on 224 for the third wicket to put the visitors very much in the driving seat. Gloucestershire declared with seven wickets down for the second time in the match, leaving us to get 295 to win in 186 minutes. At more than 90 an hour, it was a tough target, and I think they thought we would perish in the attempt.

However, we still had the benefit of a very good batting wicket and, at 250 for 2, were still on course to turn the match around and record a famous victory. With the required rate now down to a very gettable five or so an over, Alan was still going strong and getting good support from Gwyn Richards – his second promising knock in the match. Roger Davis, sharing an opening partnership of over a hundred, and Geoff Ellis, had already helped Alan to get our chase off to a great start.

Then, out of the blue, this incident-packed contest took another quite unexpected turn. Tony Brown, Gloucestershire's experienced skipper and right-arm medium-paced bowler, took a hat-trick! In the last two balls of an over he bowled Gwyn Richards and then had Tony Cordle, promoted in the order for quick runs, lbw first ball. Worse was to follow with David Graveney catching Alan Jones, well-set on 109, off the first ball of his captain's next over.

When umpires Budd and Pepper called time, we were only 35 short of what had initially seemed an unlikely victory target but later had become one almost within our grasp. It was an exciting and unpredictable draw, full of surprise twists and changes of fortune right to the end – and with over 1,300 runs scored. It was another game that still figures prominently in the St. Helen's record-books – and in supporters' memories.

Coincidently, Lloyd Budd, the old Hampshire fast-medium right-arm bowler who had played until just after the war, stood in the matches against both Kent and Gloucestershire. He must have been something of a lucky mascot for me! Three seasons after the Gloucestershire game Budd officiated in his first international match – the controversial Test at Old Trafford when England's John Edrich and Brian Close withstood a period of sustained short-pitched bowling from the West Indian pace attack.

I saw some members of that formidable 1976 West Indies attack at first-hand when we played them in the traditional August Bank Holiday game at St. Helen's a month later. Two of the bowlers who had given England so much trouble, 22-year-old Michael Holding and 20-year-old Wayne Daniel, were included in the side that came to Swansea. Andy Roberts, at 25 the elder statesman of the pace attack, was rested for the game against us. In dismissing

Michael Holding bowling to Alan Jones at Swansea, with Clive Lloyd at first slip.

Wayne Daniel bowling to Arthur Francis. The umpire is Arthur Jepson, who once reported me to Lord's for questioning a decision!

England for 71 and 126 at Manchester, the three fast bowlers had taken all 20 wickets between them – Roberts 9 for 59, Holding 7 for 41, and Daniel 4 for 52.

Thankfully the Swansea wicket had more in it to interest the spinners, and although the pace-men were impressive, it was the batting – and particularly an innings from skipper Clive Lloyd – that was our outstanding memory of the game.

Lloyd's innings was incredible, and is still in the record books. It also forms an interesting post-script to my maiden century against Surrey in the opening fixture of the season as, when we came to entertain the tourists, mine was still this country's fastest century of the season, and was taking me towards winning the annually awarded – and prestigious – Walter Lawrence Trophy. In those days such batting milestones were measured in minutes rather than balls.

St. Helen's was obviously a favourite ground of Clive's, and I had been a member of the Glamorgan side when, in 1969, he and Basil Butcher had taken

On his 1976 visit, Clive Lloyd got his second score of 201 not out at St. Helen's.

our attack apart – especially our spinners. In the West Indians' first innings total of 419 for 5 declared, Butcher had scored 151 and Lloyd 201 not out. I got 3 for 104 – and remember it well! The power of Clive Lloyd's stroke-play was still clear in our memories when he walked down the St. Helen's steps again seven years later. We knew just how much damage he could do – and how quickly he could do it, too.

We batted first and did reasonably well, though nobody managed to go on and get a really big score after getting a decent start. I was pleased with my batting again, top-scoring with 64.

When the West Indians replied, Tony Cordle dismissed opener Roy Fredericks – the former Glamorgan player – for only two, but success was short-lived! Gordon Greenidge and Viv Richards – who would later in his career also become a Glamorgan player – put on 224 for the next wicket. Again, there wasn't much in the pitch to help 'Speedy' and me, and I went wicketless for 77 off my 12 overs. Lawrence Rowe chipped in with 88, but it was Clive Lloyd, in his favourite number five spot, and wielding an even bigger and heavier bat than on his earlier visit, who really caught the eye – and once again did considerable damage to our spin attack.

He was racing towards his century when one of the guys realised that my fastest hundred award was in danger of being snatched away. It looked as if Clive might just beat me to it by a crucial couple of minutes. Word spread round the fielders, and as the West Indian captain stroked his way through the not-very-nervous 90s there were several brief, and loyally-intended, delays in play. Not just lace-tying and ball-polishing and field-changing, but a drinks break, too. In fact, anything to ensure that he went past my 76 minutes! We succeeded – just! Clive's century was timed at 80 minutes.

The last laugh, however, was with the batsman. Several laughs, actually. Firstly, because it turned out that tourist games were not eligible for the Lawrence Trophy anyway – so we had been, quite literally, wasting our time! – and secondly, because Clive's second hundred followed in an amazing 40 minutes as he raced from a hundred off 79 balls to two hundred off 124. At the time (and for eight years afterwards) his innings was in the record books as the equal fastest double-century in the history of first-class cricket – matching to the minute Gilbert Jessop's 200 for Gloucestershire in 1903! It probably should have beaten it – the drinks break probably wasn't accounted for by the time-keeper! – and it was Clive's second successive 201 not out at St. Helen's, the West Indies declaring on 554 for 4. It was an amazing experience to be part of. He was wonderful to watch. Brutal to bowl to.

There is one final 'last laugh', and a post-script to the post-script. It is that I didn't win the 1976 Walter Lawrence Trophy anyway. In September, Alan Knott took just 70 minutes to reach 100 for Kent against Sussex at Canterbury. Pipped at the post!

So, one way or another, 1976 was a special year for batting achievements, but the next season saw another, again at St. Helen's. I played in a game in which another piece of cricket history was written when New Zealand international Glenn Turner established a very unusual record in our Championship match against Worcestershire.

Glenn was another fantastic batsman to watch, and another difficult guy to bowl to. He didn't make many mistakes and was a particularly good judge of line. Always with a straight bat, and with an exceptionally good eye, it is no accident that he is one of the distinguished group of players to have scored a hundred first-class hundreds. Century number 66, though, the second of three he scored at Swansea, was probably the strangest.

Worcestershire's Glenn Turner, one of the best opening batsmen I bowled to, got an unusual world record at Swansea in 1977.

Alan Jones was skippering Glamorgan and we batted after he won the toss. We got a decent score, too, with contributions from all the top order followed by an unbroken fifth-wicket partnership of 161 between Mike Llewellyn and Gwyn Richards that enabled a declaration at 309 for 4. This left Worcestershire with a tricky final hour or so before close of play.

As usual, Turner opened for the visitors, partnered on this occasion by newcomer Barry Jones. I trapped Barry leg before for a single, but we knew there was plenty of strong batting to come. Phil Neale was next, but he didn't last long either, caught behind off Alan Wilkins, and Jim Cumbes was sent in as night-watchman. Of Worcestershire's total of 42 for 2 at stumps, Glenn Turner had 39 of them to his name.

Next morning, Worcestershire added another 33 before Cumbes, who had defended well for his five, became my second lbw victim. His dismissal signalled a middle-order collapse with Ted Helmsley, Basil D'Oliveira, Dipak Patel and wicketkeeper David Humphries all going in quick succession as a bewildered Turner watched from the other end. He said later that he had tried to reassure the incoming batsmen that there was no problem with the wicket, but they wouldn't believe him! Our visitors had slumped to 87 for 7.

When Humphries headed off for the long climb back to the pavilion, Glenn Turner had scored 70 of those 87 runs and he looked as untroubled as ever! Fast bowler Vanburn Holder nicked a boundary through the slips before falling lbw to Tony Cordle. At 93 for 8, it appeared that Worcestershire would be very unlikely to avoid the follow-on, but skipper Norman Gifford had other ideas.

He stayed with Turner for 50 minutes, content not to score, but allowing his partner to accumulate runs. Glenn had one slice of luck, missed in the slips by Rodney Ontong off my bowling, but eventually he went on to his century – 101 out of the team total of 127 for 8. The stand was broken when Gifford fell to the spin of Barry Lloyd with Worcestershire on 150. Then it was last man Paul Pridgeon's turn to stay with Turner as the follow-on was successfully avoided. This turned out to be crucial, because rain on the third day meant that we were unable to go on and press for the win we deserved.

When Pridgeon became Tony Cordle's fifth victim, Worcestershire were all out for 169. Glenn Turner had carried his bat with 141 of them, batting for 216 minutes and scoring 20 fours and a six. The other ten batsmen made only 14 scoring shots between them. None got into double figures – the second-highest scorer in the team was Norman Gifford with seven.

The contribution of Glenn's innings to cricket history? His score was a world-record 83.4% of his side's total. A record that still stands.

Going back to the subject of my own batting milestones, the 1978 season brought some more innings to remember and celebrate.

After my back-to-back hundreds in 1976, I scored only one more century, and again it was a knock I was very proud of. It was the second-highest score of my career – and not out, too! We were playing Ray Illingworth's Leicestershire at St. Helen's early in June. You could say that this knock followed a familiar pattern. Leicestershire had declared on 303 for 7, and in our first innings reply we were once again in big trouble on 78 for 7 when I walked out to join not-out batsman Gwyn Richards.

We batted well together, and our stand of 166 for the eighth wicket was a Glamorgan-best against Leicestershire. I ended undefeated on 124 off 100 balls, and hit five sixes.

I always believed I could do something to change a game, whether with bat or ball. Often it didn't come off, of course, but every so often – as it did against Leicestershire – everything worked. I admit, too, that as well as changing a game, I liked nothing better than giving the ball a really good clout!

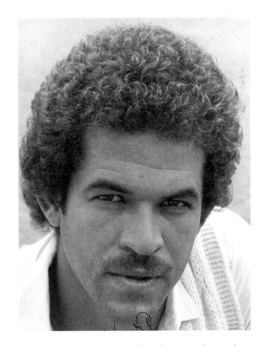

Rodney Ontong and I shared a record stand against Essex.

Frank Hayes. Could lightning strike twice?

I figured in two other Glamorgan record-breaking stands that season. Rodney Ontong and I put on 105 for the ninth wicket against Essex at Sophia Gardens – at the time, only the second occasion on which a Glamorgan pair had got over 100 for the ninth wicket. I was lbw to John Lever for 52, and Rodney went on to get an undefeated century. Then later in the season, back at The Oval against Surrey, I got 63 as Tony Cordle and I put on 74 for the ninth wicket.

One other memorable recollection of the batting summer of '78 came in our Championship game against Somerset at Taunton. It was ten years since Garry Sobers had scored his six sixes at Swansea, something I'd been reminded of just the previous year when Frank Hayes, Lancashire's England batsman, hit me for 34 in an over – again at Swansea. It was the first over after lunch and, strangely enough, I'd just cut short a telephone call from the *Daily Mirror* as we were about to take the field, asking my view on the odds of six sixes being hit at the upcoming Gillette Cup final. Frank hit my first ball for six and I must admit to being rather miffed when the second was dispatched for four. My response was to start bowling short at him but, as St. Helen's is not the ideal wicket for short deliveries, Frank swiftly hit the third, fourth, fifth and sixth balls over the boundary. If I'd let my anger get the better of me after the first ball he may well have repeated Garry's famous feat! My bowling figures for that innings – 15-5-71-0 – would have looked a whole lot better without that over.

At Taunton, I found myself with bat in hand and facing the left-arm orthodox spin of Dennis Breakwell. I hit the first ball of the over for six, and the second. Derek Taylor, the Somerset wicketkeeper, asked me what I was going to do next! "Just keep watching," I told him, as the third ball went for another six, followed by the fourth.

Taylor asked me, "Are you going for it?"

"What do you think?" I replied. I was on a roll.

Dennis was obviously keen to protect his figures – or to save his name from going into the record-books alongside mine! Perhaps he got a signal from the 'keeper – I don't know – and the next two balls were fired down the leg side. Just think how cool it would have been if I *had* been able to hit those final two balls for six! The first bowler to be hit for six sixes, and the second batsman to hit six sixes.

Now that really would have been a cricketing record.

14

Gillette and Other Close Shaves

'South Wales was gripped by cricket fever, as in almost every pub and club there was excited chatter about the final. Ticket applications were made and travel plans were finalised, and the net result was that Lord's, on the morning of the final, was alive with Welsh voices ...'
Andrew Hignell

Lord's again, and that special feeling again. I looked round the ground from the players' balcony as our skipper Alan Jones walked to the middle to toss with Mike Brearley, captain of Middlesex.

Lord's was packed, as it always was in those days for the premier event of the one-day game. It was Glamorgan's first final, and there were a lot of excited and enthusiastic Welshmen in the crowd. The Balconiers were up from Swansea, and there were placards announcing the presence of 'The Daffodil Army'. Judging from the noise in the ground, there were quite a few honorary Welshmen in the crowd, too. In fact, as if to support this theory, I spotted a banner which read 'Richie Benaud is a Welshman'. It was quite a party – and the match hadn't even begun. It gave you a real buzz of excitement.

It was the first Saturday of September, 1977. The country was coming to the end of a summer of celebrations marking the Queen's Silver Jubilee, and our day at the home of cricket seemed to fit the 'street party' mood perfectly. There'd also been a British winner at last – Virginia Wade – at Wimbledon.

Unfortunately, during the 1977 County Championship, Glamorgan's cricket could not be described as either celebratory or uplifting, with only three wins to our name.

We fared better in limited-over competitions, though. The John Player League saw us comfortably mid-table with seven wins and seven losses.

Our support at Lord's was incredible.

While in the Benson and Hedges Cup, we had three wins out of four, and an unsuccessful quarter-final match against Hampshire, who were seen home to victory by a Trevor Jesty century.

We did better still in the Gillette Cup. In fact, we did brilliantly! Our performances in all our games in this competition, like our match earlier in the season against the Australian tourists, made it a memorable summer of cricketing celebration after all. We found ourselves coming close to achieving what would have been rated as two historic outcomes.

To be honest, our Gillette Cup hopes could easily have fallen at the first hurdle – and almost did. After a bye in the first round, we found ourselves at New Road in mid-July for a game against Worcestershire. The home side batted first and found scoring difficult, eventually getting to 213 for 9 in their 60 overs. I managed to get through my 12 overs for only 26 runs, with five maidens.

We didn't find it an easy wicket to score quickly on, either. Arthur Francis, batting at three, was still there at the end and, with support from a Mike Llewellyn half-century, tied the scores off the penultimate ball of the game. I had just gone in and was the other end when Arthur hit a four off the final ball to give us a four-wicket victory – and to win the Man of the Match award. It was an exciting game to play in, as they often were against Worcestershire, and a good start for us in the competition. It was a very close shave. We could so easily have effectively ended our 1977 Gillette Cup run there and then.

In the quarter-final against Surrey at Sophia Gardens, we again fielded first and got Surrey all out in the final over. Skipper Alan Jones and our new overseas recruit, West Indian all-rounder Collis King, both got half-centuries as we chased down the total with four overs to spare. I was in the middle again, with Efion Jones this time, when the winning run came off the bowling of Geoff Arnold.

So our next Gillette Cup hurdle was the semi-final – already the furthest we'd ever progressed in this competition – against Leicestershire at Swansea. The start of the match was postponed for 24 hours because of heavy rain. Next day, when we eventually got underway, a near capacity crowd packed St. Helen's in the hope of seeing us secure a place in a one-day final for the first time. The outfield was damp and Alan won an important toss, enabling us to bowl first. Again, we did a good job in restricting the visitors to what seemed a modest 172 for 7 off their full 60 overs. David Gower top-scored with 43, supported by 40 each from captain and Rhodesian international Brian Davison and medium-pacer Peter Booth. I got opener John Steele for a single, and completed my 12-over allocation, including four maidens, for 38 runs. Alan Wilkins and Gwyn Richards bowled very tight 12-over spells too, each taking a couple of wickets. Gwyn's figures of 12-4-17-2 were exceptional.

We got our innings off to a great start with Alan and John Hopkins putting on 108 for the first wicket. That put us in a strong position, ahead of the clock, and earned John the Man of the Match award for his crucial 63. Run-making on the St. Helen's pitch was never easy, with Jack Birkenshaw in particular bowling a very tight 12 over spell of off-breaks for only 21 runs – including seven maidens. Jack could be very difficult to score off. In the end, Eifion

Arthur Francis secured a vital last-ball victory early in our Gillette Cup campaign.

Our new overseas signing Collis King and skipper Alan Jones both scored half-centuries to ease us to a win over Surrey.

Alan Wilkins (left) and Gwyn Richards (right) bowled tight spells in the semi-final.

Jones and Gwyn Richards saw us home with five wickets and 15 balls in hand. We were going to Lord's! It was the cue for more of those very special St. Helen's celebrations, including another stirring rendition of the Welsh National Anthem – *Hen Wlad fy Nhadau* – on the Swansea outfield.

The other semi-final, between Middlesex and Somerset, was also delayed by poor weather and we had to wait quite a while longer for our opponents to be decided. In the meantime, plans for a historic day out at Lord's were already being made by our very loyal, and very enthusiastic, supporters.

So to the final at Lord's, to face a strong Middlesex side, the reigning County Champions and strongly in contention for the 1977 title. They included in their ranks a good sprinkling of internationals and were led by the newly appointed England captain, Mike Brearley. The pattern of the match changed for us when Mike won an important toss and, unsurprisingly, we found ourselves batting first in what promised to be tricky conditions early on a September Saturday morning. It had rained in London earlier, and conditions were damp and overcast. We knew it wasn't a good time to be batting. It certainly wouldn't be easy.

The other negative thing about batting first was that only the two openers were in the game straight away. We'd been over to the Nursery for a net, but as our final Championship game of the season – a draw against Gloucestershire

The semi-final side at Swansea – and also the squad for the final.
Back row (left to right): Alan Lewis Jones, Tom Cartwright, Rodney Ontong, Mike Llewellyn, Collis King, Alan Wilkins, Arthur Francis, Frank Culverwell (scorer). Front row: John Hopkins, Malcolm Nash, Eifion Jones, Alan Jones, Gwyn Richards, Tony Cordle.

in Cardiff – had finished late the previous day, and we'd driven up to London in the evening, I didn't feel I needed to bowl too much. We did a lot of fielding practice, though, and I had a few throw-downs with the bat. Then we all had a look at the wicket on the way back to the dressing-room. Now we were doing things to occupy ourselves – I'd had a cup of tea and a couple of cigarettes – or were watching from the balcony, taking in the atmosphere and sense of occasion. An advantage of fielding first in an important game is that everyone is in the action from the start!

Mike Selvey, the Middlesex and England fast-medium bowler who later in his career came to Glamorgan, made the most of the helpful conditions and soon got the wickets of Alan Jones and Collis King. Another England player, all-rounder Mike Gatting, chipped in, having Rodney Ontong caught behind for a duck, and we found ourselves on a very unpromising 50 for 3. There seemed to be little for the thousands of Glamorgan supporters to cheer about.

That all changed with a powerful, counter-attacking partnership of 65 between Maesteg-born right-handed opener John Hopkins and Mike

Tickets for the final were in huge demand across Wales as Glamorgan headed to Lord's.

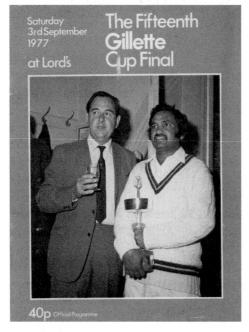

It was Glamorgan's first cup final, and the official programme was a collector's item for Welsh cricket supporters.

Llewellyn, our powerful left-hander from Clydach, in the Swansea Valley. They took the attack to the Middlesex bowlers, and the crowd loved it. Mike's first three balls from Gatting all went to the boundary – four, six, four – and he also took a liking to the bowling of yet another England bowler, off-spinner John Embury. More boundaries followed. More big hits to delight the Glamorgan supporters. One – off Embury's final ball – is still talked about at Lord's today! It was a colossal strike. A massive straight drive which almost went clean over the old pavilion – but not quite. When the ball made contact with the building, it was still going up! It finished high on the top tier, in

It was an amazing atmosphere to play in.

the guttering above the BBC's commentary box. It was a very special stroke, and prompted a special response from *Test Match Special*'s Brian Johnston who, to the crowd's delight, waved a white handkerchief out of the commentary box window.

Llewellyn eventually fell for 62 to the off-spin of Norman Featherstone – another player who would later join Glamorgan – and we lost momentum a bit after that. Batting was still not easy and several more wickets fell cheaply. I was another Featherstone victim, and we ended our 60-over allocation on 177 for 9. Not a disaster, but not as many as we would have liked. If we were going to get anything from the game, we needed to get early Middlesex wickets.

With the new ball in my hand, I prepared to bowl the first over. At the other end was Mike Brearley, just appointed to lead England in the Ashes Series against Australia, and someone I admired greatly as both a batsman and a skipper.

The first ball was in exactly the right place. From my point of view, it was the perfect away-swinger, drifting across Mike's bat. It took the edge and was enthusiastically gobbled up by Eifion behind the stumps. Mike walked.

Two 'home-grown' batsmen, John Hopkins (left) and Mike Llewellyn (right), rescued us with some powerful hitting.

It must have been a strange experience for him, leaving the field after a first-baller, and with the strains of *Hen Wlad Fy Nhadau* – sung with great gusto – accompanying him.

It was a dream start for us. Next man in was Clive Radley, and in my second over he edged a ball straight to Collis King at second slip. As slip chances go, it has to be said that it was relatively straightforward, but there was a huge groan round the ground as Collis, usually such a safe 'slipper', spilled it. They would have been 4 for 2, and nerves in the Middlesex dressing room would have been really jangling. Looking back, it was probably the main turning point in the game. Radley went on to score 85 not out and win the match with just over four overs left and five wickets in hand.

I must admit, I felt gutted to have lost. I sat in the changing room with a pint of milk! The Middlesex boys came in and we had a few beers, but it was an hour or so before I recovered enough to get stuck in! Then we had a wonderful evening celebrating with supporters back at The Clarendon hotel before driving ourselves up to Leicestershire the next morning for a Sunday League match. It was a crazy schedule! Anyway, Leicestershire had to win the

When Middlesex batted, I got us off to the perfect start, getting Mike Brearley's wicket with the first ball. It was yet another wicket in combination with wicketkeeper Eifion Jones.

match to win the League – and they did – by five wickets. It would be fair to say that we weren't at our best.

Looking back, it was a comfortable victory for Middlesex, but I honestly think things would have been a lot closer if we'd taken our catches – and if Alan had won the toss! We'll never know. Naturally, we didn't feel we'd done ourselves justice. Neither did we feel in any way disgraced. It was a great occasion and we and our wonderfully enthusiastic supporters had all enjoyed our historic final at the home of cricket.

In addition to our Gillette Cup run, that summer had already included one other important close shave! Earlier in the season we'd had another taste of excitement – and a reminder of our potential as a side – when we faced Australia again at St. Helen's.

The Australians, who had just met and defeated England in the Centenary Test at Melbourne, were over for a five-Test Ashes series preceded by three one-day internationals. With the first Test only a month away, and the first ODI in just two weeks, there was a lot of healthy competition for places. Their guys all wanted to do well at Swansea, especially because they had played hardly any cricket since their arrival, with the first four matches against county sides all being affected by rain. Skipper Greg Chappell didn't play at St. Helen's, handing the captaincy to Doug Walters, but it was a strong line-up with ten of the side going on to play in at least one of the ODIs, and six going on to appear in the first Test at Lord's. Within a month of leaving south Wales, every member of the Australian side at St. Helen's had played against England in a one-day international or Test match – or both!

The background to the Test series, and our game against Australia, was very much about matters relating to another Australian, Kerry Packer, and his plans

Doug Walters skippered the Australian side at St. Helen's.

for World Series Cricket. The tournament, to be televised on his own channel and in opposition to the Australian Board of Control, was very much the main news story in cricketing circles worldwide.

In fact, on the first scheduled day of our match, the British newspapers published the story that Tony Greig had been sacked as captain of England, though he, Derek Underwood and Alan Knott – who had all already signed up to play in the World Series – were still available for international selection later in the summer. It became clear that planning for the tournament and the recruitment of players had been going on in secret for months, but news of the World Series had only become public less than a week earlier, during Australia's game against Sussex. It was revealed at the same time that 13 of the 17-man touring squad had already signed for Packer.

The previous tour match, against Hampshire at Southampton, had been completely lost to the weather, and the rain followed the tourists west, preventing any play on the first day at Swansea – and in so doing, having a significant impact on the result. There was a bigger than usual press contingent present at St. Helen's when play eventually got underway in what was now a two-day game.

Our skipper Alan Jones found little support in the Glamorgan top order, and had watched his side subside to a depressing 61 for 4 before Alan Lewis Jones gave him any real assistance. They pulled things together, but we were all out for a disappointing 172. I'm afraid I didn't distinguish myself with the bat, being caught for nine attacking the leg-spin of Kerry O'Keeffe.

Our visitors didn't fare much better. Tony Cordle and I had some early successes, reducing them to 40 for 3 before it was their skipper's turn to perform a rescue act, Doug Walters enjoying a stand of getting on for a hundred with middle-order batsman Gary Cosier. I was bowling well and making the most of the conditions, and had taken 4 for 71 off 18 overs when Walters, in an attempt to force a result, declared 19 runs behind with four wickets in hand.

We did better the second time we batted, Alan and his opening partner John Hopkins sharing a century opening stand before both losing their wickets to the left-arm orthodox spin of Ray Bright. After two more wickets had fallen – again, both to Bright – I was promoted up the order to join Gwyn Richards and try to get some quick runs. I was 11 not-out when Alan declared, leaving the Australians 184 to win – and us just 100 minutes to get them out!

I got right into them, taking 5 for 32 in my opening spell of 12 overs. I always bowled well against Australians and I ripped through the top order, with the wickets of Ian Davis (for 12), fellow-opener and wicketkeeper Richie Robinson (a duck), Kim Hughes (a duck), Gary Cosier (five) and skipper Doug Walters (six). Not bad wickets! The top five, and all Test batsmen. Bright and O'Keeffe, batting at eight and nine, steadied the ship and were both still there when time ran out with the Australians on 86 for 6.

What wouldn't we have given for just a bit of the precious time that had been lost to rain! We had them on a piece of string and were so close to what would, at the beginning of the previous day, have seemed a very unlikely result. We were a whisker away from our third win over an Australian touring side at Swansea in five visits spanning just 14 years.

Our performance against Australia, and our Gillette Cup final were very special occasions, and games that none of us who played will ever forget.

For me, the appearance at Lord's – and the days following – was not the end of the 1977 celebrations. My season ended with wedding plans for the following spring, and also news from the club that I had been granted a benefit year for 1978. So, for me, it was very much a busy winter of preparations.

My benefit year was very successful, and I am still grateful to the club and my teammates, and to all the many other people who contributed by volunteering their time and help in so many ways. We had a network of district fundraising committees planning benefit functions of all sorts all over Wales.

One event that sticks particularly in my mind was a concert in Swansea – at the lovely Victorian (and now listed) Tabernacle Chapel, Morriston – for which I had been fortunate to secure the services of two famous opera singers, Anne Howells and Ryland Davies, as well as the Pontarddulais Male Voice Choir. It was an amazing group of performers to

Richie Robinson, one of my '5-for' that also included Ian Davies, Kim Hughes, Gary Cosier and Doug Walters. Five of Australia's first six on the score-card.

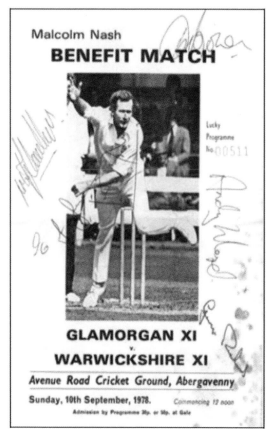

One of the many Benefit Year functions! This one, at Aberdare, was supported by double All Black Brian McKechnie. In November 1978, full-back Brian broke Welsh hearts by scoring a controversial last-minute penalty to deprive Wales of victory over the All Blacks at Cardiff. In all, he won 26 rugby caps, and appeared in 14 one-day cricket internationals.

get together, and naturally I was delighted once all the arrangements were confirmed. Compered by the BBC's Alun Williams, it promised to be an evening to remember.

So it was, in more ways than one. My planning had not been as careful as it should have been, and I was double-booked. The day of the concert was also my wedding day! I had to explain to Sue, my very patient bride-to-be, that after the wedding at 2pm, and then the reception, we would be dashing to the Tabernacle in Morriston for a concert at 7pm! For the record, it was a great evening of wonderful music.

I'd met Sue through cricket when we were introduced by mutual friends during a match at Worcester in our Championship-winning season, and I'd nearly lost her straightaway through my own carelessness. At the end of the game at New Road, very eager to see her again, I'd suggested that she might like to come to our next match just up the road at Edgbaston. To my delight, Sue agreed, and I promised to leave a ticket on the gate.

However, when my guest arrived at the Birmingham ground, there was no ticket. Nor were Glamorgan Warwickshire's opponents! A kindly gateman investigated and discovered that we were, in fact, playing in Manchester. Sue admitted later that at this point she was very tempted to return home to Worcester. Instead, several hours later, Peter Walker was putting some stuff in his car when he discovered a very attractive – but not very happy – young lady in the car park asking if Malcolm Nash was around! I'm still not sure how I got Edgbaston and Old Trafford mixed up, but I'm so thankful that Sue persevered and tracked me down. She forgave me and we never looked back!

I'm not the first or last cricketer to get confused about the detail of the busy schedule. On one occasion, on the morning of the final day of a match at Cardiff, the guys were packing their overnight stuff and civvies into cars ready to set off for Fenner's at the close of play. Another long drive lay ahead, but Lawrence Williams didn't have a bag.

"I'll pick up anything I need from the house in the morning," he reassured us. "No problem. I'm only up the road."

"But we're leaving for Cambridge tonight, Willie."

"Cambridge? Oh, bugger. I thought it was Cowbridge!"

15

Captain of Glamorgan

'A thoughtful and sensitive cricketer, he helped out as captain for a couple of difficult seasons, though from a sense of duty rather than real enthusiasm for the post. It appealed to his astute cricketing brain but not to his essentially amiable personality.'
John Arlott

I t was a very special moment for me. A very proud moment indeed.

Although this was the start of my 15th Championship season and I'd tasted most things in county cricket, I still had goose-bumps as I pulled on my club blazer and made my way out to the middle to toss-up with Essex skipper Keith Fletcher. The fact that this was at my favourite St. Helen's ground made it even more important to me.

It was the first Championship match of the 1980 season, and it was my first match as captain of Glamorgan. Official captain, that is, as I'd led the side in one game towards the end of the previous season.

I lost the toss, and half-an-hour later led the guys down the steep steps and through the old metal gate on to the playing area. Taking the new ball from umpire David Constant, I set my field and prepared to bowl to the very talented Essex opener, Graham Gooch.

Becoming captain was an honour, of course. This was genuinely a very proud moment for me, and something I shall never forget, but having the captaincy was certainly not a case of 'a dream come true' because I can honestly say that captaincy had never been my dream. John Arlott described me as 'a reluctant captain' and I suppose he was right, to a large extent, as he was about most things to do with cricket. I *was* reluctant, in that captaincy wasn't something I would have chosen to do, had not circumstances led to it. It was certainly not something I had ever hankered after.

The Glamorgan squad in 1980 – my first season as captain. Standing (l to r): John Hopkins, Barry Lloyd, Ezra Moseley, Neil Perry, Geoff Holmes and Arthur Francis. Seated: Eifion Jones, Mike Llewellyn, Malcolm Nash, Alan Jones, and a very friendly Allan (A.A.) Jones.

At that time, as a side, Glamorgan were in a mess. There was no beating about the bush. From the heady days of our successive finishes in third, first and second places – still the best run of Championship finishes in the club's history – we had sunk to finishing last in 1979 without a Championship victory to our name. The 1970s had seen us go from County Champions without a single defeat to last place without a single win. It was a dramatic, and sad, reversal of fortunes.

So I listened when Ossie Wheatley, himself an ex-captain who had worked hard at rebuilding a Glamorgan side and was now chair of the Cricket Committee – and someone who I knew, like me, always had the best interests of the club at heart – sounded me out about taking on the captaincy.

In the end, and to some extent reluctantly, I said "Yes", but being initially reluctant doesn't mean being half-hearted! Once I said, "Yes, I'll have a go," any reluctance disappeared. I went into it positively. Enthusiastically. As I always did with any new challenge. I really believed we could, and should, be doing better as a side, and I believed I could bring an energy and renewed commitment to play more adventurous cricket. I was genuinely excited at the prospect, and could see no reason why the players, committee and supporters wouldn't share

Tony Lewis – a very successful captain, leading us to three top-three Championship finishes.

my excitement, my thinking, and my enthusiasm for a new approach.

Well, not new, really. In many ways, I wanted us to think and play more like the Championship-winning side of 1969. So when we had a meeting before the season started, I told the guys I wanted us to be more adventurous. To play more attacking cricket and, at the same time, to have more impact and presence both on and off the field. I also wanted us to enjoy our cricket more, and to be proud of what we did on the pitch. Tony Lewis had achieved this in leading the side so successfully a decade earlier, himself building on Ossie's improvements and strategies developed through the 1960s.

It was an approach I'd discussed with Garry Sobers on more than one occasion. I really felt comfortable with Garry's captaincy philosophy, and am happy to admit that I was influenced by him. He always said that you needed to attack, and that sometimes this meant taking risks. To give yourself a chance of winning, you had to give the opposition a sniff as well – particularly in the case of a second innings declaration when you had to give yourselves time to bowl them out. So attack and adventure, coupled with enjoyment and pride, was the basis of my approach. OK, we don't like losing, but if we end up losing a game in making a positive effort to win, then so be it. As Garry always emphasised, with this approach and mind-set, you'll win more than you'll lose – and you'll enjoy your cricket more, too.

It sounded so straightforward. Why would anyone – in whites or a suit – not buy into it? I reckoned that there was a lot going for my captaincy plans, and to support my decision to take the job on. There seemed to be plenty of positives.

For a start, I was confident that I could read the game pretty well, and the technical side of captaincy held no great worries. At the same time, I knew the guys, and their strengths, weaknesses and preferences, and we got along well. So I didn't have to take time learning about the team and the individuals in it. We could hit the ground running. I was well aware, too, that none of us had been enjoying being beaten on a regular basis. It was thoroughly demoralising. Some wins would be welcomed with open arms.

Another positive for me was that I knew – and was known by – the supporters, and that I had their trust. They knew that I always gave things my best shot, and that I would never give up. That I felt the hurt of defeat and under-performance as keenly as they did. They wanted better days back again, too.

I saw the Glamorgan committee as a positive, too. After all, these people were asking me to take the role on and to try to improve the fortunes of the side, and they knew me well. Because I'd been around a while, and because of my work as Glamorgan's PCA rep, they knew exactly what they were getting. I didn't need to pretend to be something else!

I knew that the task ahead would not be a straightforward or easy one. I didn't under-estimate it, and I believed I could succeed. Perhaps, though, in focussing on the many

Glamorgan captain – a real honour.

positives, coupled with my belief that I could succeed, I ignored or played down any of the potential negatives.

For one thing, the side's under-performance had gone on for several seasons. Had it become too much of a habit? The resulting frustrations of supporters, committee and players alike were widely and openly acknowledged and were the subject of discussion and speculation in club yearbooks and committee reports, as well as in the local and national press. They were shared and well-understood by many of us in the dressing room.

I realised, too, that I was not inheriting the strongest side we'd ever had, and that a small number of players in the existing squad were not as offended by under-performance – individual as well as collective – as they should have been. Some seemed not to want to be challenged and, as far as I was concerned, lacked ambition.

In addition, there had been some unhelpful – though doubtless well-intentioned – committee decisions over several seasons. We lost some promising players, and we lost some absolutely top-class players, too. Some experienced and key players finished earlier than perhaps they really needed

Robin Hobbs was my predecessor as Glamorgan captain having joined us from Suffolk in 1979 specifically to take up the role.

to. The loss of top performers was more keenly felt because, in some cases, the replacements did not match in terms of either their ability, their contribution to the dressing-room, or their passion for the Glamorgan cause. At the same time, we did not always use our opportunities to benefit from overseas players as well as we could – though there were notable exceptions, of course. In fact, I would argue that in both domestic and overseas terms, we made some average signings, and some poor signings.

Robin Hobbs, my predecessor as captain, was most certainly not one of these. No-one could doubt his ability – he had a hatful of wickets to his name when he arrived, and had represented England in seven Tests. Neither could his attitude or relationship with the guys be questioned, nor his commitment to the Glamorgan cause be faulted.

Robin had joined us at the beginning of the 1979 season specifically to skipper the side. Having retired from first-class cricket after a notable career with Essex as a leg-spin and googly bowler, he was in his third season of minor counties cricket with Suffolk when head-hunted by Glamorgan. Unfortunately, he didn't enjoy any more success than his immediate predecessors. Under Hobbsy, results continued to be disappointing, with us propping up the Championship table.

This wasn't surprising really, because I don't think the over-riding issue was the captaincy as such. I'm convinced that Wilf Wooller himself would have struggled. So too would Tony or Ossie, both tremendous captains. I'm probably over-simplifying a complex situation, but as far as I was concerned, the problem was two-fold – and the two parts were related. The first was attitudes and commitment, both on and off the field. The second was management – not so much of the team by the captain, but of cricket in general, including recruitment and selection.

Looking at Robin's experiences at the conclusion of the 1979 season should have rung alarm bells for me. With hindsight, it was another obvious negative staring me immediately in the face. It was the way the people I would be working closely with – and to whom I would be answerable – had dealt with events leading up to the change of captaincy. I felt these could have been handled better, and didn't seem from the outside to bear all the hallmarks of an open relationship between captain on the one hand and committees and wider management team on the other – and these were the same people that I would be working closely with, and be reliant upon. Perhaps, if I had paused to think about it, I'd have realised that Robin's treatment didn't bode well for my own working partnerships.

Not long after Ossie, on behalf of the committee, had approached me about the possibility of taking on the captaincy, I had visited Robin in hospital in Carmarthen. He was getting over surgery on a knee injury that had caused him to miss the end of the season. He was pleased to see me, but as we chatted and put the cricketing world right, I sensed that he was in the dark about deliberations relating to the club's captaincy plans for the forthcoming season. Of course, like me he would have known that it was a committee appointment made on an annual basis, and that discussions were probably taking place.

I felt that I had to tell him about being sounded out. After all, there was no way I would take the captaincy on unless he was OK with it. I suspect, from his reaction, that it was a surprise, and not a pleasant one, but Hobbsy told me to go ahead and accept.

I was really pleased that, in the end, Robin decided to stay on and continue to play for Glamorgan, and he was a useful and loyal member of the 1980 side. He was also very helpful to me as I grew into the captaincy role, and was always willing to offer advice. His recovery from injury and inclusion in the side for the first game of my captaincy against Essex at Swansea also gave me a great boost.

This opening game saw some promising individual contributions – most notably from newcomer Javed Miandad, our attacking Pakistan Test batsman, who scored a superb 140. He had arrived late for pre-season training and had been fined. I think he was making a point!

Javed Miandad scored big centuries in his first two championship games with us – and there was plenty more to come!

I was pleased with some of the features of our collective performance, too. There were some promising signs, and as for the fate of the England opener Graham Gooch? Well, in the first innings he succumbed to the swing of Nash! – although, to be fair, he did score a century in the second.

We were in a positive frame of mind as we travelled over the Severn Bridge to our next fixture. I always relished playing against Gloucestershire, and often did well. They were an enjoyable side to play, and there were always some tough individual battles. Things didn't look promising for us at one stage, as the home side batted first and got a fairly ordinary 180 on a pretty flat, early season Bristol pitch, but we fared even worse with 125. It looked as if, on a pitch that wasn't easy to bat on, a first-innings lead of 55 was a lot to give away. Gloucestershire did a bit better second time round, with 220. That left us to get 276 to win. It would be the highest total of the match.

Javed did us proud again, and showed his class, with a second successive score of 140 to see us home with only three wickets down. It was an emphatic victory, and a very important one for us psychologically. Our more attacking approach had paid off. There was a new sense of belief – and enjoyment – in the dressing room. Almost 21 months had passed since our last Championship win – against Sussex at Swansea in August 1978. That was 25 games without a win!

The Gloucestershire match was an important game for me personally, too. I made a significant contribution to the outcome with a '5-for' and a '6-for' to give me match figures of 11 for 130. My wickets included Zaheer on 93, when he looked as if he was taking the game away from us, and danger-man Mike Proctor in both innings. It was great tussling with 'Proccie'. I always looked forward to our battles, whether I was bowling to him or he was bowling to me.

It was always an enjoyable tussle with Mike Proctor, batting or bowling.

I scored well in our first innings at Bristol, including some fours off Mike! I got a few just right and he started grumbling. "It's OK," I said. "You keep running in and I'll keep whacking it!"

That didn't cheer him up. "My son can bat better than you", he informed me.

"That's fine. Bring him along. I bet you couldn't get *him* out, either."

We always loved the battles and the banter – and a beer together over some cricket yarns at the end of the day.

I especially enjoyed the beer I had at the end of *this* game. I felt I deserved it. As well as leading Glamorgan to our first Championship victory for ages, I'd made significant personal contributions with ball and bat, too. Things were looking up.

Getting a win early on was a massive boost for the side. We felt pretty good about it, and the guys were walking a bit taller. I decided to strike while the iron was hot!

"Look," I said, "we've already achieved some of the things we talked about pre-season, including starting to have a greater presence on and off the field. Let's keep it going. In fact, let's step it up. If we can't always play the part, at least let's always look the part."

There were nods and murmurs of agreement.

"Guys, we're going to be wearing our club blazers here, there, and everywhere. You'll look good and feel good, and you'll have a bit of extra pride with the badge on your breast pocket. Let's keep the flag flying."

Not everyone was nodding now. My suggestion didn't go down well with some of the guys, especially one or two of the newer recruits. There were some grumbles, and reminders that it was 1980. "It's not necessary these days," I was told, but I really wanted us to do it. So I stopped them going to lunch unless they were wearing a blazer! "If you're too lazy to put your blazer on to go down for lunch, that's tough! Go without, and don't try to get the 12th man to bring your food to the dressing room, because that's not going to happen either."

A few of the players dug their heels in and went without lunch for a couple of days. In the end I had no alternative really but to compromise with those who were unhappy about it. I was more concerned about what we were doing on the field and in continuing to improve performances and results – but at least the message had got out that I was a bit 'old school'. Some of the team actually did wear their blazers more – and enjoyed doing so.

It is safe to say, though, that our game against Gloucestershire was a significant one for many reasons, and there were more Championship wins after Gloucestershire, too.

We beat a strong Warwickshire side in a low-scoring game at Sophia Gardens, where I got so excited that I managed to run myself out going for the winning run!

Canterbury was the venue for our third win, fighting hard again after Kent had got a decent first-innings lead, and had declared twice in the match to try to force a win. Scores in the seventies from Alan Jones and Arthur Francis helped us to knock off the 242 target.

We also won the return fixture against Gloucestershire at Swansea. A fine century by Norman Featherstone had put us in a good position and secured a first-innings lead of 66. Although Proctor and Zaheer again got runs for

Gloucestershire in their second innings, they weren't able to set a challenging target and we got home with the loss of only two wickets. A great double!

This was a particularly good match for me as I got skipper Mike Proctor twice, clean bowling him for 88 second time round. My second innings figures of 7 for 79 off 24.5 overs were the best for our side that season. They also took me past 100 career wickets taken against Gloucestershire – I told you I always enjoyed playing against them! Apparently I was only the fourth Glamorgan bowler to take 100 wickets against a single county. The match also has a special memory and significance for another reason.

When Eifion Jones caught Chris Broad early in the Gloucestershire second-innings, he set a new Glamorgan wicketkeeping career record for dismissals, beating the previous record held by the legendary Haydn Davies. When Eifion eventually stopped playing a couple of seasons later he had a staggering 933 first-class dismissals to his name, 840 caught and 93 stumped. You can add 223 League dismissals to those, making a career total of well over 1,000.

Eifion was an outstanding wicketkeeper and a great teammate. He was unlucky not to have been selected for England, coming particularly close to selection for the Ashes tour in 1970-71, after a season that had seen him

Efion Jones set a new Glamorgan record for dismissals, beating the previous record held by Haydn Davies (right). My partnership with Eifion brought us 173 first-class victims.

top the national wicketkeeping table with 94 first-class dismissals. He had also had an exceptional season the year before, playing a huge part in our Championship success. I think that in several ways he was technically a better glove-man than either Alan Knott or Bob Taylor, the two wicketkeepers who toured that winter.

Eifion Jones and I were a formidable double-act! Over the time we played together, we combined as bowler/keeper to get 173 first-class dismissals – 166 caught and seven stumped. We had a great working understanding. He'd move up to the stumps if the batsman tried to negate the swing by standing outside the crease. He'd check with me: "Look, I'm going to stand up. I might miss a couple here, OK?" – but he didn't ever miss much, and he'd catch them standing up, too.

When Eifion was up close, he was great at sensing if batsmen were starting to get uncomfortable or almost over-balancing to my late in-swing. He'd spot signs that their weight distribution wasn't particularly good, then he would give me a signal. We had a little code that we'd change. It might be an arm movement or a scratch of the head – whatever it was we had agreed on – and we'd go from there. Sometimes he'd just say, "Nashy, full-length, leg stump." Let everyone know! Anyway, once I'd got the word or the signal, I'd get it up there full-length and we'd do them down the leg-side, sure as eggs were eggs!

I'm so glad that Eifion broke the record off my bowling, and on his local ground. It was appropriate that it was in a game we won, too.

Our four wins – and only four losses – gave us a joint 12th place finish in the table, a significant improvement on our 17th place the season before. It was a tight table, too. Sussex also had four wins, but finished fourth! While Somerset, one place behind them, had only three wins against their name – one less than us. It would have taken very little for at least one of our 14 draws to be turned into a win and for us to finish significantly higher in the final table. Also, some of them were very close calls – 'attacking draws' – with us in a position to press for victory given just a little more time and, perhaps, a little more good fortune. Of course, some better weather would have helped – we had a number of games spoilt by rain.

I'd tried hard to pursue the attacking policy we had all agreed on at the beginning of the season and had, from time to time, gambled to try to force a victory. In a rain-affected match against Northamptonshire at Cardiff, I forfeited our first innings to make a game of it. In the next match, at Derby, I declared behind to encourage them to set a target – and both we and Derbyshire came close to forcing an exciting win. Later in the season, in two other weather-affected but exciting games against Leicestershire and Worcestershire, I collaborated with opposing skippers Brian Davison and Norman Gifford in making declarations and setting competitive targets.

As well as frustrations with the weather, there were also some crucial issues of player availability – or, unavailability – towards the end of the season.

One of the games we nearly won – and should have won – was against Warwickshire at Edgbaston in the last week of August. We'd already beaten them at home earlier in the season, and we arrived in Birmingham full of confidence from our double over Gloucestershire.

Bob Willis won the toss and decided to bat on what looked like a decent pitch, but we got into them straight away. I trapped opener David Smith leg-before for a duck, and soon after bowled Andy Lloyd to have them on 28 for 2. Dennis Amiss, the other opener, was still there steadying the Warwickshire ship with Alvin Kallicharran, but wickets continued to fall and it wasn't long before Ezra Moseley joined in the wicket-taking and polished off the tail. We had them all out for 235 soon after tea. I'd had a long day with the ball, bowling 35 overs, including 12 maidens, and getting 6 for 105. Ezra and I shared the Warwickshire wickets, seven of them clean bowled!

Ezra Moseley and I shared the first innings wickets at Edgbaston, with seven clean bowled! We headed the Glamorgan bowling table at the end of the 1980 season.

Alan Jones and John Hopkins saw our innings off to a bright start before Alan was bowled by Bob Willis one short of his half-century. Unfortunately, Arthur Francis went right at the end of the day, but overnight we were a respectable 96 for 2, with John Hopkins looking good on 38 and Javed Miandad yet to score.

He soon did! Next morning, he and John batted beautifully and added 264 for the third wicket. It was a great stand, and potentially match-winning. John was eventually caught behind off Steve Rouse, Warwickshire's Merthyr-born left-arm medium-pacer who would later go on to become head groundsman at Edgbaston, for 112, and Javed fell to the same bowler for a brilliant 181 (which included a century before lunch). Norman Featherstone joined in the run-making with 84, and Ezra added a breezy 31 not out before I declared on 524 for 9 – a healthy lead of 289 and with plenty of time to get some of them back in the pavilion before close of play.

The plan worked beautifully! Smith and Lloyd went quickly again. The scoreboard read 17 for 2. Then I got Kallicharran and wicketkeeper Geoff Humpage. Now it was 44 for 4, which soon became 57 for 5 when Ezra dismissed the dangerous Amiss.

Philip Oliver and John Whitehouse saw the home side safely through to the end of the day, but at 98 for 5 they were still 191 in arrears and we had the whole of the third day to finish them off. Even more encouraging was the fact that Javed's three overs of leg breaks and googlies had looked very promising, and the wearing wicket would probably be even more responsive to him on the final day. Now it was just a question of us completing the task for a second successive victory.

Unfortunately, that wasn't as straightforward as it sounded! The third day saw us struggle on a wicket that was getting progressively flatter and easier. Whitehouse grafted on, supported first by Oliver and then by Rouse, in the end falling to the left-arm spin of Neil Perry for 197, in what turned out to be one of his final games for the club – a memorable way to finish! When the match ended, Warwickshire were 402 for 9. We were so close! Across their two innings, I bowled a total of 81 overs, finishing with match figures of 10 for 216. Their second innings had seen me bowl a mammoth 46 overs, 20 of them maidens, but they held out, resisting everything we could throw at them.

However, Warwickshire's obstinate batsman didn't resist everything we *could* have thrown at them. Javed should have been a key part of our attack on the final day. Unfortunately, he wasn't there! In the dressing room at the end of the second day's play I noticed that he was changing quicker than usual, and seemed to be packing his kit. I thought perhaps he was meeting some friends for an evening out in Birmingham, but his announcement to the changing room revealed another destination altogether.

"Good luck tomorrow, lads. See you in Cardiff."

My jaw dropped.

"What? Where are you going?"

"Pakistan."

"You're kidding."

"No, really, I'm flying to Pakistan this evening. I'm getting married on Saturday."

I couldn't believe my ears. "Javed, who on earth said you could go to Pakistan in the middle of a match?" – or words to that effect! – but Javed was already out of the door, anxious not to miss his flight.

Tom Cartwright, now our team manager, was in the dressing room, and naturally I asked him what was going on. It seems that earlier in the season Javed had approached Tom, who had in turn approached the chairman and committee, and that our star overseas player had indeed been given permission to take some time off to return home for his wedding. We were to play the last day at Edgbaston using our '12th', and Javed would also miss the following game away to Somerset at Taunton before rejoining us for the final Championship fixture of the season in Cardiff. If the travel plans worked out, that is.

Of course, I was furious. Naturally I was pleased for Javed and his bride-to-be, but on that day, in that dressing-room, I had steam coming out of my ears! I was dumbfounded, and disappointed. I felt let down. Why hadn't anyone in the know thought to tell me? Our international player was such a significant part of the team and our team plans. If nothing else, it seemed discourteous. I felt that my captaincy was being undermined – not for the first time – and I still feel that way.

To this day, I still think Javed's absence, on that third-day strip at Edgbaston, cost us a hard-earned victory. We just needed that extra variety in the bowling attack.

We drew the game at Taunton, and the next day arrived at Sophia Gardens to start the final match against Middlesex. The poor weather that had spoilt the Taunton fixture was still around, and the Cardiff toss – and naming of the side – was delayed. There was no sign of Javed. Telephone calls told us that he had been delayed in Pakistan. Then, that he was in the air. Then, that he had landed, but was delayed in London. A final message assured us that he would be with us by lunchtime. At the ground, I kept making noises about the uncertain weather and the poor light, delaying things as much as I dared. Eventually, I had no option but to name the team and with no further news of Javed's whereabouts we left him out and got started after taking an early lunch – with still no sign of the new groom.

For the record, Mike Brearley got a second-innings century and we lost a low scoring match by 72 runs. I was not a happy man! Yet despite these end-of-season frustrations, I felt that, all things considered, 1980 hadn't turned out too badly.

The committee's view that, in 1980, Glamorgan had been 'a more attractive and stable side', and that under my captaincy 'there were positive efforts to play good cricket and win games', was both welcome and justified. The fact that we hadn't consistently done as well, in the end, in one-day competitions wasn't an issue. We had agreed that improvement in the Championship would be our first priority and we'd delivered that. The rest could come later.

Javed Miandad and Norman Featherstone had made a big difference to our batting during the season. They took some of the pressure off the ever-reliable

Alan Jones. Javed finished the season with an average of over 50, and Alan and Norman weren't too far behind.

The bowling honours for the season also showed three key contributions to our better form. Allan (A.A.) Jones, who had set an unusual record of being the first player to represent four counties when he joined us at the beginning of the season from Middlesex (the other two being Sussex and Somerset), finished with a very useful 41 wickets, even if he was a bit more expensive. Ezra, with 51 wickets at an average of 26, and me with 74 wickets at a bit over 23, headed the Glamorgan averages.

I was relieved that the captaincy didn't seem to have adversely affected my bowling – or batting, come to that. It had been something I'd wondered about when taking on the job. One thing that was starting to concern me, though, was knowing when to put myself on – and for how long. I was probably thinking about it too much, and missed having someone make that decision for me!

Norman Featherstone made a big difference to our batting performance in 1980, and was a great support to Javed Miandad, John Hopkins, and the ever-reliable Alan Jones.

There was no reason to expect that the 1981 season would see anything other than a continuation of our improvement as a side, with even better Championship results, and a more sustained and consistent one-day campaign.

I'm convinced that it would have been, too, but for the fact that we got off to a sluggish start with some awful weather, and later lost a key player, Ezra Mosely, for a long run of games. We also missed Tony Cordle, who had retired at the end of 1980. I wished afterwards – and still do – that the club had played him more towards the end, and done more to persuade him to stay on.

Two out of our first three Championship matches in 1981 were abandoned – the first without a ball being bowled due to a flooded Cardiff square. So it was the fourth game, against Worcestershire at Hereford's Racecourse Ground (one of only five first-class matches ever played there) before we got even a draw! It was certainly not the start to the season that we wanted or expected. With a third of the season gone, it was three losses, no wins.

Our fortunes changed at Cardiff with a decisive win – by an innings – against Warwickshire. Javed Miandad and John Hopkins made big scores again, supported by a half-century from Ezra Moseley – himself no mug with a bat. We got them all out for 100 in the second innings, with our pace attack of Ezra, Allan Jones and me doing all the damage. The improvement in our form continued in the next match, a high-scoring draw against Somerset at St. Helen's with Javed again showing his immense class with a century in each innings.

John Hopkins was the batting star in our second victory, a month later, over Yorkshire at Sophia Gardens. This century was one of four he got in the season. He and Javed, whose eight centuries – including two double-hundreds – beat Gilbert Parkhouse's Glamorgan record of seven in a season, were the

Javed Miandad scored an amazing eight centuries in 1980, beating the previous Glamorgan record of seven set by Gilbert Parkhouse.

key to our batting. Javed's season was phenomenal, especially considering that the team's performance was average at best. Javed became the first Glamorgan player to score over 2,000 runs in a season, and his average of 69.43 was another record – the best ever by a Glamorgan player.

Our only other win in this disappointing season was at Edgbaston where we completed the double over Warwickshire in a high-scoring game, with Javed again in superb form with 153 and 96, and Norman Featherstone also contributing with a second-innings hundred. Norman, John, Alan Jones and, of course, Javed all passed 1,000 runs for the season.

There is another big Glamorgan name – a future captain – that figures as a footnote in the 1981 batting records. In our penultimate game against Leicestershire at Sophia Gardens we included a 17-year-old schoolboy called Hugh Morris! Hugh, a very promising left-handed batsman, found himself making his first-class debut against his great hero David Gower. I can remember that Hugh was cross with me for getting David out – twice – because he was looking forward to watching him bat at close quarters! At least David got 62 in the first innings, and was clearly a good role-model for Hugh who went on to score over 18,000 elegant Championship runs, and a further 8,000 one-day runs, in a long and distinguished playing career with Glamorgan that included two spells of captaincy and three Test caps.

Just as the season had got off to a poor start, though, it ended badly, too. In the final match at Trent Bridge, Nottinghamshire beat us by ten wickets after we were all out for an embarrassing 60 in our first-innings. Not the way to end the season, and we finished in 14th place, one lower than the season before. Although we managed only one less win than in my first season as skipper, we had a lot more losses – ten against four – but a number of these were at the end when, significantly, we were without Ezra.

He was injured in our game against Lancashire at Cardiff in early August, bowling only five and three overs, respectively, in the two innings. He didn't play again for the rest of the season. That

Hugh Morris made his first-class debut in the home match against Leicestershire – and his hero David Gower.

In the absence of tour captain Kim Hughes, Rod Marsh skippered the Australian side at St. Helen's.

was another seven Championship games – a third of the fixtures – and we lost most of them, as well as the Lancashire game. So six losses out of the final eight matches, when we'd lost only four in the whole of the rest of the season to that point, shows how important Ezra's contribution was to side and how much we missed him.

One of my favourite memories of Ezra – and a classic example of his bowling at its very best – was in the match against the 1981 Australian tourists at St. Helen's.

With Greg Chappell unable to tour, Kim Hughes was captain but, not for the first time, an Australian touring skipper didn't play at Swansea, and the side was led instead by Rod Marsh, their combative wicketkeeper. It was still in the early days of a tour that was scheduled to be shorter than usual, and the previous two games against county sides had been spoilt by late-May rain. Our match followed the same pattern, with no play at all possible on the first day.

It was a very proud moment for me when I walked out to the St. Helen's square as captain of Glamorgan to toss-up with Rod. I shall always remember the sense of occasion, standing out there in my club blazer, together with one of the Australian Test regulars – already with ten years of international cricket to his name, and well on his way to his world record 355 Test dismissals – in his green touring blazer. Rod called correctly and decided to bat. It was a decision I thought he might come to regret, and it wasn't long before I was proved right!

I opened the bowling from the Mumbles Road end and soon had right-handed Queenslander Martin Kent, who played all his three Tests later in that summer, caught behind by Eifion. Australia 6 for 1. Ezra was bowling an amazing spell the other end. With the tourists' score on 12, he took the prize wickets of Alan Border and Trevor Chappell, both clean bowled, and had Graham Yallop, who had captained Australia in their unsuccessful 1978-79 Ashes series, caught behind. Australia 12 for 4. I had to pinch myself when I looked at the score-board!

Ezra's spell wasn't over, and soon he had Dirk Wellham, who later in the summer would score a century in his first Test, caught by Mike Llewellyn. Australia 16 for 5.

John Dyson, the other opener, was still there and top-scored with 44, but wickets continued to fall. Rodney Ontong and Barry Lloyd chipped in with one apiece, and Ezra got tail-ender Ray Bright to keep the Australians in trouble on 103 for 9 and give himself innings figures of 6 for 23 off 22 overs. It was an inspired spell from a very talented bowler.

The tail-ender 'quicks', Geoff Lawson and Terry Alderman, improved the Australian situation a bit with an irritating last-wicket stand of 44, but when I had Alderman caught they were all out for a still very modest 147. We were delighted, of course, though disappointed not to have nailed the final wicket sooner.

In the 25 overs we faced at the end of the day, we lost three wickets, all to the left-arm orthodox spin of Ray Bright, in reaching 84. I declared overnight in an attempt to make a game of it and try to force a result, but the weather had the last word and the third day went the same way as the first. We didn't get back on the field again. It was such a pity when we had started so well and – not for the first time – had a touring side on the back foot.

Ezra's performance against the Australians was a demonstration of his huge ability with the ball, and of his importance to us as a team. When he went back to his home in Barbados for some sunshine and recuperation after his end-of-season injury, we knew how vital it was that he was fully fit and ready to start the new season.

However, when Alan Jones was in the West Indies that autumn, he went to see Ezra – and returned with some alarming news. Ezra was struggling to walk, never mind play cricket. He didn't seem to have made much progress with the injury. Would he be fit for the beginning of the 1982 season? Naturally, I was concerned that we had either a fully-fit Ezra or a suitable replacement ready for April. I also shared my concerns, as skipper, with club officials – more than once.

Each time I was reassured that the club's contacts in the Caribbean were keeping an eye on Ezra's progress. That the situation was being monitored, and all concerned were confident that our star overseas international bowler would be ready for action. I'm afraid I wasn't as confident, and urged that Ezra be requested to come over for a proper assessment and any necessary treatment. I think it's fair to say that my anxiety didn't seem to be shared by either the cricket committee or the team manager. I had the impression – and still do – that they felt I was fussing unnecessarily.

Looking back, I can see that from my point of view doubts surrounding Ezra's injury, and the club's apparent lack of action and concern, marked a significant deterioration in an already uneasy relationship with the powers that be. For me, it was another example of being side-lined. Another example of a captain not being treated as one would expect while preparations for a new and crucial season were underway. We would already be without some key players. Robin Hobbs was moving back to Suffolk, and two other recent acquisitions, Allan Jones and vice-captain Norman Featherstone, were both retiring – in Norman's case, unexpectedly to pursue a business opportunity. This was on top of having already lost Tony Cordle to retirement the previous winter. I knew we were already light on bowling, and the end of the previous season had shown very clearly how much we needed Ezra or his equivalent. We would be starting the season at a huge disadvantage without him.

More time passed. As winter progressed, and the new season loomed, the issues around Ezra's injury – and doubts over his availability – became the final straw for me. You could say that, ironically, Ezra's back injury was the straw that broke this particular camel's back. This captain's anyway! I felt that proper captaincy was being made increasingly difficult, if not impossible. It was like rowing against the tide. An ebb tide!

I indicated that I did not wish to continue in the post for the new season and, sadly, my spell as captain of Glamorgan was over.

When we took the field against Warwickshire at Edgbaston in the first week of May, 1982, Javed Miandad was the new Glamorgan skipper. He, in turn, would give way to Barry Lloyd when he was called up to the Pakistan squad at the end of June for their tour and three-Test series against England.

Ezra, however, was not in the side. He had eventually arrived in Cardiff for the pre-season nets, but we could all see straight away that he was still in considerable difficulty with his back. On the first day he managed only three or four balls at half pace before pulling up in severe pain. Investigation showed a stress fracture that would require surgery and, in the end, cause him to miss the whole season.

Winston Davis was recruited to replace the injured Ezra Mosely as our overseas quick bowler.

Winston Davies (left), Ezra Moseley (in a very 1970s T-shirt), and Bill Edwards in front of Bill's famous sports shop in King Edward's Road, Swansea, adjacent to the St. Helen's ground.

We were, as I had feared, in big trouble. The committee did source a replacement – Ezra's fellow West Indian pace bowler, Winston Davis. Winston, who was knocking on the door of the West Indian side and would go on to make his international debut the following winter, was certainly a quick and very useful performer, but as far as I was concerned we had started the search for a replacement for Ezra too late and it was mid-July before Winston made his first appearance in a Glamorgan shirt. This was in what was already our tenth Championship game – out of the scheduled 22. The damage had already been done – six draws and three defeats. Winston's debut saw us slide to another defeat, and the pattern continued, our only Championship win of a depressing season coming in the penultimate game against Gloucestershire.

16

Bolt From The Blue

'County cricket clubs have been notoriously bad at ending players' careers with dignity and compassion, and Glamorgan was no exception.'
Douglas Miller

I couldn't believe it. It was like a dagger in my heart, and I didn't see it coming. Looking back, perhaps I should have, but I didn't. Perhaps I should have been prepared, but I wasn't.

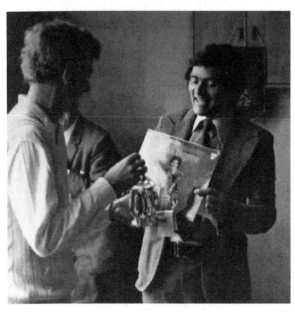

Max Boyce presented me with my 1974 Balconiers Player of the Year award, and a copy of his bestselling LP.

The St. Helen's ground had become a great favourite of mine. I always enjoyed playing there, partly because it was compact and so atmospheric, and also because we were always so well supported. The crowd, and in particular the St. Helen's Balconiers, always made the Swansea welcome a very special one. It meant a lot to me that I had been voted their Player of the Year two seasons running, in 1974 and 1975.

St. Helen's had also been the venue for my first game as captain, as well as the setting for a lot of our outstanding games, and both team and personal achievements – including beating the Australians! It was also associated with lots of other happy times. Visiting sides being entertained at Sunday night sing-songs at The Fountain in Pontarddulais. Or just sitting on the balcony at the end of a day's play, sharing a few beers with the opposition and looking out to sea.

It was here, too, that I had been presented with my Glamorgan cap. Before all that, Swansea CC, based at St. Helen's, had been the first local league club I'd been attached to after signing for Glamorgan. Now I was here again, all these years later, playing for the 2nd XI against Worcestershire 2nd XI in a three-day game. I felt at home. This was my patch!

I had found myself an empty seat – not too difficult – in the stand in front of the dressing rooms and was enjoying some very pleasant August sunshine. St. Helen's was looking good, and just over the top of Fred's Bar the sea was sparkling and there were yachts racing in Swansea Bay. There aren't many grounds in the world with a better view – cricket and sea framed together!

My calm was disturbed by the approach of the new Glamorgan secretary, Philip Carling. I was surprised, to say the least. A key member of the Club's management team was a rare sighting at a 2nd XI game. He settled into the seat next to me.

I don't know how the detail and direction of the conversation that followed was recorded in the official documents of the time, but it is a conversation I've played back in my head many times in the intervening years, and my own recollection of it is along the following lines:

One of the best views in cricket! St. Helen's from in front of the players' balcony.

"I've got some bad news for you," the secretary announced, coming straight to the point.

"What's that?"

"Well, the committee has decided that you don't fit into our future plans, either short-term or long-term."

I couldn't take the words in. It was right out of the blue. There had been no discussion – not with me, anyway. It was so abrupt. So stark.

I wished it was Ossie Wheatley giving me this news, or someone else that I knew. Someone who had been on my Glamorgan journey with me. I suppose the message would have been the same, but somehow it might have been easier to accept – perhaps to discuss. It somehow seemed worse coming from a stranger. We'd hardly met since Carling's arrival from Trent Bridge at the beginning of the year, although we'd played against each other once when Glamorgan met Cambridge University at Fenner's in 1970!

"So are you saying that I'm no longer required?" I asked. "You won't be renewing my contract."

"Yes, that's more or less it, I'm afraid, but the committee wondered what it would take to keep your registration for another season and to use you in one-day cricket."

"Well, the same contract and money that I'm getting now."

"That's not going to happen. You won't be playing Championship cricket again."

The conversation was going from bad to worse. I was having trouble taking it in properly.

"So, just to clarify things. You're telling me my services are no longer required?"

"No, they're not."

"Well, I'll go then. Now. I'll pack my stuff. Please let the skipper know, and if you change your mind, you know where to find me." Then, as an afterthought, "Please contact Lord's and cancel my registration immediately."

Whatever the intention of the meeting had been, it felt to me as if I had been dismissed. Sacked. I know that what followed was an extreme reaction, but I gathered my kit from the dressing room, packed my bag, walked to the car, and drove. I'm not sure that I knew where I was going, but it turned out to be Langland Bay – and some much-needed thinking time! I suppose I was in shock. It was a bolt from the blue. I felt humiliated. Worthless. Hurt. It was an awful way to finish my career with the club. Cricket with Glamorgan had been the main part of my whole adult life, and suddenly – in one brief conversation – it had ended. It still hurts thinking about it again all these years later, but I often do.

Looking back, I suppose 1983 felt different right from the start. I had missed the final two games of the 1982 season – the first occasion for a long time that mine had not been an 'automatic' name on the team-sheet – and now here I was, at the beginning of the new season, playing in what seemed a very new and different set-up, both on and off the field.

Tom Cartwright's newly created role as cricket manager, which I confess I had always found confusing, was done away with after my spell of captaincy had ended, and Tom had taken over the new and larger role of chief coach. This continued into the 1983 season, after which – although we didn't know it at the time – it would pass to Alan Jones on his retirement as a player.

Phil Clift, who had been an important member of the support staff during and since my early days as a Glamorgan player, had retired after 46 years of loyal service in a range of roles. With him went a huge amount of Glamorgan knowledge and know-how. Phil's most recent role had been as secretary, and he was replaced by Phil Carling from Nottinghamshire.

On the playing side, left-arm medium-pace bowler Alan Wilkins rejoined us after three years with Gloucestershire. (Sadly, a shoulder injury, which had already interrupted his career, meant that this would be his only season back with us before being forced into retirement.) Hard-hitting batsman Mike Llewellyn, another member of the 1977 Gillette Cup final side, was not retained for 1983, and fast-medium right-arm bowler Simon Daniels, who had joined only two seasons earlier, called it a day with a recurring knee injury.

However, the most significant change on the playing side was the arrival as captain of another right-arm fast-medium bowler, the experienced Mike Selvey, from County Champions Middlesex. Mike had won England caps in two matches against the West Indies in 1976, and another against India the following winter. He had played against us in the Gillette Cup final the next season, taking the important early wickets of Alan Jones and Collis King, and conceding only 22 runs from his 12 overs.

Phil Clift, pictured with Alan Jones in 1978.

So, as John Billot of the *Western Mail* noted in 1983, Glamorgan were 'under new management'. As we started the new campaign, hopeful of an improvement on the disappointing performances of the previous season, it very much felt like the changing of the guard. What I didn't realise at the time was that I was inked in to be part of the change!

As we did our pre-season training, I knew I was bowling well after the winter break. I felt fit as a fiddle. I was approaching my 38th birthday, but was in good shape and felt I still had some more cricketing miles on the clock! A couple of years, I reckoned. My appetite for the game, and for competing, was as keen as ever. In the pre-season friendly against Cambridge University I got one of their openers in the second innings, and bowled 10 very tight overs for just 12 runs. I was in the groove, and wasn't surprised to be included in the side for the first Championship game of the season a week later at Old Trafford. I was, however, surprised and a bit disappointed to find myself batting at number ten. My successes with a bat in the past seemed to be either unknown or irrelevant to the new regime.

If aspects of the set-up at Glamorgan felt a bit different, the early pre-season wet weather was all too familiar. In another rain-affected draw, Lancashire

Greg Thomas - my young new-ball partner in the first game of the 1983 season.

posted a 400-plus first innings total, but I was pleased that my spell of 11 overs went for only 27 runs (with one wicket), and was disappointed not to be named in the side for the next two Championship matches – another draw against Essex and an innings defeat by Middlesex.

Local student Greg Thomas and I had opened the bowling against Lancashire, with Mike Selvey taking over from me as first change. Greg kept his place for the Essex game, this time opening with Alan Wilkins and with Mike first change. Then, in the thumping defeat by his old county, Middlesex, Mike Selvey had opened with Rodney Ontong, Alan coming on as first change. It seemed as if we were searching for the right combinations, the right balances, across the side. Meanwhile, success continued to be elusive.

The pattern of change continued when I was recalled for the fourth game against Gloucestershire at Swansea. I was to open the bowling with the new skipper the other end, and Rodney and Alan were also in the side. More rain, with three declarations required to get a positive result – though unfortunately, from our point of view, the wrong one! We got off to a good start with an opening partnership between Alan Jones and John Hopkins, who got a century. The visitors reached half of our 250 for 5 before they also declared without losing a wicket. We then chased quick runs and having moved up to bat at number six, I was 27 not out when Mike Selvey declared, leaving Gloucestershire to score 300 for victory. This they did for the loss of seven wickets, thanks largely to a century by Zaheer Abbas, their experienced right-handed Pakistan international with a hatful of Tests and ODIs already against his name.

I thought I'd had a decent game, but lost my place for the next two Championship matches. The first of these was a draw against Yorkshire at Middlesbrough, this time with Steve Barwick opening the attack with Greg Thomas and Mike Selvey coming on as first change. The other was a defeat by Warwickshire at Cardiff. Again, the scorecard shows Thomas and Barwick opening, followed by Selvey and Ontong. I was finding life frustrating, but felt that, when I had chances, I was still playing some decent cricket.

Between the first and fourth Championship matches I had a variety of cricketing experiences! I played at Old Trafford again, this time for the 2nd XI, and then for the 1st XI in all four Benson and Hedges Cup matches – two of which were spoilt by the weather, one being abandoned without a ball being bowled. I did get in some decent spells, though. My 11 overs got me 2 for 21 against Surrey, and an eight-over spell against Kent yielded 1 for 33, but my best Benson and Hedges Cup figures came in the game against Combined Universities at Fenner's: 11-7-9-3.

I also played in the John Player League win over Lancashire at Swansea on the weekend of the Gloucestershire Championship match, and against Sri Lanka in their World Cup practice match against Glamorgan at Cardiff the day after the Gloucestershire match. The tourists lost only three wickets chasing down our modest 153 off 40 overs, but at least I had the satisfaction of getting all three and seeing them tottering at 11 for 3 at one stage.

I had another couple of John Player League games – two more victories, over Nottinghamshire and Yorkshire – and another three-day game for the 2nd XI against Gloucestershire's 2nd XI at Usk, before being recalled to Championship action against Somerset at St. Helen's. This time I opened the bowling attack, again with 22-year-old Greg Thomas, with two other very promising young local products, 22-year-old Steve Barwick and 20-year-old John Derrick, also in our attack in the absence through injury of Mike Selvey. Barry Lloyd was back as skipper for this game. Another draw. Another match interrupted by rain. In Somerset's only innings, I had a long bowl, sending down 28 overs for 69 runs and getting the wicket of skipper Peter Roebuck. We followed on – and I was back batting at number ten!

After another John Player League game against Somerset at Bath, I kept my place for the next Championship match of the season, against Worcestershire at Abergavenny. It was Glamorgan's eighth Championship outing of 1983, and my fourth. This time I was opening the attack with returning skipper Selvey, supported by Rodney Ontong. Hugh Morris was getting his first first-team outing of the season in our batting line-up.

It was great to be back at Abergavenny, playing in the familiar surroundings of the Avenue Road ground – the ground that had always meant so much to me as a child and teenager, and which was such an important part of my cricketing past. Worcestershire, skippered by Phil Neale, made us work hard, openers Alan Ormrod and Martin Weston putting on 136 for the first wicket, and the skipper himself going on to get a century with support from Basil D'Oliveira and Mark Scott.

I didn't have a great day with the ball, returning figures of 1 for 45, but I did bowl Dipak Patel who would go on to play in seven Tests for New Zealand. Dipak's turned out to be my last first class wicket – number 993 – and taken, with a wonderful symmetry, on the ground where I had played my first competitive 'adult' cricket as a teenager, and against Worcestershire, who I

Steve Barwick (left) and John Derrick (right), two more promising young additions to our pace bowling attack.

June 1983 saw me back at the Pen-y-Pound ground, Abergavenny, playing in what turned out to be my final Championship game.

Alan Ormrod pictured opening the batting for the visitors at Abergavenny – and I opened the bowling.

Dipak Patel, my final Championship wicket.

had so nearly joined and with whom I had enjoyed so many exciting tussles over the years.

After the rain-ruined draw at Abergavenny, the next six weeks saw me play only two other games in Glamorgan colours. Both were three-day games for the 2nd XI – encounters with Lancashire's 2nd XI at BP Llandarcy, and Gloucestershire's 2nd XI at Bristol, the scene of my England trial seven years earlier. Both were draws. In the first of these, my first-innings figures were a very respectable 24-10-48-3, and my wickets included England's David 'Bumble' Lloyd – also playing in what turned out to be his final first-class season.

I got a couple of wickets against Gloucestershire, too, sharing the new ball with Geoff Holmes and a very promising 18-year-old called Steve Watkin! Part of the sense of 'all change' at Glamorgan was that my good friend Eifion Jones was now also in the 2nd XI having lost his place to Terry Davies mid-season. My second wicket against Gloucestershire – Richard Doughty – was, very appropriately, caught Jones, (E). It was the last time we combined to take a wicket.

This game was also memorable for an unbroken stand of 334 between John Derrick and Steve Henderson, the latter (who had just arrived from Cambridge University after several seasons with Worcestershire) scoring a double-century before our skipper Barry Lloyd had the luxury of declaring on 400 for 2!

It was then on to another outing for the 2nd XI, against Worcestershire's 2nd XI at Swansea. Another memorable game, but for quite different reasons. That unexpected visit from the new secretary, and the sudden end of my life in county cricket.

Why didn't I feature in the first team again after successive (and rain affected) matches against Somerset and Worcestershire? You'd have to ask somebody else. I wasn't bowling at my best, but I wasn't bowling badly, either. Also, and crucially from my point of view, I wasn't bowling enough overs. I still think to this day that I could have been a useful member of the 1st XI, especially alongside some of the young fast bowlers who were coming through at that time.

Geoff Holmes (left) and Steve Watkin (right), two more very promising young cricketers making their way in the second team.

From the beginning of July our overseas bowler Winston Davis rejoined the side. Having played for us the previous season, Winston had then been unavailable for the first half of the 1983 season while making his Test debut – alongside the formidable fast bowling trio of Holding, Roberts and Marshall – in the fifth match of the West Indies home series against India in Antigua, and then staying with the West Indian squad for the third World Cup in June. Once available, he slotted straight back into the Glamorgan side, sharing the new ball with Mike Selvey. This became the new usual opening pairing, with Messrs. Thomas, Wilkins and Barwick also getting occasional first-team opportunities. The only two Glamorgan victories of another disappointing summer were in successive mid-season matches against Worcestershire and Surrey, with Steve Barwick getting what remained a career-best 8 for 42 in the first. We ended a disappointing 15th in the Championship table.

While I didn't – and still don't – agree with his assessment of my potential future usefulness to the side, I have to admit that Philip Carling was certainly right about one thing. I didn't play another Championship match for Glamorgan. In fact, I didn't play in Glamorgan colours again.

It was announced that I had decided to retire. In fact, the Glamorgan Yearbook for the new 1984 season included a few paragraphs confirming my departure. It stated that I had 'taken up an appointment with an insurance company in South Wales', and went on to wish me 'a prosperous and happy retirement'.

So, as far as supporters and public were concerned, I *had* retired, and the decision would seem to have been mine. As far as I was concerned, however, I hadn't retired. I hadn't even thought of retirement – except, as most players probably do at some stage, having vague thoughts about what I might turn my hand to once the day came.

Looking back, perhaps I should have been more proactive about things. Perhaps I should have been exploring coaching or mentoring possibilities. There was, after all, a crop of very promising young bowlers emerging, and coaching was certainly an aspect of the game I'd enjoyed since my time in South Africa. Perhaps I could have linked a bowling development role with some years playing in the 2nd XI. Of course, I don't know what the club's reaction might have been to such a suggestion. In truth, I hadn't looked further than life in the 1st XI – and getting my regular place back.

Again, with the benefit of hindsight, perhaps I should have been looking round for a different cricketing environment and new challenges, seeking out another county side at the end of the 1982 season, or a year later when I finished at Glamorgan. Perhaps someone like Somerset or Gloucestershire or even Worcestershire would have been interested in offering me a one or two-year deal – who knows? – but I didn't do that. Why? Well, possibly the unexpected turn of events at St. Helen's had dented my confidence. Maybe I was just too confused and upset. I'm still not sure. At the end of the day, once the smoke is out of the bottle it's hard to get it back, isn't it?

All in all, the events of the late summer of 1983 proved a painful and stressful experience but, as far as I was concerned, it was typical of how many clubs operated in those days. They could be fairly ruthless, and seemingly ungrateful. There was little room for sentiment. I suppose I shouldn't have been too surprised. It reminded me of aspects of the experiences of former players like Don Shepherd, Peter Walker, Len Hill, Roy Fredericks and Tony Cordle towards the end of their careers. The brutal truth is that you reach a stage when you are no longer part of the plan.

Maybe the less said about it now, the better. It was certainly sad, the way it happened, but it didn't stop me appreciating the good times – so many of them – that I'd had over the years with Glamorgan, and the wonderful opportunities and experiences I'd enjoyed with a great set of guys. I can look back and remember getting the wickets of some of the best batsmen in the world! I can also look back at the sense of genuine achievement I'd got from my work on the wider cricket stage with the Professional Cricketers' Association. I'm really proud of that, too.

In the weeks after that awful day at St. Helen's, I became increasingly determined to show that I still had some decent cricket left in me. That I could still produce the goods, with ball and bat. That I was still hungry to play the game. In short, that I had *not* retired. So I signed for Shropshire and played minor counties cricket for a couple of seasons.

I really did want to keep playing, and to prove to myself that I could still get people out, which I did for my new club. I'm not saying I was the star of the side or anything, but I got some wickets and felt quite comfortable. I don't want to be disrespectful to minor counties cricket, but it was very different to first-class cricket. The intensity is not the same. The length of the game, the physical demands, the mental approach of some of the players – there were, quite understandably, a number of differences. So it was a complete change.

I had some good times, and Shropshire was a friendly club with talented players. Most of the names would not be well-known outside the area, but one very famous and familiar face was that of Mushtaq Mohammad. 'Mushy' had a long and very successful career with Pakistan as a powerful right-handed batsman and useful leg-spin bowler, playing 57 Tests and ten One-Day Internationals and captaining his country for three years. I'd come across him playing for Northants, who he'd played for from 1966 to 1977, so we had been on opposite sides many times!

Stephen Gale, who went on to become a first-class umpire, was another member of the Shropshire side. So, too, was Steve Ogrizovic. In the summer of 1984, Steve was a young goalkeeper leaving Shrewsbury Town to join Coventry City where he went on to achieve

Now Mushtaq Mohammad and I were teammates with Shropshire.

legendary status – and win an FA Cup winners' medal! – but Oggy was also a very handy cricketer, bowling medium-fast.

All three were alongside me in the Shropshire side when we met Yorkshire at Telford in the first round of the NatWest Trophy in July 1984. It was a great occasion with a lot of local interest and an enthusiastic crowd at the St. George's Recreation ground. You can imagine how exciting it was for some of the minor counties players to be taking on England players like Geoff Boycott and visiting skipper David Bairstow.

We batted first and got a respectable 60-over total of 229 for 5 – respectable in those days, anyway! Mushy top-scored with 80, but there were some other very useful contributions, too. Unfortunately from my point of view, I didn't get a bat. When Yorkshire batted, we got into them early on. Oggy had Martyn Moxon (who would soon be another Yorkshire international, winning the first of his ten England caps two years later against New Zealand) caught to put them on 21 for 1. Then I got Ashley Metcalfe, Yorkshire's promising young right-handed batsman in his second first-class season, for a duck. They were 22 for 2, and before long had slumped to 81 for 6. I had a good spell of 12 overs – half of them maidens – for just 16 runs, and helped put them well behind the clock. I could still do it against high-quality opposition.

Although there were some late-order runs, our visitors never properly recovered and were all out for 192 in 57.5 overs. It was a great victory, and cause for significant celebrations! The national press was full of it, of course, with the toppling of a first-class county, and there was a great deal of interest in our second round encounter two weeks later with Warwickshire at Edgbaston.

What a special day, and for a number of guys in our side it was their first – and quite possibly only – experience of playing on a Test ground. Great excitement, and from my own point of view a welcome opportunity to again pit my skills against some top class batsmen. I didn't have to wait long, opening the bowling with Steve Ogrizovic at the other end when Warwickshire batted. I soon had success, trapping the very experienced Dennis Amiss, with 50 England caps and 11 Test centuries to his name, lbw for just six. Then Oggy had Alvin Kallicharran leg before for three, and Warwickshire were in some early and unexpected difficulty at 33 for 2. Robin Dyer (with a century) and wicketkeeper Geoff Humpage then rescued them with a big stand, and they closed on 305 for 8 off their 60-over allocation. Perhaps it wasn't a massive score in one day terms, but it was very formidable target for a minor counties outfit faced with first-class bowling!

Warwickshire had a very impressive bowling attack. It included Bob Willis, Chris Old, Gladstone Small, Paul Smith and Norman Gifford. A few of our players got good starts with the bat, but we fell behind the asking-rate and wickets continued to fall. I went in at 110 for 6 and scored 36 not out in helping to get us up to 202 all out with two balls left. We were sorry to lose, but hadn't been disgraced. It was an enjoyable day – and I'd got Dennis out!

The following year I called time on my cricketing life. I had some great times with Shropshire but it was, perhaps, the wrong ending to my playing career. Minor counties cricket just couldn't replace the intensity and day-to-day involvement of the first-class game and, after almost 20 years as a professional, I knew it was the right thing to do.

It was time for a fresh challenge and I found it in North America where I headed for a new life in the world of commercial sports promotion – cricket and golf – firstly in Canada and then in the United States.

It's certainly a small world, as in the early days my work took me to Barbados fairly regularly, and to meetings with Wes Hall, Minister for Tourism, and his staff, and whenever I was in Barbados I'd give

Garry and I enjoyed our golf.

Garry Sobers a ring and we'd enjoy a game of golf at the beautiful Sandy Lane Club in Bridgetown. Sometimes we'd chat about cricket and cricketers, but we didn't talk about 'that over' and the world-record at St. Helen's in 1968.

Garry and I were both well aware that, as far as a lot of people were concerned, those six balls defined our careers, but we both knew that there had been so much more to our cricketing lives and achievements.

It had certainly been a memorable journey, from school cricket in Abergavenny to playing golf in the Caribbean with my boyhood hero Garry Sobers, via St. Helen's on that Bank Holiday Monday in 1968 that neither of us will ever forget.

SELECTED CAREER STATISTICS

First-Class Career Batting & Fielding (1966-1983)								
M	Inns	NO	Runs	H/S	Av	100	50	Catches
336	469	67	7,129	130	17.73	2	25	148

First-Class Career Bowling (1966-1983)										
Balls	Mdns	Runs	Wkts	BB	Ave	5wI	10wM	SRate	Econ
55,380	2,433	25,698	993	9-56	25.87	45	5	55.77	2.78

List A Career Batting & Fielding (1967-1985)								
M	Inns	NO	Runs	H/S	Av	100	50	Catches
272	226	43	2,303	103	12.58	1	4	48

List A Career Bowling (1967-1985)										
Balls	Mdns	Runs	Wkts	BB	Ave	4wI	5wI	SRate	Econ
12,527	372	6,910	325	6-29	21.26	6	4	38.54	3.30

Additional Bowling Information

- My total of 993 first-class wickets (991 in Championship matches for Glamorgan, and two for 'The Rest' in the 1976 England Trial, included: 197 bowled, 261 lbw, 527 caught, 7 stumped, and 1 hit-wicket.
- I took an additional 20 wickets for D.H. Robins' XI, but these matches have not been given first-class status

- There were only three counties against whom I didn't get a five-wicket innings return at least once – Kent, Lancashire and Yorkshire (though I got '4-for' against them!).
- The teams I got most wickets against were Gloucestershire and Hampshire.
- In 12 seasons I got 50 or more wickets
- The highest number of wickets I took in a single season was 85 in 1975, followed by 81 in 1977, and 80 in 1969 and 1973.
- I played for Glamorgan against every Test-level cricket-playing nation except South Africa – India, Pakistan, New Zealand, Australia, West Indies and Sri Lanka.
- I played against Australian touring sides on five occasions, finishing on the winning side once (1968), the losing side once (1975) with three games drawn.
- If pressed to name the best opening batsmen I bowled to – and the most difficult to get out – I'd come up with Barry Richards, Gordon Greenidge, Glenn Turner and Geoff Boycott, but it's a difficult call, with so many factors to take into account, and there are so many other outstanding batsmen that I would want to mention if space permitted.

Additional Batting Information

- My highest score of 130 was against Surrey, and included a century before lunch (off 61 balls in 76 minutes).
- My other first-class century was against Leicestershire (124 not out).
- I scored what is still (and will always be) the fastest century in Benson and Hedges Cup competition (in 63 minutes, off 53 balls, against Hampshire).
- In 1971, I scored the fastest televised half-century in the John Player Sunday League.

BIBLIOGRAPHY

Allen, D. R. [Ed.], *Arlott on Cricket: His Writings on the Game*, William Collins (1984)

Arlott, J., Malcolm Andrew Nash, *Glamorgan CCC 1978 Yearbook*

Arlott, J. 'Five the game can ill afford to lose', *Wisden Cricket Monthly*, April 1984

Bailey, T. *Sir Gary: An Autobiography*, Collins (1976)

Cairns, R. and Turner, G., *Glenn Turner's Century of Centuries*, Hodder and Stoughton (1983)

Chambers, D., Unattributed cricket reports published in the *Abergavenny Chronicle* (1960-66)

Green, B. [Ed.] *Wisden Anthology 1963-82*, Queen Anne Press (1983)

Hignell, A., *Glamorgan CCC: 100 Greats*, Tempus Publishing (2000)

Hignell, A., *Glamorgan CCC: Fifty of the Finest Matches*, Tempus Publishing (2001)

Hignell, A., *Glamorgan Grounds: The Homes of Welsh Cricket*, Tempus Publishing (2002)

Hill, J., 'If the cap fits let all-rounder Nash wear it', *Daily Express* (May 12th, 1976)

Lloyd, G., *Six of the Best*, Celluloid Ltd (2008)

Miller, D., *Born to Bowl: The Life and Times of Don Shepherd*, Fairfield Books (2004)

Newbon, G., *Sporting Heroes* (interview with Gary Sobers) Sky Sports (December 13th, 2015)

Phelps, G. [Ed.], *Arlott and Trueman on Cricket*, BBC (1977)

Preston, N. [Ed.], *Wisden Cricketers' Almanack 1969*, Sporting Handbooks/John Wisden (1969)

Preston, N. [Ed.], *Wisden Cricketers' Almanack 1970*, Sporting Handbooks/John Wisden (1970)

Preston, N. [Ed.], *Wisden Cricketers' Almanack 1976*, Sporting Handbooks/John Wisden (1976)

Shepherd, D. with Foot, D., *Shep: My Autobiography*, Orion (2001)

Sobers, G. with Scovell, B., *Sobers: Twenty Years at the Top*, MacMillan (1988)

Sussex, P. and Wallace, R., *Abergavenny Cricket Club: A celebration of 175 years*, Abergavenny Cricket Club (2009)

Trueman, F., *Freddie Trueman's Book of Cricket*, Pelham Books (1964)

Vockins, M., *Arthur Milton: Last of the Double Internationals*, Sports Books Ltd. (2011)

Walker, P., *Cricket Conversations*, Pelham Books (1978)

Walker, P., *It's Not Just Cricket*, Fairfield Books (2006)

Wynne-Thomas, P., *The Complete History of Cricket Tours at Home and Abroad*, Hamlyn (1989)

ACKNOWLEDGEMENTS

I am grateful to all those individuals and organisations who have supported this project in a number of ways, including supplying pictures and other archive material from their collections.

In particular, my thanks go to Glamorgan County Cricket Club, the Glamorgan Cricket Archives, and the cc4 Museum of Welsh Cricket. The support of Glamorgan's Chief Executive, Hugh Morris, and their Heritage and Education Co-ordinator, Dr Andrew Hignell, has been invaluable.

Thanks also go to Abergavenny CC, Nottinghamshire CCC Library, St. Helen's Balconiers, Media Wales Ltd. (publishers of the South Wales Evening Post), and CricketArchive.

A number of individuals have also helped the project in various important ways. These include Mike Brearley OBE, Tony Lewis CBE, Paul Sussex, John Williams, Chris Peregrine, Daniel Lightman QC, Jeff Smith, Peter Wynne-Thomas, Sally Bentley Read and Victoria Macleod.

I would also like to put on record my gratitude to Dr Richard Bentley for helping me to recapture and organise my recollections – and, together with Joy, for making me so welcome while we were lost in our cricketing world! The hours of taped discussion and research have brought back so many memories – mostly very happy ones – of my life in the game, and of being part of the wonderful community of cricket.

Malcolm Nash
April 2018

INDEX

ST DAVID'S PRESS

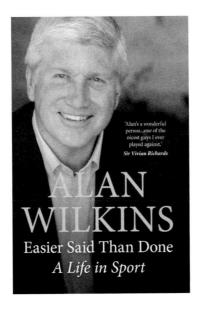

'Alan was an excellent county cricketer ... He may be Cardiff born and Cardiff bred but, in a broadcasting sense, Alan is 'a citizen of the world'.'
Tony Lewis

'Easier Said Than Done reads the same way as our chats, so enjoy the book in the same way as I am fortunate to enjoy his friendship - with a warm smile!'
Vijay Amritraj

'Alan Wilkins has to be the nicest man in broadcasting. There is nobody who is so gentle, so kind, so generous with his time and someone who laughs at himself as much as Wilko does.'
Sunil Gavaskar

'Alan epitomises what sport is all about'
Clive Lloyd

With great honesty and humility, Alan Wilkins tells the fascinating story of his seven years as a professional cricketer with Glamorgan and Gloucestershire – taking over 370 wickets and playing in the 1977 Gillette Cup final – and how his career was brought to a devastating end in 1983 by a debilitating shoulder injury.

Determined that his *Life in Sport* would not end after his enforced retirement, Alan Wilkins then embarked on a new and successful career in sports broadcasting, which has made him one of the most recognisable faces and voices in sports broadcasting in SE Asia, South Africa and in his native Wales.

hb - 978 1 902719 610   £20   304pp + 32pp of illustrations & photographs

ST DAVID'S PRESS

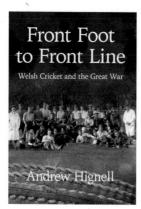

CRICKET IN WALES

Front Foot to Front Line
Welsh Cricket and the Great War
Dr. Andrew Hignell

'We must never forget what these people did, either at the crease or in the trenches. As a tribute to their deeds either on the Front Foot or on the Front Line, this book is a most fitting one.' **Hugh Morris, from his Foreword**

Front Foot to Front Line commemorates Welsh cricket's contribution to the Great War by chronicling the lives of 55 professional and amateur cricketers who left the friendly rivalry of the crease for the brutality and horror of the trenches, and lost their lives as servicemen on the bloody battlefields of Europe.

The cricket clubs featured in *Front Foot to Front Line* include:
Blaina, Barry, Brecon, Bridgend Town, Briton Ferry, Cardiff, Cowbridge, Crickhowell, Denbighshire, Ferndale, Garth, Glamorgan, Llancarfan, Llandovery College, Llandudno, Llanelli, Monmouthshire, Neath, Newport, Pontypridd, Radyr, Swansea, Usk Valley, and Ystrad Mynach.

978-1-902719-42-9   209pp   £16.99   PB

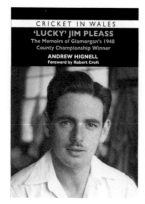

CRICKET IN WALES

'Lucky' Jim Pleass
The Memoirs of Glamorgan's 1948 County Championship Winner
Dr. Andrew Hignell

'I can but only admire Jim's contributions during Glamorgan's Championship-winning summer of 1948 or his efforts with the bat against the 1951 South Africans at Swansea...[without him] I can only wonder at how different the course of Glamorgan's cricketing history might have been'. **Robert Croft, from his Foreword**

In 2014 Jim Pleass was the longest surviving member of Glamorgan's County Championship winning team of 1948, the first time the Welsh team won the highest honour in county cricket.

Jim was a very lucky man, as the book explains his narrow escape from certain death when he stormed the Normandy beaches on D day in 1944. If it wasn't for the over-exuberance of a driver on another landing craft, Jim would never have graced the cricket field wearing the daffodil of Glamorgan County Cricket Club.

978-1-902719-36-8   128pp   £14.99   PB